Honolulu

Glenda Bendure
Ned

Honolulu

2nd edition

Published by
Lonely Planet Publications
Head Office: PO Box 617, Hawthorn, Vic 3122, Australia
Branches: 155 Filbert St, Suite 251, Oakland, CA 94607, USA
10 Barley Mow Passage, Chiswick, London W4 4PH, UK
71 bis rue du Cardinal Lemoine, 75005 Paris, France

Printed by
Pac – Rim, Kwartanusa Printing
Printed in Indonesia

Photographs by
Glenda Bendure   Ned Friary
Hawaii State Archives   David Russ

Front cover: surfboards, Waikiki, Cheyenne Rouse

First Published
June 1995

This Edition
November 1997

Although the author and publisher have tried to make the information as accurate as possible, they accept no responsibility for any loss, injury or inconvenience sustained by any person using this book.

National Library of Australia Cataloguing in Publication Data

Bendure, Glenda.
Honolulu.

2nd ed.
Includes index.
ISBN 0 86442 490 6.

1. Honolulu (Hawaii) – Guidebooks. I. Friary, Ned.
II. Title.

919.69310441

Glenda Bendure & Ned Friary

Glenda grew up in California's Mojave Desert and first traveled overseas as a high school AFS exchange student to India.

Ned grew up near Boston, studied Social Thought & Political Economy at the University of Massachusetts in Amherst and upon graduating headed west.

They met in Santa Cruz, California, where Glenda was completing her university studies. In 1978, with Lonely Planet's first book *Across Asia on the Cheap* in hand, they took the overland trail from Europe to Nepal. They spent the next six years exploring Asia and the Pacific from a home base in Japan where Ned taught English and Glenda edited a monthly magazine.

The first of many extended trips to Hawaii was in 1980, when they went straight from Osaka to the green lushness of Hawaii, a sight so soothing for concrete-weary eyes that a two-week vacation turned into a four-month sojourn.

Ned and Glenda have a particular fondness for islands and tropical climates. They are the authors of Lonely Planet's *Hawaii*, *Micronesia* and *Eastern Caribbean* guides. They have also written the Norway and Denmark chapters of LP's *Scandinavian & Baltic Europe on a Shoestring*.

They now live on Cape Cod in Massachusetts – at least when they're not on the road.

From the Authors

Many thanks to the people who helped us on this project: State Parks archaeologist Martha Yent; Linda Delaney from the Office of Hawaiian Affairs; Christina Meller, Na Ala Hele Program Manager; Jon Giffin of the Division of Forestry & Wildlife; Honolulu astronomer Ted Brattstrom; marine biologist Lisa King; and the Hawaii Visitors Bureau. Thanks also to those friends and travelers who have shared insights and experiences with us along the way.

From the Publisher

This book was edited by Tom Downs (the Jack Lord of Oakland), Laini Taylor and Sacha Pearson. Kate Hoffman proofed. A special 'mahalo' to Don 'The Mon' Gates for setting the tone.

Maps were drawn by Beca Lafore and Alex Guilbert. Illustrations were drawn by Hayden Foell and Mark Butler.

Design and typesetting were by Scott Summers and the cover was designed by Hugh D'Andrade.

Thanks

Thanks to the following travelers for writing to us about their travel experiences in Honolulu (apologies if we've mispelled your name): Kristen Caven, Dan Fowler, Trish & Bruce Murray, Darren Scott, Mike Tuggle, Jodie Wesley.

Warning & Request

Things change – prices go up, schedules change, good places go bad and bad places go bankrupt – nothing stays the same. So, if you find things better or worse, recently opened or long since closed, please tell us and help make the next edition even more accurate and useful.

We value all of the feedback we receive from travelers. A small team reads and acknowledges every letter, postcard and email, and ensures that every morsel of information finds its way to the appropriate authors, editors and publishers. Everyone who writes to us will find their name in the next edition of the appropriate guide and will also receive a free subscription to our quarterly newsletter, *Planet Talk*. The very best contributions will be rewarded with a free Lonely Planet guide.

Excerpts from your correspondence may appear in updates (which we add to the end pages of reprints); in new editions of this guide; in our newsletter, *Planet Talk*; or in the Postcards section of our Website – so please let us know if you don't want your letter published or your name acknowledged.

Contents

Map Legend

BOUNDARIES

International Boundary

Provincial Boundary

AREA FEATURES

Park

NATIONAL PARK — National Park

National Forest, Watershed Area

HYDROGRAPHIC FEATURES

Water

Reef

Coastline

Beach

Swamp

River, Waterfall

Mangrove, Spring

ROUTES

Freeway

Primary Road

Secondary Road

Tertiary Road

Dirt Road

Trail

Ferry Route

Railway, Train Station

ROUTE SHIELDS

(H1) Interstate Freeway

(99) State Highway

SYMBOLS

✪	NATIONAL CAPITAL	✚	Airfield	⬮	Gas Station	)(	Pass
◉	State Capital	✈	Airport	ʅ	Golf Course	┯	Picnic Area
●	City	∴	Archaeological Site, Ruins	●	Hospital, Clinic	★	Police Station
●	City, Small	⑤	Bank, ATM	❶	Information	▭	Pool
●	Town	⬭	Baseball Stadium	🛉	Lighthouse	▾	Post Office
		🮲	Beach	☀	Lookout	⚲	Shipwreck
■	Hotel, B&B	⚖	Buddhist Temple	☷	Mine	❖	Shopping Mall
▲	Campground	◖	Bus Station, Bus Stop	▲	Monument	⚡	Skiing, Downhill
⬗	Hostel	⊞	Cathedral	▲	Mountain	𝆏	Skiing, Cross-country
⚏	RV Park	⌢	Cave	🏛	Museum	🏛	Stately Home
⬘	Shelter, Refugio	✝	Church	✔	Music, Live	☎	Telephone
▾	Restaurant	⬢	Dive Site	←	One-Way Street	◼	Tomb, Mausoleum
⬛	Bar (Place to Drink)	◔	Embassy, Consulate	⬡	Observatory	🏃	Trailhead
⬛	Cafe	⋈	Foot Bridge	▲	Park	⚚	Winery
		⁙	Garden	▣	Parking	🐘	Zoo

Note: Not all symbols displayed above appear in this book.

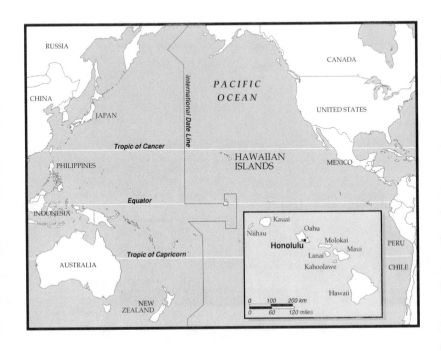

Introduction

Honolulu is Hawaii's capital and its center of business, culture and politics. It's also one of the prime tourist destinations in the Pacific and an increasingly popular place for business conventions.

To most visitors, the very name Honolulu conjures up romantic images of hula dancers, swaying palm trees and balmy weather. Indeed, it's the only US city located in the tropics and the only one that can claim to equally blend Western, Asian and Polynesian influences.

As home to people from throughout the Pacific, Honolulu is a city of minorities and has no ethnic majority. This diversity can be seen on almost every corner – the sushi shop next door to the Vietnamese bakery, the Catholic church around the block from the Chinese temple, and schoolchildren of every hue waiting for the bus.

The city has an intriguing variety of things to see and do. Cultural offerings range from Japanese tea ceremonies and traditional hula performances to a symphony orchestra and good museums. Honolulu has the only royal palace in the USA, fine city beach parks and some great hilltop views.

Downtown Honolulu has government offices and the state's highest concentration of historic buildings, while adjacent Chinatown is a delightful mélange of Asian influences.

Almost all of Honolulu's tourist facilities are centered in Waikiki. As a world-class vacation destination, Waikiki has all the pluses and minuses of mass tourism: seaside restaurants, excellent hotels, lively entertainment and beach activities are all close at hand, although city noise and congestion are present as well.

Still there's much more to Honolulu than its urban quarters. The valleys above the city have lush forest reserves, and quiet, lightly trodden hiking trails are just 15 minutes from the city center.

Within an hour's drive of Honolulu are numerous worthwhile excursions, including the Nuuanu Pali Lookout, with its sweeping views, and scenic Hanauma Bay, with fine opportunities for snorkeling. In winter a popular touring area is Oahu's North Shore, which boasts the world's top surfing action.

Facts about Honolulu

HISTORY

The Hawaiian Islands are the northernmost point of a huge triangle of Pacific Ocean islands known as Polynesia; the southwestern extreme of Polynesia is New Zealand, while the southeastern point is Easter Island.

Because the long path of migration ran from Southeast Asia east through the islands of the South Pacific before extending north, Hawaii was the last Polynesian island chain to be settled. While parts of southern Polynesia had been colonized as early as 1000 BC, it was another 1500 years before the first settlers arrived in Hawaii.

Archaeological evidence indicates that the first settlers arrived from the Marquesas around 500 AD. They were followed by Tahitians, who arrived in Hawaii in about 1000 AD. Unlike the Marquesans, who had sparse settlements at the northwestern end of the Hawaiian chain, the Tahitians settled all of the main islands.

The Tahitians were thorough colonizers, arriving in double-hulled canoes that were loaded with pigs, chickens, dogs and staple food plants such as taro and bananas.

Adept seafarers who used ocean currents and star patterns to navigate, the Tahitians were not only capable of making the 2700-mile journey north but were also able to memorize the route and retrace it. Vast waves of Tahitian migration occurred throughout the 13th and 14th centuries and archaeologists now believe that Hawaii's population probably reached a plateau of approximately 250,000 by the year 1450. The voyages back and forth continued until around 1500, when all contact between Tahiti and Hawaii appears to have stopped.

Ancient Hawaii

The earliest Hawaiians had simple animistic beliefs. Good fishing, a safe journey and a healthy child were all the result of being in tune with the spirits of nature. Their offerings to the gods consisted of prayers and a share of the harvest.

Around the 12th century, a powerful Tahitian *kahuna* (priest), Paao, arrived in Hawaii. Convinced that the Hawaiians were too lax in their worship, Paao introduced the concept of offering human sacrifice to the gods and he built the first *luakini heiau*, a type of temple where these sacrifices took place. He also established the *kapu* system, a practice of taboos which strictly regulated all social interaction.

The kapus forbade commoners from eating the same food or even walking the same ground as the *alii*, or royalty, who were thought to be representatives of the gods. A commoner who crossed the shadow of a king could be put to death. Kapus prohibited all women from eating coconuts, bananas, pork and certain varieties of fish.

This strict system of kapus and social delineation remained intact until after the arrival of the first Westerners in the late 18th century.

Westerners Arrive

Hawaii was the last of the Polynesian islands to be 'discovered' by the West, since early European explorers, who entered the Pacific around the tips of Africa or South America, concentrated their initial explorations in the Southern Hemisphere. Indeed, the great British explorer Captain James Cook spent the better part of a decade exploring and charting most of the South Pacific before chancing upon Hawaii as he sailed north from Tahiti in search of a northwest passage to the Atlantic.

On January 18, 1778, Captain Cook sighted the islands of Oahu, Kauai and Niihau. The winds favored approaching Kauai and on January 19 Cook's ships, the *Discovery* and the *Resolution*, sailed into Kauai's Waimea Bay. Cook named the Hawaiian archipelago the Sandwich

Islands in honor of the Earl of Sandwich. The captain, who received a friendly reception, was surprised to find that the islanders had a strong Tahitian influence in their appearance, language and culture. After two weeks of stocking provisions, Cook's expedition continued its journey north.

Failing to find the fabled passages through the Arctic, Cook returned to Hawaii the following year, where he lost his life in a freak melee with the Hawaiians. Despite the tragedy, Cook's men returned home with enthusiastic accounts of the Hawaiian Islands and in the decades that followed Honolulu became a common port of call for European and American ships.

The Battle for Oahu

At the time of the first European contact with Hawaii, the Hawaiian Islands were under the control of a handful of chiefs who were engaged in a struggle for dominance of the island chain.

The main rivals were Kamehameha the Great, chief of the island of Hawaii, and Kahekili, the aging king of Maui, who in the 1780s had killed his own stepson in order to take control of Oahu.

After Kahekili died at Waikiki in 1794 a power struggle ensued and his lands were divided between two quarreling relatives. His son, Kalanikupule, got Oahu, while his half-brother, King Kaeokulani of Kauai, gained control of Maui, Lanai and Molokai. The two ambitious heirs immediately went to battle with each other, creating a rift that Kamehameha the Great set out to exploit.

In 1795 Kamehameha swept through Maui and Molokai, conquering those islands before crossing the channel to Oahu. On the quiet beaches of Waikiki he landed his fleet of canoes and marched up towards Nuuanu Valley to meet Kalanikupule, the king of Oahu.

The Oahu warriors were no match for Kamehameha's troops. The first heavy fighting took place around the Punchbowl, where Kamehameha's men quickly circled the fortress-like crater and drove out the Oahuan defenders. Scattered fighting continued up Nuuanu Valley, with the last big battle taking place near the current site of Queen Emma's summer palace.

The Oahuans, who were prepared for the usual spear-and-stone warfare, panicked when they realized Kamehameha had brought in a handful of Western sharpshooters with modern firearms. Under Kamehameha's command the foreigners picked off the Oahuan generals and blasted into their ridge-top defenses.

What should have been the high-ground advantage turned into a death trap for the Oahuans when they found themselves wedged up into the valley, unable to redeploy. Fleeing up the cliffsides in retreat, they were forced to make their last stand at the narrow precipitous ledge along the current-day Nuuanu Pali Lookout. Hundreds of Oahuans were driven over the top of the *pali* (cliff) to their deaths.

Some Oahuan warriors, including King Kalanikupule, escaped into the upland forests. When Kalanikupule surfaced a few months later Kamehameha, as an offering to his war god, made a human sacrifice of the fallen king. Kamehameha's taking of Oahu marked the last battle ever fought between Hawaiian troops as well as Hawaii's emergence as a united kingdom.

The Founding of Honolulu

In 1793 the English frigate *Butterworth* became the first foreign ship to sail into what is now called Honolulu Harbor. Its captain, William Brown, named the protected harbor Fair Haven. Ships that followed called it Brown's Harbor. Over time the name Honolulu, which means 'Sheltered Bay,' came to be used for both the harbor and the seaside district that the Hawaiians had called Kou.

As more and more foreign ships found their way to Honolulu a harborside village of thatched houses sprang up. The port soon became a focal point for merchant ships plying the seas between the USA and Asia. In 1809 Kamehameha, who had been living at his royal court in Waikiki, decided to move to the Honolulu Harbor area, which by then had grown into a village of almost

The Sandalwood Trade

In the early 1790s American sea captains discovered that Hawaii had great stocks of sandalwood, which were worth a premium in China.

A lucrative three-way trade developed. From Honolulu the ships sailed to Canton and traded loads of the fragrant sandalwood in exchange for Chinese silk and porcelain, which were then carried back to New England ports and sold at high profit. In New England the ships were reloaded with goods to be traded to the Hawaiians.

Hawaii's forests of sandalwood were so vast at that time that the Chinese name for Hawaii was Tahn Heong Sahn – the 'Sandalwood Mountains.'

To try to maintain the resource, Kamehameha took total control over the sandalwood forests, but even under his shrewd management the bulk of the profits ended up in the sea captains' pockets. Payment for the sandalwood was in overpriced goods, originally cannons and rifles, and later exotic items such as European furniture.

While Kamehameha was careful not to use up all his forests or overburden his subjects, his successor, Liholiho, allowed local chiefs to get in on the action. These chiefs began purchasing foreign luxuries by signing promissory notes to be paid in future shipments of sandalwood.

To pay off the rising 'debts,' commoners were forced into virtual servitude. They were used like packhorses to haul the wood, which was strapped to their backs with bands of ti leaves. The men who carted the wood were called *kua leho*, literally 'calloused backs' after the thick permanent layer of calluses which they developed. It was not uncommon for them to carry heavy loads 20 miles from the interior to ships waiting on the coast. Missionaries recorded seeing caravans of as many as 3000 men carting wood during the height of the trade.

Within a few short years after Kamehameha's death Hawaii's sandalwood forests were exhausted. In a futile attempt to continue the trade, Oahu's Governor Boki, who had heard of vast sandalwood reserves in New Hebrides, set sail in November 1829 with 500 men on an ill-conceived expedition to harvest the trees. Boki's ship was lost at sea and the expedition's other ship, not too surprisingly, received a hostile welcome in New Hebrides.

In August 1830, 20 emaciated survivors sailed back into Honolulu Harbor. Boki had been a popular if troubled leader in a rapidly changing Hawaii. Hawaiians grieved in the streets of Honolulu when they heard of Boki's tragedy, and his death marked the end of the sandalwood trade. ■

1800 people. Intent on keeping an eye on all the trade that flowed in and out of the harbor, Kamehameha set up residence near the waterfront on what today is the southern end of Bethel St. With Kamehameha's move, Honolulu was firmly established as Hawaii's center of commerce.

Kamehameha traded sandalwood, which was shipped to China, in exchange for weapons and luxury goods. As the trade grew, Kamehameha built harborside warehouses to store his goods and he introduced wharfage fees to build up his treasury. New England Yankees, who dominated the sandalwood trade, quickly became the main foreign presence in Honolulu. In 1820 the population of Honolulu had grown to nearly 3500 people and it would continue to boom as more foreigners arrived on Hawaiian shores.

Missionaries & Sinners

By 1820 whaling ships plying the Pacific had begun to pull into Honolulu for supplies, liquor and women. To meet their needs, taverns and brothels sprung up around the harbor.

Much to the ire of the whalers, their arrival was soon followed by that of Christian missionaries. The first missionary ship to land in Hawaii, the *Thaddeus*, sailed into Honolulu on April 14, 1820. The minister in charge of the Honolulu mission was Hiram Bingham, a staunch Calvinist who was set on putting an end to the heathen ways of the Hawaiians.

The missionaries befriended Hawaiian royalty and made their inroads quickly. After Queen Kaahumanu became seriously ill, Hiram's wife, Sybil Bingham, nursed the queen back to health. Shortly after, Kaahumanu showed her gratitude by passing a law forbidding work and travel on the Sabbath.

Although both the missionaries and the whalers hailed from New England they had little else in common and were soon at odds, with the missionaries intent on saving souls and the whalers intent, after months at sea, on satisfying more earthly desires.

In January 1826 the captain of the American warship USS *Dolphin*, having arrived in Honolulu to investigate trade issues, raised a stir with the missionaries by advocating for prostitution. In response Bingham convinced the island chiefs to put a kapu on women, forbidding them to board ships in the harbor. After the sailors stoned Bingham's house, the women were allowed to go aboard but the struggles continued.

In time the missionaries gained enough influence with Hawaiian royalty to have more effective laws enacted against drunkenness and prostitution. By the peak whaling years of the mid-1800s, most whaling boats had abandoned Honolulu, preferring to land in Lahaina on Maui, where the whalers had gained an upper hand over the missionaries.

Interestingly, both groups left their marks on Honolulu. To this day the headquarters of the Protestant mission sits placidly in downtown Honolulu, while only minutes away Honolulu's red-light district continues to attract sea-weary sailors and wayward souls.

Downtown Honolulu also became the headquarters for the emerging corporations that eventually gained control of Hawaii's commerce. It's no coincidence that their lists of corporate board members – Alexander, Baldwin, Cooke and Dole – read like a roster from the first mission ships, for indeed it was the sons of missionaries who became the power brokers in the new Hawaii.

By the mid-1800s Westerners had managed to take over most of Hawaii's land, establishing sugar plantations throughout the islands. To work the plantations, they imported tens of thousands of laborers from Japan, the Philippines, China, Korea, Portugal and other countries, changing the face of Hawaii forever.

Honolulu as Capital

In 1845 Kamehameha III, the last son of Kamehameha the Great, moved the capital of the Kingdom of Hawaii from Maui to Honolulu. Kamehameha III, who ruled from 1825 to 1854, established Hawaii's first national legislature, provided for a Supreme Court and passed the Great Mahele land act, which established religious freedom and gave all male citizens the right to vote.

Hawaii's only 'invasion' by a foreign power occurred during Kamehameha III's reign. In 1843, George Paulet, an upstart British commander upset about a petty land deal involving a British national, sailed into Honolulu commanding the British ship *Carysfort* and seized Oahu for six months. In that short period, he Anglicized street names, seized property and began to collect taxes.

To avoid bloodshed, Kamehameha III stood aside as the British flag was raised and the ship's band played 'God Save the Queen.' Queen Victoria herself wasn't flattered. After catching wind of the incident, she dispatched Admiral Richard Thomas to

The Great Mahele

The Great Mahele of 1848, which was introduced under the urging of influential missionaries, permanently altered Hawaiian concepts of land rights. For the first time, land became a commodity that could be bought and sold.

Through the provisions of the Great Mahele, the king, who had previously owned all land, gave up title to the majority of it. Island chiefs were allowed to purchase some of the lands which they had controlled as fiefdoms for the king. Other lands, which were divided into three-acre farm plots called *kuleana*, were made available to all Hawaiians. In order to retain title, chiefs and commoners alike had to pay a tax and register the land.

The chiefs had the option of paying the tax in property and many did so. Commoners had no choice but to pay the taxes in cash. Although the act was intended to turn Hawaii into a country of small farms, in the end only a few thousand Hawaiians carried through with the paperwork and received kuleanas.

In 1850 land purchases were opened to foreigners. Unlike the Hawaiians, the Westerners jumped at the opportunity and before the native islanders could clearly grasp the concept of private land ownership, there was little land left to own.

Within a few decades the Westerners, who were more adept at wheeling and dealing in real estate, owned 80% of all privately held lands. Even many of the Hawaiians who had gone through the process of getting their own kuleana eventually ended up selling it off for a fraction of its real value.

Contrary to the picture the missionaries had painted for Kamehameha III, the Hawaiians suddenly became a landless people, drifting into ghettos in the larger towns. With a bitter twist, many of the missionaries themselves ended up with sizable tracts of land and more than a few of them left the church to tend their new estates.

Although Hawaiian commoners had no rights to the land prior to the Great Mahele, they were free to move around and work the property of any chief. In return for their personal use of the land they paid the chief in labor or with a percentage of their crops. In this way they lived off the land. After the Great Mahele, they were simply *off* the land. ■

restore Hawaiian independence. Admiral Thomas re-raised the Hawaiian flag at the site of what is today Honolulu's Thomas Square. As the flag was raised Kamehameha III uttered the words '*Ua mau ke ea o ka aina i ka pono,*' meaning 'The life of the land is perpetuated in righteousness,' which remains Hawaii's official motto.

In an 1853 census, Honolulu registered 11,450 residents, a full 15% of the Hawaiian kingdom's population. Though still a frontier town with dusty streets and simple wooden buildings, Honolulu had established itself as both the commercial and political center of the kingdom. In the decades that followed, Honolulu began to take on a modern appearance as the monarchy erected a number of stately buildings in the city center, including St Andrew's Cathedral, Iolani Palace and the Supreme Court building Aliiolani Hale.

By the mid-19th century Honolulu had a prominent foreign community comprised largely of American and British expatriates. These foreigners were not only active in missionary endeavors but were also opening schools and starting newspapers and, more importantly, landing powerful government positions as ministry officials and consuls to the king. As the city continued to grow and Westerners wrested increasing control over island affairs from the Hawaiians, the powers of King Kamehameha's successors eroded.

King Kalakaua

King David Kalakaua, who reigned from 1874 to 1891, was Hawaii's last king. He was a great Hawaiian revivalist who brought back the hula, reversing decades of missionary repression against the 'heathen dance,' and composed the national anthem *Hawaii Ponoi*, which is now the state song. He also tried to ensure some self-rule for native Hawaiians, who had become a minority in their own land.

Although he was unwaveringly loyal to the interest of native Hawaiians, Kalakaua was realistic about the current-day realities he faced. The king proved himself a successful diplomat by traveling to Washington, DC, and persuading president Ulysses Grant to accept a treaty giving Hawaiian sugar growers tariff-free access to US markets. In so doing Kalakaua gained, at least temporarily, the support of the sugar plantation owners, who controlled most of Hawaii's agricultural land.

The king became a world traveler, visiting India, Egypt, Europe and Southeast Asia. Kalakaua was well aware that Hawaii's days as an independent Polynesian kingdom were numbered. To counter the Western powers that were gaining hold of Hawaii, he made a futile attempt to establish a Polynesian-Pacific empire. On a visit with the emperor of Japan, he even proposed a royal marriage between his niece Princess Kaiulani and a Japanese prince, but the Japanese declined.

Visits with other foreign monarchs gave Kalakaua a taste for royal pageantry. He returned to build Iolani Palace for what the business community thought was an extravagant $360,000. To many influential whites, the king was perceived as a lavish spender who was fond of partying and throwing public luaus.

As Kalakaua incurred debts, he became increasingly less popular with the sugar barons whose businesses were now the backbone of the economy. They formed the Hawaiian League in 1887 and developed their own armies which stood ready to overthrow Kalakaua. The league presented Kalakaua with a list of demands and forced him to accept a new constitution strictly limiting his powers. It also limited suffrage to property owners, which by then excluded the vast majority of Hawaiians.

On July 30, 1889, a group of about 150 Hawaiians attempted to overthrow the new constitution by occupying Iolani Palace. Called the Wilcox Rebellion after its part-Hawaiian leader, it was a confused and futile attempt and the rebels were forced to surrender.

Kalakaua died in San Francisco in 1891.

HAWAII STATE ARCHIVES

King Kalakaua

Overthrow of Queen Liliuokalani

In January 1893, Queen Liliuokalani, Kalakaua's sister and successor, was preparing to proclaim a new constitution strengthening the throne when a group of armed US businessmen occupied the Supreme Court and declared the monarchy overthrown. They announced a provisional government, led by Sanford Dole, son of a pioneer missionary.

A contingent of US sailors came ashore, ostensibly to protect the property of Americans, but instead of parading to neighborhoods where Americans lived, they marched on the palace and positioned their guns at the queen's residence. The queen opted to avoid bloodshed and stepped down.

The provisional government immediately appealed to Washington for annexation, while the queen appealed to the same powers to restore the monarchy. To the dismay of Dole's representatives, the timing seemed to be to the queen's advantage. Democrat president Grover Cleveland had just replaced a Republican administration and his sentiments favored the queen.

Cleveland sent an envoy to investigate the situation and received Queen Liliuokalani's niece, Princess Kaiulani, who, at the time of the coup, had been in London being prepared for the throne. The beautiful 18-year-old princess eloquently pleaded the monarchy's case. She also made a favorable impression with the American press, which largely caricatured those involved in the overthrow as dour, greedy buffoons.

Cleveland ordered that the US flag be taken down and the queen restored to her throne. However, the provisional government, now firmly in power, turned a deaf ear, declaring that Cleveland was meddling in 'Hawaiian' affairs.

On July 4, 1894, Dole stood on the steps of Iolani Palace and announced that Hawaii was now a republic and he was its president. A disapproving Cleveland initially favored reversing the situation, but he realized the US public's sense of justice was thin and that ousting a government of white

Americans and replacing them with native Hawaiians could backlash on his own political future. Consequently, his actions were largely limited to rhetoric.

Weary of waiting for outside intervention, in early 1895 a group of Hawaiian royalists attempted a counterrevolution that was easily squashed. Liliuokalani was accused of being a conspirator and placed under arrest.

The queen was tried in her own palace, fined $5000 and sentenced to five years of hard labor, later reduced to nine months of house arrest at the palace. Liliuokalani spent the rest of her life in her husband's residence, Washington Place, one block from the palace.

The Spanish-American War of 1898 and the acquisition of the Philippines marked the arrival of American expansionism in the Pacific. In short order the annexation of Hawaii was adopted by the US Congress and, in 1900, US President McKinley appointed Sanford Dole the first governor of the Territory of Hawaii.

World Wars & Statehood

Soon after annexation, the US Navy set up a huge Pacific headquarters at Pearl Harbor and in central Oahu built Schofield Barracks, the largest US military base anywhere. The military quickly became the leading sector of Oahu's economy.

The islands were relatively untouched by WWI, even though the first German prisoners of war 'captured' by the USA were in Hawaii. They were escorted off the German gunboat *Grier* which had the misfortune to be docked at Honolulu Harbor when war broke out.

WWII had a much more dramatic effect on Hawaii. On December 7, 1941, the Japanese staged a surprise attack on Pearl Harbor that sunk or seriously damaged 21 ships, killed more than 2300 people and catapulted the USA into the war.

After the smoke cleared, Hawaii was placed under martial law and Oahu took on the face of a military camp. Already heavily militarized, vast tracts of Oahu's land were turned over to the US armed forces for expanded military bases, training and weapons testing. Much of that land would never be returned. Throughout the war, Oahu served as the command post for the USA's Pacific operations.

WWII also brought Hawaii closer to the center stage of American culture and politics. On August 21, 1959, after 61 years of territorial status, and following a plebiscite in which 90% of islanders voted for statehood, Hawaii became the 50th state of the USA.

GEOGRAPHY

Honolulu extends along the south-central shore of Oahu, the third-largest Hawaiian island. Urban Honolulu occupies 84 sq miles, nearly 15% of Oahu's total land mass. The island's extreme length is 44 miles, its width 30 miles.

Two separate volcanoes arose to form Oahu's two mountain ranges, Waianae and Koolau, which slice the island from the northwest to the southeast. Oahu's highest point, Mt Kaala at 4020 feet, is in the Waianae Range.

Honolulu is south of the tropic of Cancer, 1470 miles north of the equator, and shares the same latitude as Hong Kong, Calcutta and Cuba. It is 2557 miles from Los Angeles, 3847 miles from Tokyo and 5070 miles from Sydney.

CLIMATE

Honolulu's climate is typically warm and sunny. It's unusually pleasant for the tropics, as near-constant trade winds prevail throughout the year. Although there can be spells of stormy weather, particularly in the winter, much of the time the rain falls as short daytime showers accompanied by rainbows.

In Honolulu the average daily maximum temperature is 84°F and the minimum is 70°F. Temperatures are a bit higher in summer and a few degrees lower in winter. The highest temperature on record is 94°F and the lowest is 53°F.

Rainfall varies greatly with elevation, even within the city. Waikiki has an average annual rainfall of only 25 inches, whereas the Lyon Arboretum in the upper Manoa Valley, at the north side of Honolulu, aver-

ages 158 inches. Mid-afternoon humidity averages 56%.

Average water temperatures in Waikiki are 77°F in March, 82°F in August.

The National Weather Service provides recorded weather forecasts for Honolulu (☎ 973-4380) and all Oahu (☎ 973-4381). They also have recorded tides and surf conditions (☎ 973-4383) and a marine forecast (☎ 973-4382).

ECOLOGY & ENVIRONMENT

Situated 2500 miles from the nearest continental land mass, Hawaii has one of the world's most isolated and fragile ecosystems. Over 90% of Hawaii's native flora and fauna are found nowhere else on earth.

Hawaii's native species have been highly sensitive to habitat degradation and over the past century numerous species have become extinct, including more than a third of all native forest birds. Today fully half of Hawaii's native flora and fauna is either threatened or endangered.

Vast tracts of native forest have long been buried under to give way to the monocrop cultures of sugar cane and pineapple. In the 1960s the advent of mass tourism posed new challenges to the environment, most notably in the rampant development of land-hungry golf courses. In the past two decades the number of golf courses on Oahu has jumped from just a handful to 32 and the total acreage given over to these golf courses now rivals that used for plantation agriculture.

In terms of air quality Oahu has no polluting heavy industry. However Honolulu, being on the dry and less windy leeward side of the island, occasionally has moderate levels of vehicle-related pollution. As for general aesthetics, roadside billboards are not allowed and overall the level of environmental awareness is more advanced than on much of the US mainland.

There are more than 150 environmental groups in Hawaii, ranging from chapters of international organizations fighting to save the rainforest to neighborhood groups working to protect local beaches from impending development.

One of the broadest based is the Hawaii chapter of the Sierra Club, whose activities range from political activism on local environmental issues to weekend outings for eradicating invasive plants from native forests.

A sister organization, the Sierra Club Legal Defense Fund (SCLDF), is in the forefront pressing legal challenges against abuses to Hawaii's fragile environment. For instance, in conjunction with Greenpeace Hawaii, they've forced the state to prohibit jet skis in waters used by endangered humpback whales.

A different approach is taken by the Nature Conservancy of Hawaii, which protects Hawaii's rarest ecosystems by buying up vast tracts of land and working out long-term stewardships with prominent landholders. On Oahu the Nature Conservancy manages a crater above Hanauma Bay.

FLORA

Honolulu is abloom year round with colorful tropical flowers.

Perhaps no flower is more closely identified with Hawaii than the hibiscus, whose blooms are commonly worn by women tucked behind their ears. Thousands of varieties of hibiscus bushes grow in Hawaii; on most, the flowers bloom early in the day and drop before sunset. The variety most frequently seen is the red (or Chinese) hibiscus, which is used as a landscape hedge throughout Honolulu.

Other flowers seen in gardens and yards are blood-red anthuriums, brilliant orange birds of paradise, colorful bougainvilleas, red ginger, torch ginger, shell ginger, fragrant jasmine and gardenia and various heliconias with bright orange and red bracts.

Native coastal plants include *pohuehue*, a beach morning glory with pink flowers that's found on the sand just above the wrack line; beach *naupaka*, a shrub with oval leaves and a small white five-petaled flower that looks as if it's been torn in half; and Oahu's official flower, the low-growing *ilima*, which has delicate yellow-orange blossoms.

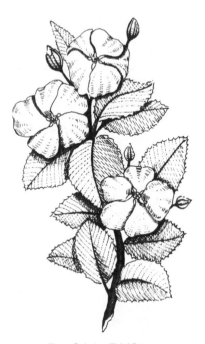

Ilima, Oahu's official flower

Common trees include fruiting varieties such as papaya, mango, guava and coconut and those planted for their lovely flowers, such as monkeypod, plumeria and poinciana.

Honolulu has some excellent botanical gardens. Foster Garden in the Chinatown area and the Lyon Arboretum at the north side of the city both have unique native and exotic species, some of which have disappeared in the wild.

FAUNA

The most prominent urban birds are pigeons, doves, red-crested cardinals and common mynas. The myna, introduced from India, is a brown, spectacled bird that congregates in noisy flocks, walks rather than hops, and is plentiful even around hotels.

For those who get into the woods, Oahu has a few native forest birds worth seeking out. The *elepaio*, a brownish bird with a white rump, and the *amakihi*, a small yellow green bird, are the most common endemic forest birds on Oahu. The *apapane*, a vivid red honeycreeper, and the *iiwi*, a bright vermilion bird, are less common.

Most of the islets off Oahu's windward coast are sanctuaries for seabirds, including terns, noddies, shearwaters, Laysan albatrosses, tropicbirds, boobies and frigate birds. Moku Manu ('Bird Island') off Mokapu Peninsula has the greatest variety of species. (Because the nesting birds on Moku Manu are sensitive to human disturbance, visitors are not allowed on the island.)

Oahu has an endemic genus of tree snail, the achatinella. In former days the forests were loaded with these colorful snails, which clung like gems to the leaves of trees. They were too attractive for their own good, however, and hikers collected them by the handfuls around the turn of the century. Even more devastating has been the deforestation of habitat and the introduction of a cannibal snail and predatory rodents. Of 41 achatinella species, only 19 remain and all are endangered.

Oahu has wild pigs and goats in its mountain valleys. A more interesting introduced species is the brush-tailed rock wallaby, accidentally released in 1916 and now residing in the Kalihi Valley, north of Honolulu. Although rarely seen, the wallabies are of keen interest to zoologists because they may be the last members of a subspecies that's now extinct in their native Australia.

Hawaii has a rich and varied marine life. Almost 700 fish species live in Hawaiian waters, with nearly one-third of those found nowhere else in the world. Oahu's near-shore waters harbor large rainbow-colored parrotfish, some 20 different kinds of butterfly fish, numerous varieties of wrasses, bright yellow tangs, odd-shaped filefish and ballooning pufferfish, just to list a few. There are also green sea turtles, manta rays and moray eels.

Several types of whales frequent Hawaiian waters, though it is the migrating humpback, with its acrobatic breaches and tail flips, that everyone wants to see. Luckily for whale watchers, humpback whales are coast-huggers, preferring waters with depths of less than 600 feet. They can sometimes be seen in winter from the beaches along Oahu's west coast. Other migratory whales in Hawaiian waters include the fin whale, minke whale and right whale; all are baleen whales.

Hawaii's year-round resident whales, which are all toothed whales, include the sperm whale, false killer whale, pigmy killer whale, beaked whale, melon-head whale and, most common of all, the pilot whale. The latter is a small whale that often travels in large pods and, like most whales, prefers deep offshore waters.

Numerous dolphins – including spinner, bottlenose, slender-beaked, spotted, striped and rough-toothed varieties – are found in the waters around Hawaii. One of the rarest marine creatures is the Hawaiian monk seal, so named for the cowl-like fold of skin at its neck and for its solitary habits. It exists only in Hawaii, with about 1000 seals remaining. Although their prime habitat is the uninhabited Northwestern Hawaiian Islands, monk seals do occasionally haul up on Oahu's more remote northwest beaches, near Kaena Point.

GOVERNMENT & POLITICS

Honolulu is the capital of the state of Hawaii and the administrative center for the island of Oahu.

For local administration, Hawaii is divided into four county governments. Unlike the mainland states, Hawaii has no separate municipal governments, so the counties provide services, such as police and fire protection, that elsewhere in the USA are usually assigned to cities.

The City & County of Honolulu is the unwieldy name attached to the single political entity governing all of Oahu. It is administered by a mayor and a nine-member council, elected for four-year terms.

ECONOMY

Oahu has a 5% unemployment rate. Tourism is the largest sector of the economy, accounting for about 30% of Oahu's jobs. It's followed by defense and other government employment which together account for 22% of all jobs.

Nearly one-fifth of Oahu is still used for agricultural purposes, mostly for growing pineapples. Sugar production, no longer profitable on Oahu, was phased out entirely in 1996.

POPULATION & PEOPLE

Honolulu is home to nearly 400,000 people, which is about a third of the population of the entire state of Hawaii.

There is no ethnic majority – everyone belongs to a minority. Honolulu's ethnic breakdown is 24% Caucasian, 21% Japanese, 17% mixed ancestry other than part-Hawaiian, 16% part-Hawaiian (less than 1% pure Hawaiian), 7% Filipino and 6% Chinese, with numerous other Pacific and Asian minorities.

Hawaii's people are known for their racial harmony. Race is generally not a factor in marriage. On average, islanders have a 50/50 chance of marrying someone of a race different than their own and the majority of children born in Hawaii are *hapa*, or of mixed blood.

ARTS
Hula

Perhaps no art form is more uniquely Hawaiian than the hula. There are many different schools of hula, all very disciplined and graceful in their movements.

Most ancient hula dances expressed historical events, legendary tales and the accomplishments of the great alii. Facial expressions, hand gestures, hip sway and dance steps all conveyed the story. They were performed to rhythmic chants and drum beatings, serving to connect with the world of spirits. Eye movement was very important; if the story was about the sun the eyes would gaze upward, if about the netherworld they would gaze downward.

One school, the *hula ohelo*, was very sensual, with movements suggesting the act of procreation.

Hula dancers wore tapa cloth – not grass skirts, which were introduced from Micronesia only a hundred years ago.

The Christian missionaries found the hula too licentious and suppressed it. The hula might have been lost forever if not for King David Kalakaua, the 'Merrie Monarch,' who revived it in the latter half of the 19th century.

Hula *halaus* (schools) have experienced an influx of new students in recent years. Some practice in public places, such as school grounds and parks, where visitors are welcome to watch. Although many of the halaus rely on tuition fees, others receive sponsorship from hotels or shopping centers and give weekly public performances in return.

There are also numerous island-wide hula competitions, one of the biggest being the Prince Lot Hula Festival held each July at the Moanalua Gardens.

Music

Contemporary Hawaiian music gives center stage to the guitar, most prominently the steel guitar, an instrument designed in 1889 by Joseph Kekuku, a native Hawaiian. The steel guitar is one of only two major musical instruments invented in what is now the USA. (The other is the banjo.) The steel guitar is usually played with slack-key tunings and carries the melody throughout the song.

The ukulele, so strongly identified with Hawaiian music, was actually derived from the braginha, a Portuguese instrument introduced to Hawaii in the 1800s. The word 'ukulele' is Hawaiian for 'jumping flea.'

Both the ukulele and the steel guitar were essential to the light-hearted, romantic music popularized in Hawaii from the 1930s to the 1950s. *My Little Grass Shack, Lovely Hula Hands* and *Sweet Leilani* are classic examples. Due in part to the 'Hawaii Calls' radio show, which for more than 30 years was broadcast worldwide from the Moana Hotel in Waikiki, this music became instantly recognizable as Hawaiian, conjuring up images of beautiful hula dancers swaying under palm trees in a tropical paradise.

Some of Hawaii's more renowned slack-key guitar players include Raymond Kane, Peter Moon and Atta Isaacs Jr, and the late Gabby Pahinui and Sonny Chillingworth.

One of the more current sounds in Hawaii is Jawaiian, a blending of Hawaiian music and Jamaican reggae. Some of the better-known island musicians who incorporate Jawaiian elements include Bruddah Waltah and Hoaikane. Other popular contemporary Hawaiian musicians include soulful vocalist-composer Henry Kapono; Hapa, the duo of Kelii Kanealii and Barry Flanagan, who fuse folk, rock and traditional Hawaiian elements; and the Hawaiian Style Band, who merge Hawaiian influences with rock.

The hottest recording star of the day is Kealii Reichel, a charismatic vocalist and hula dancer who sings Hawaiian ballads, love songs and poetic chants.

Painting & Sculpture

Many artists draw inspiration from Hawaii's rich cultural heritage and natural beauty.

Well-known Hawaiian painter Herb Kawainui Kane creates detailed oil paintings that focus on the early Polynesian settlers and King Kamehameha's life. His works are mainly on display in museums and at gallery collections in resorts.

Another notable native Hawaiian artist is Rocky Kaiouliokahihikoloehu Jensen, who does wood sculptures and drawings of Hawaiian gods, ancient chiefs and early Hawaiians with the aim of creating sacred art in the tradition of *makaku*, or 'creative artistic mana.'

Honolulu artist Pegge Hopper paints traditional Hawaiian women in relaxed poses using a distinctive graphic design style and bright washes of color. Her work has been widely reproduced on posters and postcards.

Traditional Musical Instruments

The *pahu hula*, a knee drum carved from a breadfruit or coconut log, with a sharkskin drum head, was traditionally used solely at hula performances. Other hula musical instruments include *ke laau* sticks, used to keep the beat for the dancers; *iliili*, stone castanets; *puili*, rattles made from split bamboo; and *uliuli*, gourd rattles decorated with colorful feathers.

The early Hawaiians were a romantic lot. Instruments used for courting included the *ohe*, a nose flute made of bamboo, and the *ukeke*, a musical bow with a couple of strings. ∎

Crafts

Some of Hawaii's most impressive crafts are ceramics, particularly raku work, a style of Japanese earthenware; bowls made of native woods, such as koa and milo; and baskets woven of native fibers.

Hawaiian quilting is another unique art form. The concept of patchwork quilting was introduced by the early missionaries, but the Hawaiians, who had only recently taken to Western cotton clothing, didn't have a surplus of cloth scraps – and the idea of cutting up new lengths of fabric simply to sew them back together again in small squares seemed absurd. Instead, the Hawaiian women created their own designs using larger cloth pieces, typically with stylized tropical flora on a white background.

A more transitory art form is the creation of leis. Although the type of leis most widely worn by visitors are made of fragrant flowers such as plumeria and tuberose, traditional leis (garlands) of mokihana berries and maile leaves were more commonly worn in old Hawaii. Both types are still made today.

Ancient Crafts

Tapa Weaving In ancient Hawaii, women spent much of their time beating *kapa* (tapa cloth) or preparing *lauhala* for weaving.

Tapa made from the *wauke* (paper mulberry tree) was the favorite. The bark was carefully stripped, then pounded with wooden beaters. The beaters were carved with different patterns, which then became the pattern of the tapa. Dyes were made from charcoal, flowers and sea urchins.

Tapa had many uses in addition to clothing, from food containers to burial shrouds. After the missionaries introduced cotton cloth and Western clothing, the art of tapa making slowly faded away. These days most of the tapa for sale in Hawaii is from Samoa and has bold designs. Hawaiian tapa was different, with more delicate patterns.

Lauhala Weaving Lauhala weaving uses the *lau* (leaves) of the *hala* (pandanus) tree. Preparing the leaves for weaving is hard, messy work as there are razor-sharp spines along the leaf edges and down the center.

In old Hawaii, lauhala was woven into mats and floor coverings, but these days smaller items like hats, placemats and baskets are most common.

Wooden Bowls The Hawaiians had no pottery and made their containers using either gourds or wood. Wooden food bowls were mostly of kou or milo, two native woods which didn't leave unpleasant tastes.

Hawaiian bowls were free of designs and carvings. Their beauty lay in the natural qualities of the wood and in the shape of the bowl alone. Cracked bowls were often expertly patched with dovetailed pieces of wood. Rather than decrease the value of the bowl, patching suggested heirloom status and such bowls were amongst the mostly highly prized.

Featherwork & Leis The Hawaiians were known for their elaborate featherwork. The most impressive items were the capes worn by chiefs and kings. The longer the cape, the higher the rank. Those made of the yellow feathers of the now extinct *mamo* bird were the most highly prized.

The mamo was a predominately black bird with a yellow upper tail. An estimated 80,000 mamo birds were caught to create the cape that King Kamehameha wore. It's said that bird catchers would capture the birds, pluck the desired feathers and release them unharmed. Feathers were also used to make helmets and leis.

The *lei palaoa*, a necklace traditionally worn by Hawaiian royalty, was made of finely braided human hair hung with a smoothly carved whale tooth pendant shaped like a curved tongue. ■

Literature

A Hawaiian Reader, edited by A Grove Day & Carl Stroven (Mutual Publishing, Honolulu, 1959), is an excellent anthology with 37 selections, both fiction and nonfiction. It starts with a log entry by Captain James Cook and includes writings from early missionaries as well as Mark Twain, Jack London, Somerset Maugham, David Malo, Isabella Bird, Martha Beckwith and others. If you only have time to read one book about Hawaii this inexpensive paperback is a great choice.

OA Bushnell is one of Hawaii's best-known contemporary authors. The University of Hawaii Press has published his titles

The Return of Lono (1971), a historical novel of Captain Cook's final voyage; *Kaaawa* (1972), about Hawaii in the 1850s; *The Stone of Kannon* (1979), about the first group of Japanese contract laborers to arrive in Hawaii, and its sequel *The Water of Kane* (1980).

Stories of Hawaii (Mutual Publishing, Honolulu, 1990) is a collection of 13 of Jack London's yarns about the islands.

Talking to the Dead by Sylvia Watanabe (Doubleday & Company, New York, 1992) is an enjoyable read that portrays a sense of growing up as a second-generation Japanese-American in post-war Honolulu.

SOCIETY & CULTURE

In many ways, contemporary culture in Hawaii resembles contemporary culture in the rest of the USA.

Hawaiians listen to the same pop music and watch the same TV shows as Americans on the mainland. Honolulu has discos and ballroom dancing, rock bands and classical orchestras, junk food and nouvelle cuisine. The wonderful thing about Hawaii, however, is that the mainland influences largely stand beside, rather than engulf, the culture of the islands.

Not only is traditional Hawaiian culture an integral part of the social fabric, but so are the customs of the ethnically diverse immigrants who have made the islands their home. Honolulu is more than just a meeting place of East and West; it's also a place where the cultures merge, typically in a manner that brings out the best of both worlds.

The 1970s saw the start of a Hawaiian cultural renaissance that continues today. Hawaiian language classes are thriving and there is a concerted effort to reintroduce Hawaiian words into modern speech. Hula classes are concentrating more on the nuances behind hand movements and facial expressions than on the dramatic hip-shaking that sells dance shows. Many Hawaiian artists and craftspeople are returning to traditional mediums and themes.

Certainly the tourist centers have long been overrun with packaged Hawaiiana, from plastic leis to theme-park luaus, that seems almost a parody of island culture. But fortunately for the visitor the growing interest in traditional Hawaiiana is having an impact on the tourist industry and authentic performances by hula students and contemporary Hawaiian musicians are increasingly easier to find.

RELIGION

Honolulu's population is religiously diverse. In addition to the standard Christian denominations, the city has numerous Buddhist temples and Shinto shrines. There are also Hindu, Taoist, Tenrikyo, Jewish and Muslim houses of worship.

Christianity has the largest following, with Catholicism being the predominant religious denomination. Interestingly, the United Church of Christ, which includes the Congregationalists who initially converted the islands, now claim only about half as many members as the Mormons and one-tenth as many as the Catholics.

LANGUAGE

The main language of Hawaii is English, although it's liberally peppered with Hawaiian phrases, loan words from the various immigrant languages and pidgin slang. However, it's not uncommon to hear islanders speaking in other languages, as the first language in one out of every four Hawaiian homes is a tongue other than English.

The Hawaiian language itself is still spoken among family members by about 9000 people, and Hawaiian is, along with English, an official state language.

Closely related to other Polynesian languages, Hawaiian is melodic, phonetically simple and full of vowels and repeated syllables.

Some 85% of all place names in Hawaii are in Hawaiian and often have interesting translations and stories behind them.

The Hawaiians had no written language until the 1820s when Christian missionaries arrived and wrote down the spoken language in roman letters.

Pronunciation

The written Hawaiian language has just 12 letters. Pronunciation is easy and there are few consonant clusters.

Vowel sounds are about the same as in Spanish or Japanese, more or less like this:

a ah, as in 'father' or uh, as in 'above'
e ay, as in 'gay' or eh, as in 'pet'
i ee, as in 'see'
o oh, as in 'go'
u oo, as in 'noon'

Hawaiian has diphthongs, created when two vowels join together to form a single sound. The stress is on the first vowel, although in general if you pronounce each vowel separately, you'll be easily understood.

The consonant *w* is usually pronounced like a soft English *v* when it follows the letters *i* and *e* (the town Haleiwa is pronounced Haleiva) and like the English *w* when it follows *u* or *o*. When *w* follows *a* it can be pronounced either *v* or *w* – thus you will hear both Hawaii and Havaii.

The other consonants – h, k, l, m, n, p – are pronounced about the same as in English.

Glottal Stops & Macrons

Written Hawaiian uses both glottal stops and macrons, although in modern print they are often omitted.

The glottal stop (') indicates a break between two vowels producing an effect similar to saying 'oh-oh' in English. A macron, a short straight line over a vowel, stresses the vowel.

Glottal stops and macrons not only affect pronunciation, but can give a word a completely different meaning. For example *ai* can mean 'sexual intercourse' or 'to eat,' depending on the pronunciation.

All this takes on greater significance when you learn to speak Hawaiian in depth. If you're using Hawaiian words in an English-language context ('this *poi* is *ono*'), there shouldn't be much problem.

Compounds

Hawaiian may seem more difficult than it is because many proper names are long and look similar. Many begin with *ka*, meaning 'the,' which over time simply became attached to the beginning of the word.

When you break each word down into its composite parts, some of which are repeated, it all becomes much easier. For example: *Kamehameha* consists of the three components Ka-meha-meha. *Humuhumunukunukuapuaa*, which is Hawaii's state fish, is broken down into humu-humu-nuku-nuku-a-pu-a-a.

Some words are doubled to emphasize their meaning. For example: *wiki* means 'quick,' while *wikiwiki* means 'very quick.'

There are some easily recognizable compounds repeatedly found in place names and it can be fun to learn a few. For instance, *wai* means 'freshwater' – Waikiki means 'spouting water,' so named for the freshwater springs that were once there. *Kai* means 'seawater' – Kailua means 'two seas.' *Lani* means 'heavenly' – Lanikai means 'heavenly sea.' *Hana* means 'bay' – Hanalei means 'crescent bay.'

Common Hawaiian

Learn these words first: *aloha* and *mahalo*, which are everyday pleasantries; *makai* and *mauka*, commonly used in giving directions; and *kane* and *wahine*, often on toilet doors.

aikane – friend

aina – land

akamai – clever

alii – chief, royalty

aloha – love, welcome, goodbye

aloha aina – love of the land

hale – house

hana – work; or bay, a compound in place names

haole – Caucasian

hapa – half; or person of mixed blood

hapa haole – half-white, used for a person, thing or idea

Hauoli Makahiki Hou – Happy New Year

heiau – ancient Hawaiian temple

holoholo – to walk, drive or ramble around for pleasure

holoku – a long dress similar to the muumuu, but more fitted and with a yoke at the shoulders

hui – group, organization

hula – traditional Hawaiian dance

imu – underground earthen oven used in traditional luau cooking

kahuna – wise person in any field, commonly a priest, healer or sorcerer

kalua – traditional method of baking in an underground oven

kamaaina – native-born Hawaiian or a long-time resident; literally 'child of the land'

kane – man

kapu – taboo, part of strict ancient Hawaiian social system; today often used on signs meaning 'Keep Out'

kaukau – food

keiki – child, children

koa – native hardwood tree often used in woodworking

kokua – help, cooperation; 'Please Kokua' on a trash can is a gentle way of saying 'don't litter'

kona – leeward, or a leeward wind

lanai – veranda

lauhala – leaves of the hala plant used in weaving

lei – garland, usually of flowers, but also of leaves or shells

lilikoi – passion fruit

lolo – stupid, crazy

lomilomi – massage

luau – traditional Hawaiian feast

mahalo – thank you

makai – towards the sea

malihini – newcomer, visitor

manini – convict tang (a reef fish); also used to refer to something small or insignificant

mano – shark

mauka – towards the mountains, inland

mele – song, chant

Mele Kalikimaka – Merry Christmas

muumuu – long, loose-fitting dress introduced by the missionaries

nene – Hawaii's state bird, a native goose

ohana – family, extended family

ono – delicious; also the name of the wahoo fish

pakalolo – marijuana; literally 'crazy smoke'

pali – cliff

paniolo – Hawaiian cowboy

pau – finished, no more; *pau hana* means quitting time

puka – any kind of hole or opening

pupu – snack food, hors d'oeuvres; shells

tutu – aunt, older woman

ukulele – stringed musical instrument

wahine – woman

wikiwiki – hurry, quick

Pidgin

Hawaii's early immigrants communicated with each other in pidgin, a simplified, broken form of English. It was a language born of necessity, stripped of all but the most needed words.

Modern pidgin is better defined as local slang. It is extensive, lively and ever-changing. Whole conversations can take place in pidgin, or often just a word or two is dropped into a more conventional English sentence.

Even Shakespeare's *Twelfth Night* has been translated (by local comedian James Grant Benton) to *Twelf Nite O Wateva*. Malvolio's line 'My masters, are you mad?' becomes 'You buggahs crazy, o wat?'

Shaka Sign
Islanders greet each other with the shaka sign, which is made by folding down the three middle fingers to the palm and extending the thumb and little finger. The hand is then usually held out and shaken in greeting. It's as common as waving. ■

Short-term visitors will rarely win friends by trying to speak pidgin. It's more like an insider's code that you're allowed to use only after you've lived in Hawaii long enough to understand the nuances.

Some characteristics of pidgin include: a fast staccato rhythm, two-word sentences, dropping the soft 'h' sound from words that start with 'th,' use of loan words from many languages (often Hawaiian) and double meanings that trip up the uninitiated.

Some of the more common words and expressions:

blalah – big Hawaiian fellow

brah – brother, friend; also used for 'hey you'

broke da mouth – delicious

buggah – guy

chicken skin – goose bumps

coconut wireless – word of mouth

cockaroach – steal

da kine - that kind of thing, whatchamacallit etc; used whenever you can't think of the word you want but you know the listener knows what you mean

geev em – go for it, beat them

grinds – food, eat; *ono grinds* is good food.

haolefied – become like a *haole*

how you stay? – how are you?

howzit? – hi, how's it going?

humbug – a real hassle

like beef? – wanna fight?

mo' bettah – much better, the best

slippahs – flip-flops, thongs

stick – surfboard

stink eye – dirty look, evil eye

talk story – any kind of conversation, gossip, tales

tanks – thanks; more commonly *tanks brah*.

tree – three

Facts for the Visitor

WHEN TO GO

Honolulu is a great place to visit any time of the year.

Although the busiest tourist season is in winter, that has more to do with weather *elsewhere*, as many visitors are snowbirds escaping cold winters back home. Essentially the weather in Honolulu is agreeable all year round. It's a bit rainier in the winter and a bit hotter in the summer but there are no extremes as cooling trade winds modify the heat throughout the year.

In terms of cost, spring through fall can be a bargain, as many hotels drop prices significantly around the first of April and most don't climb back up again until mid-December.

Naturally, for certain activities there are peak seasons. For instance, if you want to go board surfing, you'll find the biggest waves in winter, whereas if you're a windsurfer you'll find the best wind conditions in summer.

WHAT TO BRING

Honolulu has balmy weather and a casual attitude towards dress so, for the most part, packing is a breeze.

It's essentially summer all year round. For tourist activities, shorts, sandals and a cotton shirt are the standard day dress. A light jacket or sweater will be the warmest clothing you'll need.

Pack light. You can always pick up something with a floral Hawaiian print when you get there and dress island style.

An aloha shirt and lightweight slacks for men, and a cotton dress for women, is pretty much regarded as 'dressing up' in Hawaii. Only a few of the most exclusive restaurants require anything dressier.

If you have plans for excursions to the Neighbor Islands, note that both Maui and the Big Island have cool 'upcountry' areas that can get quite nippy and warrant an extra layer of clothing.

If you plan on camping on Oahu, public campgrounds require tents (and because of mosquitoes they're a good idea anyway), but you won't need anything more than the lightest sleeping bag. If you don't want to pack camping gear, it can be rented in Honolulu.

You won't regret bringing binoculars for watching dolphins, whales and birds. We always carry a snorkel, mask and fins, but you can also buy or rent them in Honolulu. Actually, you don't need to worry too much about what to bring, as just about anything you forget to pack you can easily buy in Honolulu.

ORIENTATION

Visitors to Oahu land at Honolulu International Airport, the only civilian airport on the island. It's at the outskirts of Honolulu, nine miles west of Waikiki.

H-1, the main south shore freeway, passes from east to west through Honolulu, connecting the airport with the rest of the city. All other freeways on the island connect to H-1. Rush-hour traffic is heavy heading towards Honolulu in the mornings and away from it in the evenings.

By the way, H-1 is a US *interstate* freeway – an amusing designation for a road on an island state in the middle of the Pacific.

Directions on Oahu are often given by using landmarks. If someone tells you to go 'Ewa' (a land area west of Honolulu) or 'Diamond Head' (east of Waikiki) it simply means to head in that direction. Two other commonly used directional terms that you can expect to hear are *mauka*, meaning inland side, and *makai*, meaning ocean side.

Maps

Simple island maps can be found in the ubiquitous free tourist magazines, but if you're going to be renting a car and doing any exploring at all it's worth picking up a good road map, especially for navigating around Honolulu.

Detailed Gousha road maps (which are recommended as they show numbered highway exits) and Rand McNally road maps are sold in stores around Honolulu for a couple of dollars. Members of AAA or an affiliated automobile club can get a free Gousha road map from the AAA office, 590 Queen St, Honolulu. Most comprehensive – but more detailed than most visitors will need – is the 150-page *Bryan's Sectional Maps Oahu* atlas, which shows, names and indexes virtually every street on the island.

The University of Hawaii (UH) Press publishes a relief map of Oahu which not only covers roads but also beaches, historical sites and major hiking trails. This map costs $4 and is available in bookstores and shops frequented by tourists.

The United States Geological Survey (USGS) publishes topographical maps of Oahu (and the rest of Hawaii), both as full-island and detailed sectional maps. Maps can be ordered by mail from the US Geological Survey, Box 25286 Denver Federal Center, Denver, CO 80225. Prices per map range from $2.50 to $4.

In Honolulu, USGS maps can be purchased at the Pacific Map Center (☎ 545-3600), 560 N Nimitz Hwy, Suite 206A.

TOURIST OFFICES

The Hawaii Visitors Bureau (HVB) provides free tourist information on all of Hawaii. On request they'll mail out a little packet containing general information and booklets listing member hotels and restaurants.

Local Tourist Offices

The administrative office of the HVB (☎ 923-1811, fax 922-8991), which is in Waikiki at 2270 Kalakaua Ave, Suite 801, Honolulu, HI 96815, can mail out general tourist information on Oahu and the rest of the state.

To order brochures from the US mainland, contact the HVB office (☎ 415-248-3800, 800-353-5846; fax 415-248-3808) at 180 Montgomery St, Suite 2360, San Francisco, CA 94104.

To pick up tourist brochures in person, go to the HVB's visitor information office (☎ 924-0266) in the Royal Hawaiian Shopping Center (Hibiscus Court, 4th floor) in Waikiki.

Tourist Offices Abroad

For some odd reason, the Hawaii Visitors Bureau frequently changes its overseas agents. The current addresses for HVB representatives abroad are:

Canada
c/o Comprehensive Travel Industry Services
1260 Hornby St, Suite 104
Vancouver, BC V6Z 1W2
(☎ 604-669-6691, fax 604-683-9114)

Germany
c/o American Venture Marketing
Siemen Strausse 9, 63263 Neu Isenburg
(☎ 061-02-722-411, fax 061-02-722-409)

Japan
Kokusai Building, 2nd Floor
1-1 Marunouchi 3-chome
Chiyoda-ku, Tokyo 100
(☎ 03-3201-0430, fax 03-3201-0433)

Korea
c/o Travel Press
10th Floor, Samwon Building
112-5 Sokong-Dong, Chung-ku, Seoul
(☎ 02-773-6719, fax 02-757-6783)

Malaysia
c/o Pacific World Travel
2.5 & 2.6 Angkasa Raya Building
Jalan Ampang, Kuala Lumpur 50450
(☎ 03-244-8449, fax 03-242-1129)

New Zealand
c/o Walshes World, Dingwall Building
87 Queen St, 2nd Floor, Auckland
(☎ 09-379-3708, fax 09-309-0725)

Taiwan
c/o Federal Transportation Company
8th Floor, 61 Nanking East Rd
Section 3, Taipei
(☎ 02-506-7043, fax 02-507-5816)

Thailand
c/o ADAT Sales, 8th Floor
Maneeya Center Building
518/5 Ploenchit Rd, Bangkok
(☎ 02-255-6840, fax 02-254-1271)

UK
Box 208, Sunbury on Thames
Middlesex TW16 5RJ
(☎ 0181-941-4009, fax 0181-941-4011)

DOCUMENTS

All visitors, including Americans, should keep in mind that US airlines now require travelers to present a photo ID as part of the airline check-in procedure.

All foreign visitors, other than Canadians, must bring their passport. US and Canadian citizens may want to bring along a passport as well, in the event they get tempted to extend their travels beyond Hawaii. All visitors should bring their driver's license and any health insurance or travel insurance cards.

Members of Hostelling International (HI) will be able to take advantage of lower hostel rates by bringing their membership cards. Members of the American Automobile Association (AAA) or other affiliated automobile club can get some car rental and sightseeing admission discounts with their membership cards. Divers should bring their certification cards.

It's a good idea to make photocopies of all your travel documents, including airline tickets and your passport. Keep the copies separate from the originals.

Passports & Visas

The conditions for entering Hawaii are the same as for entering any other state in the USA.

Canadians must have proper proof of Canadian citizenship, such as a citizenship card with photo ID or a passport. Visitors from other countries must have a valid passport and most visitors are also required to have a US visa.

However there is a reciprocal visa-waiver program in which citizens of certain countries may enter the USA for stays of 90 days or less without first obtaining a US visa. Currently these countries are: Andorra, Argentina, Australia, Austria, Belgium, Brunei, Denmark, Finland, France, Germany, Iceland, Ireland, Italy, Japan, Liechtenstein, Luxembourg, Monaco, the Netherlands, New Zealand, Norway, San Marino, Spain, Sweden, Switzerland and the UK. Under this program you must have a roundtrip ticket that is nonrefundable in the USA and you will not be allowed to extend your stay beyond the 90 days.

Other travelers will need to obtain a visa from a US consulate or embassy. In most countries the process can be done by mail.

Your passport should be valid for at least six months longer than your intended stay in the USA and you'll need to submit a recent photo (37 x 37 mm) with the application. Documents of financial stability and/or guarantees from a US resident are sometimes required, particularly for those from Third World countries.

Visa applicants may be required to 'demonstrate binding obligations' that will ensure their return back home. Because of this requirement, those planning to travel through other countries before arriving in the USA are generally better off applying for their US visa while they are still in their home country – rather than while on the road.

The validity period for US visitor visas depends on what country you're from. The length of time you'll be allowed to stay in the USA is ultimately determined by US immigration authorities at the port of entry.

Visa Extensions If you want, need or hope to stay in the USA longer than the date stamped on your passport, go to the local Immigration & Naturalization Service (INS) office (☎ 532-3721), 595 Ala Moana Blvd, Honolulu.

CUSTOMS

US Customs allows each person over the age of 21 to bring one quart of liquor and 200 cigarettes duty-free into the USA. Most fresh fruits and plants are restricted from entry into Hawaii and there's a strict quarantine on animals.

MONEY

There are nine banks with nearly 150 branches on Oahu. The Bank of Hawaii, Hawaii's largest bank, has a branch at the airport and at 2220 Kalakaua Ave in Waikiki. Waikiki also has a Bank of America at 321 Seaside Ave and a First Hawaiian Bank at 2181 Kalakaua Ave.

EMBASSIES & CONSULATES
US Embassies Abroad

There are numerous US embassies and consulates around the world, including the following embassies:

Australia
Moonah Place
Yarralumla, Canberra
ACT 2600
(☎ 02-6270-5000)

Belgium
27 Boulevard
du Regent
B-1000 Brussels
(☎ 2-513-3830)

Canada
PO Box 5000
100 Wellington St
Ottawa, Ontario
K1P 5T1
(☎ 613-238-5335)

Denmark
Dag Hammarskjolds
Allé 24
2100 Copenhagen 0
(☎ 31-42-31-44)

**Federated States
of Micronesia**
PO Box 1286
Pohnpei, FSM 96941
(☎ 320-2187)

Finland
Itainen Puistotie 14A
Helsinki 00140
(☎ 171931)

France
2 Avenue Gabriel
75382 Paris Cedex 08
(☎ 01.43.12.22.22)

Germany
Deichmanns Aue 29
53170 Bonn
(☎ 228-3391)

Hong Kong
26 Garden Rd
Hong Kong
(☎ 523-9011)

Indonesia
Medan Merdeka
Selatan 5, Jakarta
(☎ 360-360)

Ireland
42 Elgin Rd
Ballsbridge, Dublin
(☎ 668-7122)

Israel
71 Hayarkon St
Tel Aviv
(☎ 517-4338)

Italy
Via Veneto 119/A
00187 Rome
(☎ 6-46741)

Japan
10-5, Akasaka
1-chome
Minato-ku, Tokyo
(☎ 3-224-5000)

Korea
82 Sejong-Ro
Chongro-ku, Seoul
(☎ 397-4114)

Malaysia
376 Jalan Tun Razak
50400 Kuala Lumpur
(☎ 248-9011)

Mexico
Paseo de
la Reforma 305
Colonia Cuauhtemoc
06500 Mexico
Distrito Federal
(☎ 5-211-0042)

Netherlands
Lange Voorhout 102
2514 EJ The Hague
(☎ 70-310-9209)

New Zealand
29 Fitzherbert Terrace
PO Box 1190
Thorndon, Wellington
(☎ 4-472-2068)

Norway
Drammensveien 18
0244 Oslo 2
(☎ 22 44 85 50)

Philippines
1201 Roxas Blvd
Ermita Manila 1000
(☎ 632-521-7116)

Singapore
30 Hill St
Singapore 0617
(☎ 65-338-0251)

Sweden
Strandvagen 101
S-115 89 Stockholm
(☎ 08-783-5300)

Switzerland
Jubilaeumstrasse 93
3005 Bern
(☎ 31-357-7011)

Thailand
95 Wireless Rd
Bangkok
(☎ 2-252-5040)

UK
24/31 Grosvenor
Square
London W1A 1AE
(☎ 0171-499-9000)

Western Samoa
5th Floor, Beach Rd
Box 3430, Apia
(☎ 21-631)

Hawaii's largest bank, has a branch at the airport and at 2220 Kalakaua Ave in Waikiki. Waikiki also has a Bank of America at 321 Seaside Ave and a First Hawaiian Bank at 2181 Kalakaua Ave. Elsewhere around Honolulu, banks can easily be found in central areas and in shopping centers.

Traveler's Checks

Foreign travelers will find it easier if their traveler's checks are already in US dollars, but major currencies can be exchanged at Honolulu International Airport and larger banks.

Restaurants, hotels and most stores accept US dollar traveler's checks as if they're cash, so if you're carrying travel-er's checks in US dollars, you won't have to use a bank or pay exchange fees.

Credit Cards

Major credit and charge cards are widely accepted throughout Honolulu, including at car rental agencies and nearly all hotels, restaurants, gas stations, shops and larger grocery stores. Most recreational and tourist activities can also be paid for by credit card. The most commonly accepted cards are Visa, MasterCard and American Express, although JCB, Discover and Diners Club cards are also accepted by a fair number of businesses.

ATMs

Automatic teller machines (ATMs) are

Foreign Consulates in Honolulu

Honolulu hosts the following consulates and government liaison offices:

American Samoa
American Samoa
Office-Hawaii
401 Waiakamilo Rd
(☎ 847-1998)

Australia
Consulate-General
of Australia
1000 Bishop St
(☎ 524-5050)

Austria
Consulate of Austria
1314 S King St
Suite 1260
(☎ 923-8585)

Belgium
Consulate of Belgium
745 Fort St Mall
18th Floor
(☎ 533-6900)

Brazil
Consulate of Brazil
44-166 Nanamoana
(☎ 235-0571)

Denmark
Consulate of
Denmark
1001 Bishop St
Suite 2626
(☎ 545-2028)

**Federated States
of Micronesia**
Federated States of
Micronesia Office
3049 Ualena
Suite 408
(☎ 836-4775)

France
Consulate-General
of France
2 Waterfront Plaza
Suite 300
(☎ 599-4458)

Germany
Consulate of
Germany
2003 Kalia Rd
Suite 1I
(☎ 946-3819)

India
Consulate-General
of India
2051 Young St
(☎ 947-2618)

Italy
Consulate of Italy
737 Bishop St
Suite 201
(☎ 531-2277)

Japan
Consulate-General
of Japan
1742 Nuuanu Ave
(☎ 523-7495)

Kiribati
Consulate of the
Republic of Kiribati
850 Richards St
Suite 503
(☎ 521-7703)

Korea
Consulate-General
of Korea
2756 Pali Hwy
(☎ 595-6109)

Mariana Islands
Marianas Hawaii
Liaison Office
1221 Kapiolani Blvd
Suite 730
(☎ 592-0300)

Marshall Islands
Republic of the
Marshall Islands
Office
1888 Lusitana
Suite 301
(☎ 545-7767)

Netherlands
Consulate of the

Netherlands
345 Queen St
Suite 600
(☎ 537-1100)

Norway
Consulate of Norway
1585 Kapiolani Blvd
Suite 728
(☎ 949-6565)

Philippines
Consulate-General
of the Philippines
2433 Pali Hwy
(☎ 595-6316)

Sweden
Consulate of Sweden
737 Bishop St
Suite 2600
(☎ 528-4777)

Switzerland
Consulate of
Switzerland
4231 Papu Circle
(☎ 737-5297)

Thailand
Royal Thai
Consulate-General
287A Kalihi
(☎ 845-7332)

Tonga
Tonga Consular
Agency
220 S King St
Suite 1230
(☎ 521-5149)

charge usually works out cheaper than the 1% fee commonly charged for traveler's checks – inquire at your local bank before your trip.

Major banks such as Bank of Hawaii (Bankoh for short), First Hawaiian Bank and Bank of America have extensive ATM networks throughout Honolulu that will give cash advances on major credit cards (including MasterCard, Visa, American Express, Discover and JCB) and allow cash withdrawals with affiliated ATM cards. Most ATM machines in Hawaii accept bank cards from both the Plus and Cirrus systems, the two largest ATM networks in the USA.

In addition to traditional bank locations, you can also find ATMs at most grocery stores, mall-style shopping centers and some 7-Eleven convenience stores.

Currency

As is true throughout the USA, US dollars are the only accepted currency in Hawaii.

The US dollar ($) is divided into 100 cents (¢). Coins come in denominations of one cent (penny), five cents (nickel), 10 cents (dime), 25 cents (quarter) and 50 cents (half dollar). Notes come in one, five, 10, 20, 50 and 100 dollar denominations. There is also a one dollar coin that the government has tried unsuccessfully to bring into mass circulation and a two dollar note that is out of favor but still occasionally seen.

Currency Exchange

Foreign currency can be exchanged at Honolulu International Airport and at larger banks.

At press time, exchange rates were:

Australia	A$1	=	US$0.78
Canada	C$1	=	US$0.74
France	FF1	=	US$0.19
Germany	DM1	=	US$0.63
Hong Kong	HK$1	=	US$0.13
Japan	¥100	=	US$0.86
New Zealand	NZ$1	=	US$0.70
UK	UK£1	=	US$1.67

Costs

How much money you need for visiting Honolulu depends on your traveling style. Some people get by quite cheaply while others rack up huge balances on their credit cards.

Airfare to Hawaii is usually one of the heftier parts of the budget. Fares vary greatly, particularly from the US mainland, so shop around. (Note that Honolulu stopovers are often thrown in free, or for a nominal charge, on trips between North America and Asian or Pacific countries.)

If you want to rent a car, budget about $50 a day for the rental fee, gas and parking. However, a car is not essential to exploring the Honolulu area as Oahu has a good inexpensive bus system that will take you anywhere on the island for just $1.

The Waikiki/Honolulu area has a wide range of accommodations, including two HI-affiliated hostels and a few private hostel-style places where dormitory beds cost about $15. After that, there are rooms at Ys for $30 and a few bottom-end Waikiki hotels that start around $45. Waikiki has lots of middle-range hotels in the $65 to $100 range as well as luxury beachfront hotels for triple that rate.

Since much of Hawaii's food is shipped in, grocery prices average 25% higher than on the US mainland. While Waikiki restaurants generally reflect these higher prices, food in Honolulu's plethora of less-touristed neighborhood restaurants is an excellent value, with prices generally as cheap as you'll find on the mainland.

Tipping

Tipping practices are the same as in the rest of the USA. In restaurants, the average tip is around 15%, while 10% is generally sufficient for taxi drivers, hair stylists and the like. Hotel bellhops are typically tipped about $1 per bag.

Taxes

Hawaii has a 4.17% state sales tax that is tacked onto virtually everything, including all meals, groceries, car rentals and accommodations. An additional 6% room tax brings the total tax added to all accommodation bills to 10.17%. Another tax targeting visitors is a $2-a-day 'road use' tax imposed upon all car rentals.

DOING BUSINESS

There are a couple of organizations that provide assistance to people interested in doing business in Hawaii.

The State Department of Business, Economic Development & Tourism (☎ 586-2545, fax 586-2544), 1130 N Nimitz Hwy, Suite A254, Honolulu, HI 96817, will supply a packet that includes information on business assistance provided by state agencies, while the Chamber of Commerce of Hawaii (☎ 545-4300), 1132 Bishop St, Suite 200, Honolulu, HI 96813, provides more general background information and support.

In terms of everyday practicalities, business travelers will find that some of the larger Waikiki hotels, like Hilton Hawaiian Village, offer personal computer rentals and other specialized services for business travelers. Four Waikiki hotels in the Outrigger chain have small business centers where guests can rent work desks equipped with computers, printers and modem hookups and arrange other business services.

One modern city hotel, the Executive Centre Hotel in downtown Honolulu, is geared specifically for business travelers. The rooms at the Executive have private-line phones with voice mail, while the hotel's business center has work stations, laptop rentals and secretarial services.

Photocopying is available at numerous

A: Chess at Kuhio Beach Park
B: Pali Tunnel, Nuuanu Pali
C: USS Arizona Memorial, Pearl Harbor

D: Duke Kahanamoku statue, Waikiki
E: Coconut palms, Waikiki

A: DAVID RUSS

B: NED FRIARY

C: DAVID RUSS

D: NED FRIARY

A: Hawaii State Library
B: Iolani Barracks

C: No 1 Capitol District
D: Waikiki at night

A: Aliiolani Hale
B: King Lunalilo's Tomb

C: Iolani Palace
D: Dillingham Building reflected in Grosvenor Tower

A: NED FRIARY

D: NED FRIARY

B: NED FRIARY

C: NED FRIARY

E: GLENDA BENDURE

A: Statue of King Kamehameha I
B: Native ilima, Oahu's official flower
C: Hawaii's state flag

D: Iolani Palace gate
E: Statue of Queen Liliuokalani

places around the city. In Waikiki, the Island Printing Center (☎ 922-1225) in the Waikiki Business Plaza, 2270 Kalakaua Ave, has a convenient fast-feed self-service copier with reasonable rates. Kinko's, downtown at 1050 Bishop St (☎ 528-7171) and near the university at 1500 Kapiolani Blvd (☎ 944-8500), charges just a few cents per copy and is open 24 hours a day.

Kinko's also offers reasonably priced on-site PC and Mac rentals, with major word processing programs, scanning and color output. Kinko's doesn't have online services, however. For places that specialize in internet access, see the Fax & Internet heading in the following Post & Communications section.

Cellular phone rentals are available from Cellular Rentals of Hawaii (☎ 596-4433) and Cheetah Communications (☎ 531-2363).

If you have any last-minute business needs, the Thomas Cook Business Center (☎ 831-3600) in the main departure lobby of Honolulu International Airport offers photocopy, fax and express mail services, typewriter rentals and a conference room.

POST

The main Honolulu post office is not in town, but is at the side of the airport at 3600 Aolele St, opposite the inter-island terminal. It's open from 7:30 am to 8:30 pm Monday to Friday and from 8 am to 2:30 pm on Saturdays.

The downtown branch of the Honolulu post office is opposite Iolani Palace on the Richards St side of the Old Federal Building. It's open from 8 am to 4:30 pm weekdays except on Wednesdays when it's open until 6 pm.

Waikiki's main post office, at 330 Saratoga Rd, is open from 8 am to 4:30 pm on weekdays, except on Wednesdays when it stays open until 6 pm, and from 9 am to noon on Saturdays. There are smaller branch post offices in Waikiki at the Royal Hawaiian Shopping Center, 2233 Kalakaua Ave, and at the Hilton Hawaiian Village, 2005 Kalia Rd.

Postal Rates

Postage rates for first-class mail within the USA are 32¢ for letters up to one ounce (23¢ for each additional ounce) and 20¢ for postcards. First-class mail between Honolulu and the mainland goes by air and usually takes three to four days.

International airmail rates are 60¢ for a half-ounce letter and 50¢ for a postcard to any foreign country with the exception of Canada (46¢ for a one-ounce letter and 40¢ for a postcard) and Mexico (40¢ for a half-ounce letter and 35¢ for a postcard).

The cost for parcels airmailed anywhere within the USA is $3 for two pounds or less, $6 for five pounds. For heavier items, rates differ according to the distance mailed.

Express Mail

The US Postal Service does not offer overnight express mail service between Honolulu and the US mainland unless the package is brought directly to the main Honolulu post office at the airport by 11:30 am. Even then, overnight service is limited to major US west coast cities. All other express mail service between Honolulu and the US mainland is on a two-day basis.

Speedier service is available from the private sector. In downtown Honolulu, there's a Federal Express (FedEx) office at 841 Bishop St, open from 9 am to 5 pm Monday to Friday; the last drop time for overnight delivery to the US mainland is 2:45 pm. In Waikiki, there are both FedEx and UPS drop boxes on the 2nd-floor lobby of the Sheraton Waikiki hotel, 2255 Kalakaua Ave (take the escalator up from the main lobby and turn right towards the Convention Services Office); pickup for overnight delivery is 2 pm.

Receiving Mail

All general delivery mail sent to you in Honolulu must be picked up at the main Honolulu post office, next to the airport. Note that any mail sent general delivery to the Waikiki post office or other Honolulu branches will either go to the main post office or be returned to sender. If you're receiving mail in Honolulu, have it addressed to you c/o General Delivery, Main Post Office, 3600 Aolele St, Honolulu, HI 96820-3600. Domestic mail is generally held for 10 days, international mail for 30 days.

Most hotels will also hold mail for incoming guests. In addition, the American Express office at the Hyatt Regency hotel in Waikiki will hold mail for 30 days for American Express card and traveler's check holders. Have mail addressed to you c/o American Express, Client Mail Service, 2424 Kalakaua Ave, 2nd Floor, Honolulu, HI 96815. Their office is open from 8 am to 8 pm every day.

TELECOMMUNICATIONS

The telephone area code for all of Hawaii is 808. The area code is not used when making calls on the same island, but must be added to all Hawaiian phone numbers when calling from outside the state and when calling from one Hawaiian island to another.

All phone numbers listed in this book beginning with 800 are toll-free numbers from the US mainland, unless otherwise noted. The same numbers are sometimes toll free from Canada as well.

Pay phones can readily be found in public places such as shopping centers, hotel lobbies and beach parks. You can pump in quarters, use a phone card or make collect calls from pay phones.

Local calls within Hawaii cost 25¢ at pay phones, and there's no time limit. Any call made from one point on Oahu to any other point on Oahu is a local call. Calls from Oahu to the other Hawaiian islands are long distance.

To dial direct from one Hawaiian island to another from a pay phone, the rate from 8 am to 5 pm weekdays is $1.55 for the first minute plus 25¢ for each additional minute. From 5 to 11 pm Sunday to Friday it's $1.44 for the first minute and 16¢ for each additional minute. At all other times the rate is $1.34 for the first minute and 10¢ for each additional minute.

Most hotels add on a service charge of 50¢ to $1 for each local call made from a room phone and most also have hefty surcharges for long-distance calls.

For directory assistance on Oahu dial ☎ 1-411; for elsewhere in Hawaii dial ☎ 1-808-555-1212. To find out if there's an inter-island toll-free number for a business, dial ☎ 1-800-555-1212. In Hawaii you can make 800-number (toll-free) calls from pay phones without inserting any money.

International Calls

If you're calling Hawaii from abroad, the international country code for the USA is '1' and all calls to Hawaii are then followed by the area code 808 and the seven-digit local number.

To make an international call direct from Hawaii, dial 011 + country code + area code + number. (An exception is to Canada, where you instead dial: 1 + area code + number.) You may need to wait as long as 45 seconds for the ringing to start. For international operator assistance dial 0.

Rates vary, but most international calls dialed direct from a pay phone cost about $5 for the first minute and about $1 for additional minutes. The operator can give more specific rate information and tell you which time periods are the cheapest for the country you're calling.

Fax & Internet

Faxes can be sent and received through the front desk of most hotels. Business centers such as Kinko's also offer reasonably priced fax services on a 24-hour basis. If you're carrying a laptop you may want to check in advance with your hotel to see if the room has a phonejack that can accommodate modem hook-ups.

A number of cybercafes, where travelers can check their email or go online, have sprung up in Honolulu, including the Internet Cafe (☎ 735-5282), at 559 Kapahulu Ave near Waikiki; the Net Cafe (☎ 955-2345), at 1009 University Ave just south of the UH campus; and Cyber Cafe

(☎ 593-1664), 1311 Kapiolani Blvd, north of the Ala Moana Center.

At any of these places you can spend 15 to 30 minutes online for just a couple of dollars. In addition, Borders bookstore at the Ward Centre has a couple of computers where you can check your email for free, but there may be a long wait.

For Websites relating to Hawaii, check the Internet Directory at the back of this guide.

BOOKS
There is a wealth of books available on everything from culture and history to Oahu's best beaches and surfing spots. Information on Honolulu bookstores can be found in the Shopping chapter.

History, People & Culture
Hawaii's Story by Hawaii's Queen by Queen Liliuokalani (Mutual Publishing, 1990), written in 1897, is an autobiographical account of Liliuokalani's life and the circumstances surrounding her 1893 overthrow.

The Betrayal of Liliuokalani: Last Queen of Hawaii, 1838-1917 by Helena G Allen (Mutual Publishing, Honolulu, 1990) is an insightful account not only of the queen's life but also of missionary activity and foreign encroachment in Hawaii.

Hawaiian Antiquities by David Malo (Bishop Museum Press, Honolulu, 1992), written in 1838, was the first account of Hawaiian culture written by a Hawaiian. It gives an in-depth history of Hawaii before the arrival of the missionaries.

Shoal of Time by Gavan Daws (University of Hawaii Press, Honolulu, 1974) is a comprehensive and colorful history covering the period from Captain Cook's 'discovery' of the islands to statehood.

The Hawaiian Kingdom by Ralph S Kuykendall (University of Hawaii Press, Honolulu) is a three-volume set written from 1938 to 1967. It covers Hawaiian history from 1778 to 1893 and is considered the definitive work on that period.

Keneti by Bob Krauss (University of Hawaii Press, Honolulu, 1988) is a biography of Kenneth 'Keneti' Emory, the esteemed Bishop Museum archaeologist who over the years sailed with writer Jack London, worked with anthropologist Margaret Mead and surfed with Olympian Duke Kahanamoku. Emory, who died in 1992, spent much of his life uncovering the ruins of villages and temples throughout the Pacific, recording them before they disappeared forever.

Na Wahi Pana O Koolau Poko by Anne Kapulani Landgraf (University of Hawaii Press, Honolulu, 1994) focuses on the historical sites of Windward Oahu. The book has 82 quality duotone photographs accompanying a Hawaiian/English text.

Nana I Ke Kumu (Look to the Source) by Mary K Pukui, EW Haertig & Catherine A Lee (Hui Hanai, 1972, 2 vols) is a fascinating source of information on Hawaiian cultural practices, social customs and beliefs.

Merchant Prince of the Sandalwood Mountains by Bob Dye (University of Hawaii Press, Honolulu, 1997) tells the story of Chun Afong, Honolulu's first Chinese millionaire, in the context of the turbulent social and economic changes of the 18th century.

Mythology
The Kumulipo by Martha Beckwith (University of Hawaii Press, Honolulu, 1972) is a translation of the Hawaiian chant of creation. The chant of 2077 lines begins in the darkness of the spirit world and traces the genealogy of an *alii* (royalty) family, said to be the ancestors of humankind.

Hawaiian Mythology by Martha Beckwith (University of Hawaii Press, Honolulu, 1970) has comprehensive translations of Hawaii's old myths and legends.

The Legends and Myths of Hawaii (Charles Tuttle Co, Rutland, Vermont, 1985) is a collection of legends as told by King David Kalakaua. It has a short introduction to Hawaiian culture and history as well.

Natural History

The Many-Splendored Fishes of Hawaii by Gar Goodson (Stanford University Press, California, 1985) is one of the best of several small, inexpensive fish identification books on the market, and has good descriptions and 170 color drawings.

Hawaii's Fishes: A Guide for Snorkelers, Divers and Aquarists by John P Hoover (Mutual Publishing, Honolulu, 1993) is a more expensive and comprehensive field guide covering over 230 reef and shore fishes of Hawaii. It's fully illustrated with color photographs and gives insights on Oahu dive sites.

Hawaii's Birds (Hawaii Audubon Society, Honolulu, 1993) is the best pocket-sized guide to the birds of Hawaii. It has color photos and descriptions of all the native birds and many of the introduced species.

For something more comprehensive, there's *A Field Guide to the Birds of Hawaii and the Tropical Pacific* by H Douglas Pratt, Phillip L Bruner and Delwyn G Berrett (Princeton University Press, New Jersey, 1987). The 409-page book contains 45 pages of color plates.

Mammals in Hawaii by P Quentin Tomich (Bishop Museum Press, Honolulu, 1986) is the authoritative book on the mammals in Hawaii, with interesting stories on how they arrived in the islands. It covers whales, dolphins and such oddities as the Australian rock-wallabies that were accidentally released in 1916 and now reside in Oahu's Kalihi Valley.

Plants and Flowers of Hawaii by SH Sohmer & R Gustafson (University of Hawaii Press, Honolulu, 1987) has quality color photos and descriptions of over 130 native plants of Hawaii, including information on their habitat and evolution.

Practical Folk Medicine of Hawaii by LR McBride (Petroglyph Press, Hilo, 1975) has descriptions of many native medicinal plants and their uses.

A good general book on flora and fauna is *Plants and Animals of Hawaii* by local biologist Susan Scott (Bess Press, Honolulu, 1991). It discusses various environments, including reefs, shorelines, forests and wetlands, and details plants and animals of the islands, both native and introduced. There are interesting tidbits on medicinal uses, origins and the like.

Outdoor Activities

The Beaches of Oahu by John RK Clark (University of Hawaii Press, Honolulu, 1977) is a comprehensive book detailing the island's coastline and every one of its beaches, including water conditions, shoreline geology and local history.

Diving and Snorkeling Guide to the Hawaiian Islands by Doug Wallin (Pisces Books, New York, 1991) is a good guide to both diving and snorkeling on the four main islands. It has color photos of sites and fish.

Surfer's Guide to Hawaii: Hawaii Gets All the Breaks by Greg Ambrose (Bess Press, Honolulu, 1991) describes the top surfing spots, including Oahu's world-famous Sunset Beach and Banzai Pipeline. Written in an entertaining style, it's packed with everything you need to know about surfing in Hawaii.

The Hikers Guide to Oahu by Stuart Ball (University of Hawaii Press, Honolulu, 1993) details 53 hikes in Oahu. Ball, a former president of the Hawaiian Trail & Mountain Club, gives information on length, difficulty and direction to the trailhead for each hike. Walks are described in detail and accompanied by a topographical map.

General

From the Skies of Paradise, Oahu is a good aerial photography book with color plates by renowned photographer Douglas Peebles and text by Glen Grant (Mutual Publishing, Honolulu, 1992). All parts of Oahu – cities, beaches, mountains and fields – are beautifully photographed, with accompanying narratives that incorporate Hawaiian myths and legends.

Architecture in Hawaii by Rob Sandler (Mutual Publishing, Honolulu, 1993) is a coffee table book with striking color photographs of Hawaii's most notable buildings, the majority of which are in Honolulu. More than 150 buildings are detailed, from thatched cottages to the royal palace, covering some two centuries of island architecture. There are also biographies of Hawaii's top architects.

Reference & Travel

If you're planning to visit any of the Hawaiian islands other than Oahu, you'll want to pick up Lonely Planet's *Hawaii*, which is packed with comprehensive information on traveling throughout Hawaii.

Although it's a bit dated, the 238-page *Atlas of Hawaii* by the Department of Geography, University of Hawaii (University of Hawaii Press, Honolulu, 1983), is loaded with data, maps and tabulations covering everything from land ownership to seasonal ocean wave patterns.

Place Names of Hawaii by Mary Kawena Pukui, Samuel H Elbert & Esther T Mookini (University of Hawaii Press, Honolulu, 1974) is a glossary of 4000 Hawaiian place names. The meaning and background of each name is explained.

Hawaiian Dictionary by Mary Kawena Pukui & Samuel H Elbert (University of Hawaii Press, Honolulu, 1986) is the authoritative work on the Hawaiian language. It's in both Hawaiian-English and English-Hawaiian, with 30,000 entries. There's also a $4.95 pocket-size version with 10,000 Hawaiian words.

There are many other Hawaiian language books on the market including grammar texts, conversational self-study guides and books on pidgin.

Ordering by Mail

The following publishers will send catalogs of their titles that can be ordered by mail:

Bess Press
  3565 Harding Ave, Honolulu, HI 96816
  (☎ 734-7159, 800-910-2377; fax 732-3627; besspr@aloha.net)

Bishop Museum Press
  1525 Bernice St, Honolulu, HI 96817
  (☎ 848-4134, fax 841-8968)

Petroglyph Press
  201 Kinoole St, Hilo, HI 96720
  (☎ 935-6006, fax 935-1553)

University of Hawaii Press
  2840 Kolowalu St, Honolulu, HI 96822
  (☎ 956-8255, 800-956-2840; fax 988-6052)

NEWSPAPERS

Hawaii's two main daily papers are the *Honolulu Advertiser*, which is published daily each morning, and the *Honolulu Star-Bulletin*, which comes out in the afternoon Monday to Saturday. To order copies of either paper by mail, contact the Circulation Department (☎ 538-6397), Box 3350, Honolulu, HI 96801. A single Sunday paper sent airmail to the US mainland costs $7.40, to overseas destinations $18.80.

In addition, Oahu has several free weekly or monthly newspapers, including the *Honolulu Weekly*, a progressive paper with an extensive entertainment section, and the *Downtown Planet*, aimed at those who work in downtown Honolulu.

Several mainland and international newspapers are also widely available, including *USA Today*, the *Wall Street Journal*, the *San Francisco Examiner* and the *Los Angeles Times*. Look for them in the lobbies of larger hotels and in racks on busier Waikiki street corners.

MAGAZINES

Honolulu, *Aloha* and *Hawaii Magazine* are the largest general interest magazines about Hawaii. *Honolulu* is geared towards residents and is published monthly by the Honolulu Publishing Co, 36 Merchant St, Honolulu, HI 96813. *Aloha* (Box 469035, Escondido, CA 92046) and *Hawaii Magazine* (Box 485, Mt Morris, IL 61054) have more visitor-oriented feature articles; both are published six times a year.

There are also numerous free tourist magazines, such *This Week Oahu* and *Spotlight's Oahu Gold*, which are available at the airport and in hotel lobbies all around Waikiki. Most have simple maps, a bit of current event information, lots of ads and discount coupons for everything from hamburgers to sunset cruises.

Hawaiian Weddings

Many visitors come to Honolulu not only for their honeymoon, but to make their wedding vows as well.

Getting married in Hawaii is a straightforward process. Hawaii requires that the prospective bride and groom appear in person together before a marriage license agent and pay $25 for a license, which is given out on the spot. There's no waiting period and no residence, citizenship or blood-test requirements. The legal age for marriage is 18, or 16 with parental consent.

Full information and forms are available from the Department of Health (☎ 586-4544), Marriage License Office, Box 3378, 1250 Punchbowl St, Honolulu, HI 96813. The office is open from 8 am to 4 pm Monday to Friday.

Numerous companies provide wedding services. One of these, Affordable Weddings of Hawaii (☎ 923-4876, 800-942-4554; fax 396-0959), Box 26475, Honolulu, HI 96825, will mail out a brochure with tips on planning your wedding, choosing a location, photography services etc. The amiable Reverend MC Hansen of Affordable Weddings can provide a nondenominational service, starting at $55 for a simple weekday ceremony and going up to $700 for more elaborate packages.

For something more traditional (or nontraditional, depending on your perspective), Helemano Kauihimalaihi, wearing a ti lei, performs a ceremony entirely in the Hawaiian language. He's attempted to recreate an ancient ceremony using Hawaiian chants and proverbs, draping of the bride and groom in tapa and the like. The ceremony alone costs $150, or with flowers and photos $235. For information contact Traditional Hawaiian Weddings (☎ /fax 671-8420, 800-884-9505), 94-1054 Paha Place, Suite N2, Waipahu, HI 96797. ■

RADIO & TV

Honolulu has 17 commercial AM radio stations, 12 FM stations and three non-commercial stations. Radio station KCCN features slack-key Hawaiian guitar on 1420 AM and 'island music,' with a blend of more contemporary Hawaiian songs and reggae, on 100.3 FM. Da KINE (105.1 FM) plays classic Hawaiian music. Hawaii Public Radio is on KHPR (88.1 FM), KKUA (90.7 FM) and KIPO (89.3 FM).

Oahu has 10 commercial TV stations, including those representing public broadcasting (PBS) and the three major US networks. There are also numerous cable stations; cable channel 8 features continuous visitor information and ads geared to tourists.

For some local flavor, the evening news on Channel 2 ends with some fine slack-key guitar music by Keola and Kapono Beamer and clips of people waving the shaka sign.

PHOTOGRAPHY & VIDEO

Both print and slide film are readily available in Honolulu. If you're going to be in Hawaii for any length of time, consider having your film developed there, as the high temperature and humidity of the tropics greatly accelerates the deterioration of exposed film. The sooner it's developed, the better the results.

Kodak and Fuji have labs in Honolulu, and drug stores and camera shops usually send in to those labs. Longs Drugs is one of the cheapest places for both purchasing film and having it developed. Slides generally take two to three days, prints a day or two, and the cost is cheaper than at camera shops. While there are no branches in Waikiki, there's a Longs Drugs on the upper level of the Ala Moana Center and another next to Times Supermarket at 3221 Waialae Ave, near the university. There are also numerous places in Waikiki that do one-hour photo processing.

Honolulu is a great place for photography. However, sand and water are intense reflectors and in bright light they'll often leave foreground subjects shadowy. You can try compensating by adjusting your f-stop or attaching a polarizing filter, or both, but the most effective technique is to take photos in the gentler light of early morning and late afternoon.

Don't leave your camera in direct sun any longer than necessary. A locked car can heat up like an oven in just a few minutes.

TIME

When it's noon in Honolulu, the time in other parts of the world is: 1 pm in Anchorage, 2 pm in Los Angeles, 5 pm in New York, 10 pm in London, 11 pm in Bonn, 7 am the next day in Tokyo, 8 am the next day in Sydney and Melbourne, and 10 am the next day in Auckland.

Hawaii does not observe daylight-saving time. Therefore, the time difference is one hour greater during those months when other countries observe daylight saving. For example from April to October when it's noon in Honolulu it's 3 pm in Los Angeles and 6 pm in New York; and from November to March when it's noon in Honolulu it's 9 am in Melbourne and 11 am in Auckland.

Honolulu has about 11 hours of daylight in mid-winter and almost 13½ hours in mid-summer. In mid-winter the sun rises at about 7 am and sets about 6 pm. In mid-summer it rises before 6 am and sets after 7 pm.

And then there's Hawaiian Time, which is a slow-down-the-clock pace or a euphemism for being late.

ELECTRICITY

Electricity is 110/120V, 60 cycles, and a flat two-pronged plug is used, the same as everywhere else in the USA.

LAUNDRY

Many hotels and hostels have coin-operated washers and dryers. If there's not one where you're staying, coin laundries are easily found. The average cost is about $1 to wash a load of clothes and another dollar to dry. In Waikiki there are public coin laundries at the Outrigger West Hotel, 2330 Kuhio Ave, the Outrigger Coral Seas, 250 Lewers St, and the Outrigger Waikiki, 2335 Kalakaua Ave, all open from 7 am to 10 pm daily.

WEIGHTS & MEASURES

Hawaii, like the rest of the USA, uses the imperial system of measurement. Distances are in feet, yards and miles; weights are in ounces, pounds and tons. Gasoline is measured in US gallons (1 gallon=3.79 liters).

HEALTH

Honolulu is a very healthy place. As it's 2500 miles from the nearest industrial center, there's little air pollution. Hawaii ranks first of all the 50 US states in life expectancy, which is currently about 76 years for men and 81 years for women.

There are few serious health concerns. Hawaii has none of the nasties like malaria, cholera or yellow fever and you can drink water directly out of any tap.

No immunizations are required to enter Honolulu or any other port in the USA.

Fair-skinned people should be aware that they can quickly get first and second-degree burns in the hot Hawaiian sun, so a sunscreen is recommended, doubly so if you're not already tanned. If you're going into the water use one that's water-resistant. Snorkelers may want to wear a T-shirt if they plan to be out in the water a long time. The most severe sun is between 10 am and 2 pm.

If you're new to the heat and humidity you may find yourself easily fatigued and more susceptible to minor ailments. Acclimatize yourself by slowing down your pace and setting your body clock to the more kicked-back 'Hawaiian Time.' Drink plenty of liquids.

If you're planning on a long outing or

anything strenuous, be sure to take enough water and don't push yourself.

Be aware that there are many poisonous plants in Hawaii, so you should never taste a plant that you cannot positively identify as edible.

Health Insurance

Foreign visitors should be warned that health care in the USA is expensive, and while Hawaii is the only one of the 50 states that has an extensive health-insurance program, the coverage is limited to Hawaii residents.

Therefore, a travel insurance policy that covers medical expenses may be a wise idea. There are a wide variety of policies available and your travel agent should have recommendations. While you may find a policy that pays doctors or hospitals directly, be aware that many private doctors and clinics in Hawaii will demand payment at the time of service. If you have to make a claim later be sure to keep all documentation.

Check the fine print because some policies exclude 'dangerous activities' like scuba diving, motorcycling and anything to do with parachutes.

Medical Care

Two major hospitals with 24-hour emergency services are Queen's Medical Center (☎ 538-9011), 1301 Punchbowl St, and Straub Clinic & Hospital (☎ 522-4000), 888 S King St at Ward. Divers with the bends are sent to the UH Hyperbaric Treatment Center (☎ 587-3425), 347 N Kuakini St, Honolulu.

In Waikiki, Doctors On Call (☎ 971-6000), on the 2nd floor of the Outrigger Waikiki Hotel, 2335 Kalakaua Ave, has a 24-hour clinic, complete with X-ray and lab facilities. The minimum charge for an office visit is $68 before 10 pm, $92 after. They'll also make house calls, though this will run more than twice the office visit cost. There are branch clinics at Hilton Hawaiian Village (☎ 973-5252) and Royal Hawaiian Hotel (☎ 923-4499), both open from 8 am to around 5 pm daily.

WOMEN TRAVELERS

Women travelers are no more likely to encounter problems in Honolulu than any other US city, although the usual precautions apply. Women who have been the victims of abuse or sexual assault can call the Sex Abuse Treatment Center's 24-hour hotline on Oahu at ☎ 524-7273.

GAY & LESBIAN TRAVELERS

Gay and lesbian travelers are taking a growing interest in Hawaii, as the state has become centerstage in the movement to legalize same-gender marriages. In December 1996 a circuit court judge ruled that state prohibitions against same-sex marriages violated the equal protection clause of Hawaii's constitution, which explicitly bans gender discrimination. While it's an important round for gay activists, the implementation of the ruling has been postponed until after the state appeals the case to the Hawaii Supreme Court.

If the supreme court rules favorably, then the state will be compelled to issue marriage licenses free of gender prejudice. Should that happen, a move to amend the Hawaii state constitution, supported largely by mainland political and religious extremists, is expected to gather momentum – so the final battle in this protracted struggle may still be years away.

Gay marriages aside, Honolulu is as popular a vacation spot for gays and lesbians as it is for straights. Hawaii is a liberal state, with strong minority protections and a constitutional guarantee of privacy that extends to sexual behavior between consenting adults.

Still, most of the gay scene is low key; public hand-holding and other outward signs of affection between gays is not commonplace.

Certainly in terms of nightlife, the main gay club scene is centered in Waikiki (see the Entertainment chapter for details).

The following information sources can help gay and lesbian visitors get oriented.

The free *Island Lifestyle* (☎ 737-6400; ilm@tnight.com), Box 11840, Honolulu, HI 96828, a 48-page monthly magazine for the gay community, can be picked up at clubs in Honolulu, bookstores and other locations. The latest issue can be ordered by mail; the cost is $3 within the USA, $5 overseas. Lifestyle also sells *The Pages*, a $4 directory of clubs, B&Bs, restaurants and other businesses that are supportive to the gay community.

Pacific Ocean Holidays (☎ 923-2400, 800-735-6600; fax 923-2499; poh@hi.net), 155 Paoakalani Ave, Suite 901, Honolulu, HI 96815, arranges vacation packages for gay men and women. They also produce a small booklet called *Pocket Guide to Hawaii* which is geared to the gay community and costs $5 when ordered by mail.

The Gay & Lesbian Community Center (☎ 951-7000; glcc@aloha-cafe.com), 1820 University Ave, Honolulu, HI 96822, is a good source of information on local issues for both women and men.

Hawaii Equal Rights Marriage Project (HERMP), Box 11690, Honolulu, HI 96828, has spearheaded the fight to legalize gay marriages in Hawaii. You can plug into the latest by looking them up at their website (see the Internet Directory on page 161).

DISABLED TRAVELERS
Overall, Honolulu is an accommodating destination for travelers with disabilities, and Waikiki in particular is considered one of the more handicapped-accessible destinations in the USA. Many of Honolulu's larger hotels have wheelchair-accessible rooms and as more of them renovate their facilities, accessibility improves.

The Commission on Persons with Disabilities (☎ 586-8121), 919 Ala Moana Blvd, Room 101, Honolulu, HI 96814, distributes the three-part *Aloha Guide to Accessibility,* which contains detailed travel tips for physically disabled people. Part I has general information and covers airport access on the major islands; this section can be obtained free by mail and with it you'll get an order form for purchasing Parts II & III, which detail accessibility to beaches, parks, shopping centers and visitor attractions and list hotels with

wheelchair access or specially-adapted facilities. The entire set costs $15, postage included – or $5 if you just want the section on hotels.

In terms of getting around, about half of Oahu's modern fleet of public buses have wheelchair lifts. In addition, disabled travelers can contact the Honolulu Public Transit Authority (☎ 523-4083) for information on Handi-Van curb-to-curb service and other provisions for the disabled.

Wheelers of Hawaii (☎ 879-5521, 800-303-3750) rents accessible vans, books accessible accommodations and arranges various activities for disabled travelers visiting Honolulu.

For more general information, the Society for the Advancement of Travel for the Handicapped (☎ 212-447-7284), 347 Fifth Ave, Suite 610, New York, NY 10016, publishes a quarterly magazine for $13 a year and has various free information sheets on travel for the disabled.

SENIOR TRAVELERS
Honolulu is a popular destination for retirees and lots of discount schemes are available. The applicable age has been creeping lower as well.

For instance, Honolulu's biggest hotel chain, Outrigger, offers across-the-board discounts of 20% to anyone 50 years old or better, and if you're a member of the American Association of Retired Persons (AARP), they'll discount it another 5%. AARP discounts are available from other hotels as well, so whenever you book a reservation, be sure to inquire.

The nonprofit AARP itself is a good source for travel bargains. For information on joining this advocacy group for Americans 50 years and older, contact AARP (☎ 800-227-7737), 601 E St NW, Washington, DC 20049.

HONOLULU FOR CHILDREN
Families with children will find lots of fun things to do in Honolulu, from water sports to cool sightseeing attractions.

Waikiki offers a wide range of activities right at the beach. Older children can take surfing lessons from the pros and kids of all ages can hop aboard an outrigger canoe for an easier ride across the surf.

Young children may enjoy visiting the petting section of the Honolulu Zoo, where they can encounter some of the tamer creatures up close. Older children may want to sign up for the zoo's elephant encounter, held at least once daily, which includes a lecture by the keepers on elephant care and behavior and the opportunity, when the beasts are in a good mood, for kids to feed the elephants.

The nearby Waikiki Aquarium can be a fascinating place – not only does it have the usual colorful array of fish, as well as monk seals and sharks, but there's also a touch tank geared specifically for children.

The free Kodak Hula Show, which like the zoo and aquarium are in Kapiolani Park, offers a fun little music and dance performance and is followed by a photo opportunity where parents can snap photos of their kids posing with the hula dancers.

Older children who want to learn Hawaiian arts and crafts can take advantage of the Royal Hawaiian Shopping Center's free mini-courses, including hula lessons, lei making and coconut frond weaving.

For more details on all of these activities, see Things to See & Do.

If you're traveling with infants and need supplies, Baby's Away (☎ 261-2929), a baby supply rental company, rents cribs, strollers, play pens, infant seats, high chairs, toys and more.

For lots of insightful tips on traveling with children, pick up a copy of Lonely Planet's *Travel with Children* by Maureen Wheeler.

LIBRARIES

The main library (☎ 586-3500) of Hawaii's statewide library system is in downtown Honolulu, next to Iolani Palace. It's open from 9 am to 5 pm on Mondays, Fridays and Saturdays, from 10 am to 5 pm on Wednesdays and from 9 am to 8 pm on Tuesdays and Thursdays. The Waikiki-Kapahulu branch (☎ 733-8488), 400 Kapahulu Ave, is open from 10 am to 5 pm

Mondays, Thursdays, Fridays and Saturdays and from 10 am to 8 pm on Tuesdays and Wednesdays. Both libraries have periodical sections with local and mainland newspapers, including the *New York Times* and *Wall Street Journal*.

Visitors can check out books only after applying for a Hawaii library card; a visitor's card valid for three months costs $10.

CAMPUSES

The University of Hawaii's central campus is in Honolulu's Manoa district, just two miles north of Waikiki. Not only is UH Manoa the largest campus in Hawaii, with some 20,000 students, but it's also the site of the East-West Center, a federal government-supported postgraduate facility, with an enrollment of 2000. For details on campus tours and attending the university, see the University of Hawaii section in the Things to See & Do chapter.

CULTURAL CENTERS

The Japanese Cultural Center of Hawaii (☎ 945-7633) has recently opened a facility at 2454 S Beretania St, near the university. The center has historical displays and facilities for martial arts, tea ceremonies and a range of cultural classes. For more information, see Courses at the end of the Things to See & Do chapter.

The following cultural clubs are also active in Honolulu: Canadian Club of Hawaii, New Zealand/USA Connection, Daughters of the British Empire, Organization of Chinese Americans, Hispanic Cultural Association of Hawaii, Norway Aloha Chapter of the Nordmanns-Forbundet Club, Scandinavian Club of Hawaii, Daughters of the American Revolution and United Filipino Council of Hawaii. The 'Hobby Board' section of the Sunday *Honolulu Advertiser* lists these clubs' social outings and includes their current contact phone numbers and meeting sites.

USEFUL ORGANIZATIONS
Environmental Groups

Na Ala Hele (☎ 587-0058), Division of Forestry & Wildlife, 567 S King St, Suite

132, Honolulu, HI 96813, is reestablishing many of Hawaii's historic trails and reopening them to hikers and naturalists.

The Sierra Club (☎ 538-6616), Box 2577, Honolulu, HI 96803, helps maintain Honolulu-area trails and leads guided hikes.

The Nature Conservancy of Hawaii (☎ 537-4508), 1116 Smith St, Honolulu, HI 96817, protects some of Hawaii's endangered ecosystems by acquiring land and arranging long-term stewardships with landowners. In the Honolulu area, they manage a crater above Hanauma Bay that has a unique vernal pool and a rare fern.

Other Organizations

The Division of State Parks (☎ 587-0300), Box 621, 1151 Punchbowl St, Room 131, Honolulu, HI 96809, provides a free brochure to Hawaii state parks, with a brief description of each park including camping information.

The American Automobile Association (AAA) of Hawaii (☎ 528-2600), at 590 Queen St in downtown Honolulu, can provide AAA members (as well as members of affiliated auto clubs) information on motoring in Hawaii, including detailed Honolulu and Hawaii road maps. It also provides members with emergency road service and towing (☎ 537-5544).

The AIDS/STD Hot Line (☎ 922-1313) provides AIDS counseling and referrals.

DANGERS & ANNOYANCES
Theft & Violence

For the most part, Honolulu is a safe place to be and has lower violent crime rates than most other US cities. Still, like any city, crime does occur and reasonable precautions are advisable.

Petty theft is one crime that ranks high in Honolulu. Watch your belongings and never leave anything unattended on a beach. Most accommodations have a place where you can store your valuables.

One thing in particular to be aware of is that Hawaii is notorious for rip-offs from parked rental cars. The people who break into these cars are good at what they do;

they can pop a trunk or pull out a lock assembly in seconds to get to the loot inside. What's more, they do it not only when you've left your car in a secluded area to go for a long hike, but also in crowded parking lots where you'd expect safety in numbers.

It's certainly best not to leave anything of value in your car any time you walk away from it. If for some reason you feel you must, at least pack things well out of sight *before* you've pulled up to the place where you're going to leave the car.

Other than rip-offs, most hassles encountered by visitors are from drunks. While Waikiki Beach is well patrolled by the police, you should be tuned in to the vibes on other beaches at night and in places where young guys hang out to drink.

Touts

There's been a clampdown on the hustlers who used to push time shares and other con deals from every other street corner in Waikiki. They're not totally gone – there are just fewer of them (and some have metamorphosed into 'activity centers'). If you see a sign touting car rentals for $5 a day, you've probably found one.

Time-share salespeople will offer you all sorts of deals, from free luaus to sunset cruises, if you'll just come to hear their 'no obligation' pitch. *Caveat emptor.*

Pesky Creatures

Hawaii has no land snakes but it does have its fair share of annoying mosquitoes as well as centipedes which can give an unpleasant bite. There are also bees and groundnesting wasps which, like the centipede, generally pose danger only to those who are allergic to their stings.

This being the tropics, cockroaches are plentiful and although they don't pose much of a health problem they do little for the appetite. Accommodations with kitchens have the most problems. If you find that the place you're staying at is infested you can always call the front desk and have them spray poisons – which are no doubt more dangerous than the roaches!

While sightings are not terribly common, there are two dangerous arachnids on the islands: the black widow spider and the scorpion. If you think you've been stung by either, seek immediate medical help.

Tsunamis

Tsunamis, or tidal waves, are not common in Hawaii but when they do hit they can be severe.

Tsunamis are generated by earthquakes or other natural disasters. The largest to ever hit Hawaii was in 1946, the result of an earthquake in the Aleutian Islands. Waves reached a height of 55.8 feet, entire villages were washed away and 159 people died. Since that time, Hawaii has installed a modern tsunami warning system, which is aired through yellow speakers mounted on telephone poles. They're tested on the first working day of each month at 11:45 am for about one minute.

Although tsunamis traveling across the Pacific can take hours to arrive, others can be caused by earthquakes or volcanic eruptions within Hawaii. For these there may be little warning. Any earthquake strong enough to cause you to grab onto some-thing to keep from falling is a natural tsunami warning. If you're in a low-lying coastal area when one occurs, immediately head for higher ground.

Tsunami inundation maps in the front of the Oahu phone book white pages show susceptible areas and safety zones.

Ocean Safety

Drowning is the leading cause of accidental death for visitors.

If you're not familiar with water conditions, ask someone. Most Honolulu beaches have daytime lifeguards but if there's no lifeguard on duty, local surfers are generally helpful – they'd rather give you the lowdown on water conditions than pull you out later. It's best not to swim alone in any unfamiliar place.

Shorebreaks Shorebreaks occur where waves break close to or directly on shore. They are formed when ocean swells pass abruptly from deep to shallow waters. If they are only a couple of feet high they're generally fine for novice bodysurfers to try their hand. Otherwise, they're for experienced bodysurfers only.

STRONG CURRENT   MAN-OF-WAR   SHARP CORAL

HIGH SURF   DANGEROUS SHOREBREAK   WAVES ON LEDGE

Large shorebreaks can hit hard with a slamming downward force. Broken bones, neck injuries, dislocated shoulders and loss of wind are the most common injuries, although anyone wiped out in the water is a potential drowning victim as well.

Rip Currents Rip currents, or rips, are fast flowing currents of water within the ocean, moving from shallow nearshore areas out to sea. They are most common in conditions of high surf, forming when water from incoming waves builds up near the shore. Essentially, the waves are coming in faster than they can flow back out.

The water then runs along the shoreline until it finds an escape route out to sea, usually through a channel or out along a point. Swimmers caught up in the current can be ripped out to deeper water.

Although rips can be powerful they usually dissipate 50 to 100 yards offshore. Anyone caught in one should either go with the flow until it loses power or swim parallel to shore to slip out of it. Trying to swim against a rip current can exhaust even the strongest of swimmers.

Undertows Undertows are common along steeply sloped beaches when large waves backwash directly into incoming surf. The outflowing water picks up speed as it flows down the slopes. When it hits an incoming wave the outflow curls under the wave, creating an undertow. Swimmers caught up in an undertow can be pulled beneath the surface. The most important thing is not to panic. Go with the current until you get beyond the wave.

Rogue Waves Never turn your back on the ocean. Incoming waves don't all have equal heights or strengths. An abnormally high 'rogue wave' can sweep over shoreline ledges such as those circling Hanauma Bay. You need to be particularly cautious during high tide and in conditions of stormy weather or high surf.

Some people think rogue waves don't exist because they've never seen one. But that's the point – you don't always see them.

Coral Most coral cuts occur when swimmers are pushed onto the coral by rough waves and surges. It's a good idea to wear diving gloves when snorkeling over shallow reefs. Avoid walking on coral, which can not only cut your feet, but is very damaging to the coral.

Sea Urchins *Wana*, or spiny sea urchins, have long brittle spines that can puncture the skin and break off, causing burning and possible numbness. The spines sometimes contain a toxin and can cause an infection. You can try to remove the spines with tweezers or by soaking the area in hot water, although more serious cases may require surgical removal.

Sharks More than 35 varieties of sharks are found in Hawaiian waters, including nonaggressive whale sharks and basking sharks, which can reach lengths of 50 feet. As Hawaiian waters are abundant with fish, sharks in Hawaii are well fed and most pose little danger to humans.

Sharks are curious and will sometimes investigate divers, although they generally just check things out and continue on their way. If they start to hang around, however, it's probably time for you to go.

Outside of the rarely encountered great white shark, the most dangerous shark in Hawaiian waters is the tiger shark, which averages about 20 feet in length and is identified by vertical bars along its side. The tiger shark is not terribly particular about what it eats and has been known to chomp down on pieces of wood (including surfboards) floating on the ocean surface.

Should you come face to face with a shark the best thing to do is move casually

Portuguese man-of-war

and quietly away. Don't panic as sharks are attracted by things that thrash around in water.

Some aquatic officials suggest thumping an attacking shark on the nose or sticking your fingers into its eyes, which may confuse it long enough to give you time to escape. Indeed, some divers who dive in shark waters carry a billy club or bang stick.

Swimmers should avoid murky waters. After heavy rains sharks sometimes come in around river mouths.

Sharks are attracted by blood. Some attacks on humans are related to spearfishing; when a shark is going after a diver's bloody catch, the diver sometimes gets in the way. Sharks are also attracted by shiny things and by anything bright red or yellow, which might influence your choice of swimsuit color.

Unpleasant encounters with sharks are extremely unlikely however. According to the University of Hawaii Sea Grant College, only about 30 unprovoked shark attacks were known to have occurred in Hawaii between 1900 and 1990; about a third of these were fatal. Nevertheless, in recent years, increasing numbers of both sharks and shark attacks have been reported, with attacks throughout Hawaii now occurring on average at a rate of about two or three a year.

Jellyfish Take a peek into the water before you plunge in to make sure it's not jellyfish territory. These gelatinous creatures, with saclike bodies and stinging tentacles, are fairly common around Hawaii. They're most apt to be seen eight to 10 days after the full moon, when they come into shallow near-shore waters in places such as Waikiki. They're not keen on the sun and as the day heats up they retreat from shallow waters, so encounters by beach-goers are most common in the morning. The sting of a jellyfish varies from mild to severe, depending on the variety. Unless you have an allergic reaction to their venom, the stings are not generally dangerous.

The Portuguese man-of-war, known locally as a 'bluebottle,' is the worst type to encounter. Its sting is very painful, and you're likely to get stung more than once by clusters of incredibly long tentacles containing hundreds of stinging cells. Apply vinegar or meat tenderizer to a sting to neutralize the toxins; for serious reactions, such as chest pains or difficulty in breathing, seek medical attention.

EMERGENCIES

Dial 911 for all police, fire and ambulance emergencies. A suicide and crisis line (☎ 521-4555) operates 24 hours a day. The inside front cover of the Oahu phone book lists other vital service agencies, such as poison control and Coast Guard rescues.

If you're unfortunate enough to have

something stolen, report it immediately to the police. If your credit cards, cash cards or traveler's checks have been taken, notify your bank or the relevant company as soon as possible. For refunds on lost or stolen American Express traveler's checks, call ☎ 800-221-7282; for lost MasterCard traveler's checks dial ☎ 800-223-9920.

Foreign visitors who lose their passport should contact their consulate in Honolulu; a list of consulate phone numbers can be found earlier in this chapter.

LEGAL MATTERS
Anyone arrested in Hawaii has the right to have the representation of a lawyer, from the time of their arrest to their trial. The Hawaii State Bar Association (☎ 537-1868) can make referrals; foreign visitors may want to call their consulate for advice.

In Hawaii, anyone driving with an alcohol blood limit of .08% or greater is guilty of driving 'under the influence.'

As with most places, the possession of marijuana and nonprescription narcotics is illegal in Hawaii. Be aware that US Customs has a zero-tolerance policy for drugs; federal authorities have been known to seize boats after finding even minute quantities of marijuana on board. Even trying to slip a joint through US Customs at the airport can land a visitor a penalty of $5000.

Hawaii's Department of Commerce & Consumer Affairs offers a handy recorded information line for consumer issues. Dial ☎ 587-1234 for information on your rights regarding refunds and exchanges, timeshare contracts, car rentals and similar topics.

BUSINESS HOURS
Office hours in Honolulu are commonly from 8:30 am to 4:30 pm Monday to Friday, although there's a variance of half an hour in either direction. Shops in central areas and malls, as well as large chain stores, are usually open into the evenings and on weekends, and some grocery stores are open 24 hours.

Banks are generally open from 8:30 am to 3 pm Monday to Thursday and from 8:30 am to 6 pm on Fridays.

PUBLIC HOLIDAYS
The following are public holidays in Hawaii:

New Year's Day
    January 1

Martin Luther King Day
    third Monday in January

Presidents Day
    third Monday in February

Prince Jonah Kuhio Kalanianaole Day
    March 26

Good Friday
    the Friday before Easter, in March or April

Memorial Day
    last Monday in May

King Kamehameha Day
    June 11

Independence Day
    July 4

Admission Day
    (anniversary of Hawaiian statehood)
    third Friday in August

Labor Day
    first Monday in September

Columbus Day
    second Monday in October

General Election Day
    second Tuesday in November
    (during election years)

Veterans Day
    November 11

Thanksgiving
    fourth Thursday in November

Christmas
    December 25

Note that when holidays fall on a weekend they are often celebrated on the nearest Friday or Monday instead.

SPECIAL EVENTS
With its diverse cultural heritage and good year-round weather, Oahu has a seemingly endless number and variety of holidays, festivals and sporting events. The highlights are listed here.

As events change a bit from year to year, it's best to check activity schedules in local papers or inquire at the Hawaii Visitors Bureau. Water sports in particular are reliant on the weather and the surf, so any schedule is tentative.

January

New Year's Eve – there are fireworks displays in Honolulu and firecrackers are shot off nonstop throughout the night. Downtown Honolulu hosts a 'First Night' street fair with music, dance, theater and family-oriented activities at 50 venues.

Chinese New Year – begins at the second new moon after winter solstice (mid-January to mid-February) with lion dances and strings of firecrackers. The *Narcissus Festival*, part of the Chinese New Year celebrations, runs for about five weeks and includes arts, crafts, food booths, a beauty pageant and coronation ball. Events are held all around Honolulu; Chinatown is the center stage.

Hula Bowl – this classic East/West college all-star football game is held at Aloha Stadium on a Saturday in January.

Morey Bodyboards World Championships – at this competition on the North Shore, some of the world's top bodyboarders hit the Banzai Pipeline's towering waves.

February

Cherry Blossom Festival – this covers the entire month and spills over into March, featuring a variety of Japanese cultural events including tea ceremonies, mochi pounding and taiko drummers at various locations around Honolulu.

NFL Pro Bowl – the annual all-star game of the National Football League is held at Aloha Stadium near the beginning of February.

Hawaiian Open – this PGA tour golf tournament takes place at Waialae Country Club in mid-February. Another PGA tournament, the *Hawaiian Ladies Open*, is held at Kapolei Golf Course this month.

Great Aloha Run – a popular 8.2-mile fun run from Aloha Tower to Aloha Stadium held on Presidents Day, the third Monday in February.

Buffalo's Big Board Surfing Classic – held in late February at Makaha Beach on the Waianae Coast, this surf contest showcases old-time 12-foot longboards.

March

St Patrick's Day – March 17 is celebrated with a parade down Kalakaua Ave in Waikiki.

April

International Bed Race – this offbeat wheeled-bed race from Fort DeRussy to Kapiolani Park is held in late April.

May

May Day – the first of May is Lei Day in Hawaii. Everybody dons a lei, there are lei-making competitions and Oahu crowns a lei queen.

Bankoh Kayak Challenge – held in mid-May, this 32-mile kayak race across the treacherous Kaiwi Channel starts at Kaluakoi Resort on Molokai and finishes at Koko Marina on Oahu.

June

King Kamehameha Day – a state holiday celebrated on or near June 11. The statue of Kamehameha opposite Iolani Palace is ceremoniously draped with leis and there's a parade from downtown Honolulu to Kapiolani Park.

King Kamehameha Hula & Chant Competition – one of Hawaii's biggest hula contests is held in Honolulu near the end of June.

July

Independence Day – the Fourth of July is celebrated with fireworks and festivities.

Prince Lot Hula Festival – held at Moanalua Gardens on the third Saturday, featuring hula competitions from Hawaii's major hula schools.

Transpacific Yacht Race – on the July 4 weekend of odd-numbered years, sailboats leave southern California and arrive in Honolulu 10 to 14 days later. The race has been held since the turn of the century.

TDK/Gotcha Pro – a professional surf meet for both board surfers and bodysurfers is held at Sandy Beach in southeast Oahu, usually around mid-month.

August

Obon – observed in July and August, is marked by Japanese 'bon odori' dances to honor deceased ancestors. The final event is a floating lantern ceremony at Waikiki's Ala Wai Canal on the evening of August 15.

Hawaiian Slack-Key Guitar Festival – features Hawaii's top slack-key guitarists in a concert at Ala Moana Beach Park.

Ka Himeni Ana – a contest of old-style Hawaiian singing without amplification. All the songs are pre-WWII numbers that are sung in Hawaiian. It's held at the University of Hawaii in August or September.

September

Aloha Week – a celebration of all things Hawaiian with cultural events, contests, canoe races and Hawaiian music. Festivities, held in mid-September, include a street fair in downtown Honolulu and a parade in Waikiki.

Na Wahine O Ke Kai – Hawaii's major annual women's outrigger canoe race starts at sunrise at Kaluakoi, Molokai, and ends 40 miles later at Waikiki's Fort DeRussy Beach. It's held near the end of the month.

October

Molokai Hoe – Hawaii's major men's outrigger canoe race is held near mid-month. It starts after sunrise on Molokai and finishes at Waikiki's Fort DeRussy Beach about five hours later. Teams from Australia, Tahiti, Germany and the US mainland join Hawaiian teams in this annual competition which was first held in 1952.

November

Hawaii International Film Festival – features about 150 films from Pacific Rim and Asian nations. Films are shown throughout Oahu for a week around mid-November, with the schedule listed in the Honolulu papers.

Triple Crown of Surfing – consisting of three professional competitions that draw the world's top surfers to Oahu's North Shore, the events begin in November and run throughout December. Exact dates and locations depend on when and where the surf's up.

December

Bodhi Day – the Buddhist Day of Enlightenment is celebrated on the 8th with ceremonies at Buddhist temples.

Honolulu Marathon – the nation's second-largest marathon is run mid-month along a 26-mile course from the Aloha Tower to Kapiolani Park.

Christmas – festivals and craft fairs are held around Honolulu throughout December.

Aloha Bowl – the big collegiate football game held at Aloha Stadium on Christmas Day and televised nationally.

WORK

US citizens can pursue employment in Hawaii as elsewhere in the USA, while foreign visitors who are here for tourist purposes are not legally allowed to take up employment.

As Hawaii has had a relatively slow economy for the past few years, the job situation is not particularly rosy. Much of the economy is tied into the service industry, with wages hovering close to the minimum wage. For visitors, the most common work to land is waiting tables, and if you're young and energetic there are possibilities in restaurants and clubs.

If you're hoping to find more serious 'professional' employment, note that Hawaii is considered a tight labor market, with a lack of diversified industries and a relatively immobile labor force. Those jobs that do open up are generally filled by established Hawaiian residents.

For more information on employment in Hawaii, contact the State Department of Labor & Industrial Relations (☎ 586-8700), 830 Punchbowl St, Honolulu, HI 96813.

Getting There & Away

AIR

Honolulu is a major Pacific hub and an intermediate stop on many flights between the US mainland and Asia, Australia, New Zealand and the South Pacific. Passengers on any of these routes are usually allowed to make a stopover in Honolulu.

There are numerous airlines flying to Honolulu and a variety of fares are available. So rather than just walking into the nearest travel agency or airline office, it pays to do a bit of research and shopping around first.

You might want to start by perusing the travel sections of magazines and large newspapers, like the *New York Times*, the *San Francisco Examiner* and the *Los Angeles Times* in the USA; the *Sydney Morning Herald* or Saturday's *Age* in Australia; and *Time Out* or *TNT* in the UK.

Keeping in mind that airfares are constantly changing, the fares listed throughout this chapter should at least give you an idea of relative costs.

In addition to a straightforward round-trip ticket, Honolulu can also be part of a Round-the-World or Circle Pacific ticket.

Round-the-World Tickets

Round-the-World (RTW) tickets, which allow you to fly on the combined routes of two or more airlines, can be an economical way to circle the globe.

RTW tickets are valid for one year and you must travel in one general direction without backtracking. Although most airlines restrict the number of sectors that can be flown within the USA and Canada to four, and a few heavily traveled routes (such as Honolulu to Tokyo) are blacked out by some airlines, stopovers are otherwise generally unlimited.

In most cases a 14-day advance purchase is required. After the ticket is purchased, dates can usually be changed without penalty and tickets can be rewritten to add or delete stops for $25 to $50 each – depending upon the carrier.

There's an almost endless variety of airline and destination combinations possible. Because of Hawaii's central Pacific location, Honolulu can be included on most RTW tickets. As a general rule, travel solely in the Northern Hemisphere will be notably cheaper than travel that includes destinations in the Southern Hemisphere.

British Airways and Qantas Airways offer an RTW ticket that allows you to combine routes covering the South and Central Pacific regions, Asia and Europe. Because Qantas has a code-sharing partnership with American Airlines (which means you can book a flight through Qantas, such as New York-Los Angeles, using a Qantas ticket coupon but actually flying with American), this RTW ticket also allows some travel within the USA. From Australia the ticket costs A$3399; from the USA it's US$3249; from London it's £1930. These fares allow unlimited stopovers. Qantas and British Airways also offer a cheaper 'Global Explorer' RTW fare to those willing to restrict their stops to six; the fare is US$2995 from the USA, £1198 from the UK and between A$2669 and A$3279 (depending upon the season) from Australia.

Qantas also offers RTWs in partnership with American Airlines, Delta Air Lines, Scandinavian Airlines, Canadian Airlines, Lufthansa, Air France and KLM.

As another example, Continental Airlines links up with Malaysia Airlines, Singapore Airlines or Thai Airways for US$2570. With these airlines an itinerary could take you from the US mainland to Honolulu, Guam and Bali or Manila. From there, one possible routing would be to continue through Hong Kong, Saigon, Calcutta, Delhi, Istanbul, Rome and Paris before returning back to North America.

Circle Pacific Tickets

For Circle Pacific tickets, two airlines link up to allow stopovers along their combined Pacific Rim routes. Rather than simply fly from Point A to Point B, these tickets allow you to swing through much of the Pacific and eastern Asia taking in a variety of destinations – as long as you keep traveling in the same circular direction.

Circle Pacific routes essentially have the same fares: US$2579 when purchased in the USA, C$2979 when purchased in Canada, A$3299 when purchased in Australia and NZ$4049 when purchased in New Zealand.

Circle Pacific fares include four stopovers with the option of additional stops for US$50 each. There's a seven to 14-day advance purchase requirement, a 25% cancellation penalty and a maximum stay of six months.

Canadian Airlines has Circle Pacific fares from Vancouver in partnership with Qantas Airways, Air New Zealand, Singapore Airlines, Garuda, Cathay Pacific or Malaysia airlines.

Qantas offers Circle Pacific routes in partnership with, among others, United Airlines, Delta Air Lines, Japan Air Lines, Northwest Airlines or Continental Airlines.

Air New Zealand offers the ticket in conjunction with, among others, Japan Airlines, Thai Airlines, Cathay Pacific and Singapore Airlines. United Airlines offers the ticket in combination with more than a dozen Pacific Rim carriers.

Your itinerary can be selected from scores of potential destinations. For example, a Qantas-United ticket could take you from Los Angeles to Honolulu, on to Tokyo, south to Manila, followed by Sydney and then back to Los Angeles.

Keep in mind that Circle Pacific fares are high and you may find much better deals. Air New Zealand, for instance, has recently debuted a 'Pacific Explorer' fare roundtrip from Los Angeles for US$1099 that allows stopovers at three destinations, including New Zealand, Australia, Tahiti, Hawaii, Fiji, the Cook Islands, Western Samoa and Tonga, within a two-month period.

Honolulu International Airport

Honolulu International is a modern airport that's just completed a decade-long expansion. Although it's a busy place it's not particularly difficult to get around.

The airport has all the expected services, including fast-food restaurants, lounges, newsstands, sundry shops, lei stands, gift shops, duty-free shops, a 24-hour medical clinic and a mini-hotel for naps and showers.

There's a visitor information booth, car rental counters and hotel/condo courtesy phones in the baggage claim area. You can also pick up *This Week Oahu, Spotlight's Oahu Gold* and other tourist magazines from nearby racks.

If you arrive early for a flight and are looking for something to do, the Pacific Aerospace Museum ($3) in the main departure lobby has multimedia displays on aviation.

Money Thomas Cook has foreign exchange booths spread around the airport, including in the international arrival area and in the central departure lobby next to the barber shop. On the opposite side of the same barber shop is a Bankoh ATM that gives cash advances on major credit cards and withdrawals using Cirrus and Plus systems ATM cards. As Thomas Cook adds on some hefty transaction fees, using the ATM may be a better option.

If you're in no hurry, you can avoid needling transaction fees by going to the Bank of Hawaii on the ground level across the street from baggage claim D. It's open from 8:30 am to 3 pm Monday to Thursday and from 8:30 am to 6 pm on Fridays.

Baggage Storage There are coin-operated lockers in front of gates 13 and 24 that cost 50¢ per hour, or $3 per 24 hours, up to a maximum of 48 hours; coin changing machines are located next to the lockers.

Air Travel Glossary

Apex Apex ('advance purchase excursion') is a discounted ticket that must be paid for in advance. There are penalties if you wish to change it.

Baggage Allowance For international travelers, it's usually one 20 kg item to go in the hold, plus one item of hand luggage. Most US airlines allow passengers to check in two bags, each weighing up to 70 pounds, and carry on a third weighing 40 pounds.

Bucket Shop An unbonded travel agency specializing in discounted airline tickets.

Bumped Just because you have a confirmed seat doesn't mean you're going to get on the plane (see Overbooking).

Cancellation Penalties If you have to cancel or change a ticket there are often heavy penalties involved – insurance can sometimes be taken out against these penalties.

Check In Airlines ask you to check in a certain time ahead of the flight departure (commonly two hours on international flights). If you fail to check in on time and the flight is overbooked the airline can cancel your booking and give your seat to somebody else.

Discounted Tickets There's a complex and confusing array of discount tickets available. Some require advance purchase, while others require immediate purchase at the time of booking but no specific advance. The cheapest discount tickets may impose drawbacks, such as flying with unpopular airlines or inconvenient schedules and connections.

Electronic Ticket If you're flying from the US mainland to Hawaii, it's now possible to book your flight with an electronic ticket (also called E-ticket or ticketless travel). Essentially you get a receipt, but no ticket, from your airline or travel agent; you merely show identification at the ticket counter to get your boarding pass. One big advantage is the impossibility of losing your ticket.

Full Fares Airlines traditionally offer first class (coded F), business class (coded J) and economy class (coded Y) tickets. These days there are so many promotional and discounted fares available from the regular economy class that few passengers pay full economy fare.

Lost Tickets If you lose your ticket an airline will sometimes treat it like a bank would treat a traveler's check and issue you another one, though there may be a lengthy waiting period and a reissuance fee. Legally, however, an airline is entitled to treat a ticket like cash and if you lose it then it's gone forever. Take good care of your tickets.

No Shows No shows are passengers who fail to show up for their flight, sometimes due to unexpected delays or disasters, sometimes because they made more than one booking and didn't bother to cancel the one they didn't want. Full fare passengers who fail to turn up are sometimes entitled to travel on a later flight. The rest of us are usually penalized (see Cancellation Penalties).

Open Jaws A return ticket where you fly out to one place but return from another. If available, this can save you backtracking to your arrival point.

Overbooking Airlines hate empty seats, and since every flight has some passengers who fail to show up, airlines often book more passengers than they have seats. Usually the excess passengers balance those who fail to show up but occasionally somebody gets bumped. If this happens guess who it is most likely to be? The passengers who check in late.

Reconfirmation With some airlines it's necessary to reconfirm your reservation at least 72 hours prior to the departure of an onward or return flight. If you don't do this, in some cases an airline could delete your name from the passenger list, causing you to lose your seat.

Restrictions Discounted tickets often have various restrictions on them – advance purchase is the most usual one. Others are restrictions on the minimum and maximum period you must be away, such as a minimum of three days or a maximum of 60 days.

Standby A discounted ticket where you only fly if there is a seat free at the last moment. Standby fares are largely a thing of the past in the USA.

Tickets Out An entry requirement for many countries is that you have an onward or return ticket – in other words, a ticket out of the country. If you're not sure what you intend to do next, the easiest solution is to buy the cheapest onward ticket to a neighboring country or a ticket from a reliable airline which can later be refunded if you do not use it.

Transferred Tickets Airline tickets cannot be transferred from one person to another. Travelers sometimes try to sell the return half of their ticket, but officials can ask you to prove that you are the person named on the ticket. On international flights, tickets are usually compared with passports, and even on domestic US flights identification is commonly required for security purposes.

Travel Agencies Travel agencies vary widely. Full-service agencies handle everything from tours and tickets to hotel bookings, but if all you want is a ticket at the lowest possible price, then you may be better off with an agency specializing in discounted tickets. ∎

On the ground floor of the parking structure, opposite the main overseas terminal, there are additional coin-operated lockers as well as a baggage storage service that will hold items for $3 to $10 a day, depending on the size. It's open 24 hours a day; for information call ☎ 836-6547.

Airport Shuttle The free Wiki Wiki Shuttle (☎ 836-2505) connects the more distant parts of the airport and links the main terminal with the inter-island terminals. It can be picked up streetside in front of the main lobby (on the second level) and in front of the inter-island gates.

Airlines Serving Honolulu

The following airlines have scheduled flights to Honolulu International Airport. The numbers listed for each airline are the local Oahu numbers; those that begin with 800 can be called toll free.

Air Canada	☎ 800-776-3000
Air Marshall Islands	☎ 949-5522
Air Micronesia	☎ 800-231-0856
Air New Zealand	☎ 800-262-1234
All Nippon Airlines	☎ 695-8008
Aloha Airlines	☎ 484-1111
America West Airlines	☎ 800-235-9292
American Airlines	☎ 833-7600
Asiana	☎ 943-0200
Canadian Airlines	☎ 800-426-7000
China Airlines	☎ 955-0088
Continental Airlines	☎ 800-523-3273
Delta Air Lines	☎ 800-221-1212
Garuda Indonesia	☎ 947-9500
Hawaiian Airlines	☎ 838-1555
Island Air	☎ 484-2222
Japan Air Lines	☎ 521-1441
Korean Air	☎ 800-438-5000
Mahalo	☎ 833-5555
Northwest Airlines	☎ 955-2255
Philippine Airlines	☎ 800-435-9725
Qantas Airways	☎ 800-227-4500
Singapore Airlines	☎ 800-742-3333
Trans Air	☎ 836-8080
TWA	☎ 800-221-2000
United Airlines	☎ 800-241-6522

US Mainland

Domestic airfares are constantly in flux. Fares vary with the season you travel, the day of the week you fly, your length of stay and the flexibility the ticket provides for flight changes and refunds. Still, nothing determines fares more than business, and when things are slow, regardless of the season, airlines will drop fares to fill the empty seats. There's a lot of competition to Honolulu from the major mainland cities and at any given time any one of the airlines could have the cheapest fare.

The airlines each have their own requirements and restrictions which also seem to be constantly changing. For the latest deals, either find a knowledgeable travel agent or start calling the different airlines and compare.

When you call it's important to ask for the lowest fare, as that's not always the first one they'll quote. Each flight has only a limited number of seats available at the cheapest fares. When you make reservations the agents will generally tell you the best fare that's still available on the date you give them, which may or may not be the cheapest fare that the airline is currently offering. If you make reservations far enough in advance and are a little flexible with dates, you'll usually do better.

Typically the lowest roundtrip fares from the US mainland to Honolulu are about $550 to $800 from the east coast and $300 to $450 from the west coast. Although conditions vary, the cheapest fares are generally for midweek flights and have advance purchase requirements and other restrictions. They are usually nonrefundable and nonchangeable, at least on the outbound flight (although most airlines make allowances for medical emergencies).

The following airlines fly to Honolulu from both the US east and west coasts:

American	☎ 800-433-7300
Continental	☎ 800-525-0280
Delta	☎ 800-221-1212
Northwest	☎ 800-225-2525
TWA	☎ 800-221-2000
United	☎ 800-241-6522

In addition, Hawaiian Airlines (☎ 800-367-5320) flies nonstop to Honolulu from Seattle, San Francisco and Los Angeles. Depending on the season and current promotional fares, a roundtrip ticket from

Seattle is usually around $425. The standard fares from Los Angeles and San Francisco are $388 roundtrip, though Hawaiian often offers discounted fares from those cities for around $300.

Flight time to Honolulu is about 5½ hours from the west coast, 11 hours from the east coast.

Canada

The cheapest standard fares to Honolulu with Canadian Airlines are around C$450 from Vancouver, C$650 from Calgary or Edmonton and C$900 from Toronto. These fares are for mid-week travel, allow a maximum stay of 22 days and generally have a seven-day advance purchase requirement.

Tickets that allow longer maximum stays generally add about C$100 more on to the fares. The toll-free number for Canadian Airlines in Canada is ☎ 800-665-1177.

Central & South America

Most flights to Hawaii from Central and South America go via Houston or Los Angeles, though a few of those from the eastern cities go via New York.

Continental has flights from about 20 cities in Mexico and Central America, including San Jose, Guatemala City, Cancún and Mérida. Their lowest roundtrip fare from Mexico City to Honolulu is US$900 and allows a maximum stay of 60 days. It sometimes works out cheaper to buy two separate tickets, one to Los Angeles and then a second ticket from Los Angeles to Honolulu.

Australia

Qantas flies to Honolulu from Sydney or Melbourne (via Sydney but no change of plane), with roundtrip fares ranging from A$1210 to A$1479, depending on the season. These tickets have a 14-day advance purchase requirement, a minimum stay of seven days and a maximum stay of 60 days. There are currently no US carriers providing service between Australia and Honolulu, though United and Continental have done so in the past.

New Zealand

Air New Zealand has Auckland-Honolulu roundtrip fares ranging from NZ$1369 to NZ$1519, depending on the season. These tickets, which have to be purchased at least seven days in advance, allow stays of up to six months. Stopovers are permitted for an additional NZ$100 per stop. The one-way fare, which allows a free stopover in Fiji, is NZ$1049.

Fiji

Air New Zealand has a one-way fare from Nadi to Honolulu for F$916 (US$660) and a six-month excursion ticket for F$1306 (US$940).

Other South Pacific Islands

Hawaiian Airlines flies to Honolulu from Tahiti and American Samoa. From American Samoa the fare is US$403 one way, with no advance purchase required, and from US$799 roundtrip. From Tahiti to Honolulu the standard one-way fare is a steep US$1056 but there's a seven-day 'Shoppers Special' excursion ticket with no advance purchase requirement that costs US$744.

Air New Zealand flies to Honolulu from Tonga, the Cook Islands and Western Samoa. The lowest roundtrip fare from Tonga to Honolulu costs T$1125 (US$947), requires a seven-day advance purchase and allows a stay of up to 45 days. A one-way ticket costs T$647 (US$532).

From Rarotonga on the Cook Islands, Air New Zealand's cheapest roundtrip fare to Honolulu is NZ$1269 (US$888), while the one-way fare costs NZ$999 (US$699) year round.

From Apia in Western Samoa, Air New Zealand's roundtrip fare to Honolulu is WS$1355 (US$540) with no advance purchase requirement and a 90-day maximum stay. The one-way fare is WS$940 (US$375).

Micronesia

Continental, Northwest and United fly from Guam to Honolulu with roundtrip fares of around US$950. The Northwest and United flights are via Japan, while Continental offers direct flights. The tickets generally allow a stay of up to one year.

A more exciting way to get from Guam, however, would be Continental Air Micronesia's island hopper, which stops en route at the Micronesian islands of Chuuk, Pohnpei, Kosrae and Majuro before reaching Honolulu. It costs US$632 one way with no advance purchase requirement and has free unlimited stopovers. If you're coming from Asia this is a good alternative to a nonstop transpacific flight and a great way to see some of the Pacific's most remote islands without having to spend a lot of money.

Japan

Fares in this section are in yen; there are approximately 115 yen to one US dollar.

Japan Air Lines flies to Honolulu from Tokyo, Osaka, Nagoya, Fukuoka and Sapporo. Excursion fares vary a bit with the departing city and the season but, except at busier holiday periods, they're generally about ¥135,000 for a ticket valid for three months, with a three-day advance purchase requirement. The one-way fare from Tokyo is ¥144,600.

Two American carriers, United Airlines and Northwest Airlines, also have daily flights to Honolulu from Tokyo and Osaka. Their fares are competitive with JAL's.

An interesting alternative if you're only going one way would be to fly from Japan to Guam (¥69,400) and then pick up a Continental Air Micronesia ticket that would allow you to island hop through much of Micronesia on your way to Honolulu – for less than the cost of a direct one-way Japan-Honolulu ticket.

Southeast Asia

There are numerous airlines flying directly to Hawaii from Southeast Asia. The fares given below are standard published fares, though bucket shops in places like Bangkok and Singapore should be able to come up with much better deals. Also, if you're traveling to the USA from Southeast Asia, tickets to the US west

coast are not that much more than tickets to Hawaii and many allow a free stopover in Honolulu.

Northwest Airlines flies to Honolulu from Hong Kong, Bangkok, Manila, Seoul and Singapore. Thai Airlines, Korean Air and Philippine Airlines also have numerous flights between Southeast Asian cities and Honolulu. While there are some seasonal variations, the standard return fares average about US$1100 from Manila, US$1200 from Seoul and Bangkok, US$1500 from Hong Kong and US$1800 from Singapore.

Europe

The most common route to Hawaii from Europe is west via New York or Los Angeles. If you're interested in heading east with stops in Asia, it may be cheaper to get a Round-the-World ticket instead of returning the same way.

American Airlines has a roundtrip fare from London to Honolulu for US$1025 that allows a stay of up to 30 days. American's cheapest roundtrip fare from Paris to Honolulu is US$1075 and allows a stay of up to three months. From Frankfurt to Honolulu the lowest fare is US$1157 for a stay of up to 30 days. All of these fares are for travel between Monday and Thursday.

United, Delta and Continental airlines have similarly priced service to Honolulu from a number of European cities.

You can usually beat the published airline fares at bucket shops and other travel agencies specializing in discount tickets. London is arguably the world's headquarters for bucket shops and they are well advertised. Two good, reliable agents for cheap tickets in the UK are Trailfinders (☎ 0171-937-5400), 194 Kensington High St, London W8 7RG, and STA (☎ 0171-937-9962), 86 Old Brompton Rd, London SW7 3LQ.

Within Hawaii

There are frequent flights from Honolulu to the Neighbor Islands of Maui, Kauai, the Big Island, Molokai and Lanai.

The two main carriers, Hawaiian Airlines and Aloha Airlines, both have a standard one-way fare of $69 for flights between Honolulu and the major airports of Lihue (on Kauai), Kahului (on Maui), Kona and Hilo (both on the Big Island). Hawaiian Airlines and Island Air (an Aloha Airlines affiliate) also fly to the islands of Molokai and Lanai for the same fare.

In addition, there's an upstart airline, Mahalo Air, which has flights from Honolulu to all the Neighbor Islands except Lanai; one-way fares are $55.

Hawaiian Airlines offers a good-value air pass allowing unlimited air travel in Hawaii. The cheapest pass, which is good for five consecutive days, is $189; a one-week pass costs $209, a two-week pass $284. Note that the one-week pass is written to allow travel between one day of the week and the same day of the next week (ie, Monday to Monday) so it actually allows eight days of travel.

Aloha Airlines offers American Automobile Association (AAA) members a 25% discount off all of its standard fares and on some Island Air flights.

There are also other schemes that come up from time to time so always ask what promotional fares are currently being offered when you call to make reservations. Reservation numbers for inter-island airlines are:

Aloha Airlines	☎ 484-1111, 800-367-5250
Hawaiian Airlines	☎ 838-1555, 800-367-5320
Island Air	☎ 484-2222, 800-323-3345
Mahalo Air	☎ 833-5555, 800-462-4256

Discount Fares from Honolulu

Honolulu is a good place to get discounted fares to virtually any place around the Pacific. Fares vary according to the month, airline and demand, but often you can find a roundtrip fare to Los Angeles or San Francisco for around $250; to Tokyo for $500; to Hong Kong or Manila for $575; to Singapore or Fiji for $650; and to Auckland, Sydney or Saigon for $800.

If you don't have a set destination in mind you can sometimes find some great on-the-spot deals. The travel pages of the Sunday *Honolulu Advertiser* are loaded with ads by travel agencies advertising discounted overseas fares.

CRUISES

Travel agents, or shops that sell discount cruise tickets, are the best sources of information for transpacific cruises, though Hawaii-bound cruises are rare.

Once a year, usually in January, Cunard (☎ 800-221-4770) books the *Queen Elizabeth II* on a world cruise that stops in Hawaii. The boat can be picked up in Ensenada (Mexico) for a five-day cruise to Hawaii; the cost for just that segment starts at $2300, including airfare from Honolulu back to the US mainland.

TRAVEL AGENTS

Honolulu has scores of travel agents. A complete list can be found in the Oahu phone book yellow pages.

American Express has several travel service offices in Honolulu, including one in Waikiki at the Hyatt Regency hotel. Its main Honolulu office (☎ 946-7741) is at 1440 Kapiolani Blvd, Suite 104. A handful of other travel agencies and airline offices can be found in the nearby Ala Moana Center.

Some of the more significant agencies in Honolulu that specialize in discount travel are:

Cheap Tickets
   Kapiolani Blvd at Atkinson Drive
   (☎ 947-3717, 800-377-1000)

King's Travel
   725 Kapiolani Blvd (☎ 593-4481)

Pali Travel
   1304 Pali Hwy (☎ 533-3608, fax 524-2483)

Panda Travel
   1017 Kapahulu Ave
   (☎ 734-1961, fax 732-4136)

ORGANIZED TOURS

There are a slew of package tours available to Hawaii. The basic ones just include airfare and accommodations, while others can include car rentals, sightseeing tours and all sorts of recreational activities. If you're interested, travel agents can help you sort through the various packages.

For those with limited time, package tours can be the cheapest way to go. Costs vary, but one-week tours with airfare and no-frills Waikiki hotel accommodations usually start around $500 from the US west coast, $700 from the US east coast, based on double occupancy. If you want to stay somewhere fancy or island hop, the price can easily be double that.

LEAVING HAWAII
Departure Tax
There are no departure taxes to pay when leaving Hawaii.

Agricultural Inspection
All luggage and carry-on bags leaving Honolulu for the US mainland are checked by an agricultural inspector using an X-ray machine. You cannot take out gardenia, jade vine or roses, even in leis, although most other fresh flowers and foliage are permitted. You can take out pineapples and coconuts, but most other fresh fruits and vegetables are banned. Other things not allowed to enter mainland states include plants in soil, fresh coffee berries, cactus and sugar cane. Seeds, fruits and plants which have been certified and labeled for export aren't a problem.

WARNING
The information in this chapter is particularly vulnerable to change: prices for international travel are volatile, routes are introduced and canceled, schedules change, special deals come and go, and rules and visa requirements are amended.

Airlines and governments seem to take a perverse pleasure in making price structures and regulations as complicated as possible. You should check directly with the airline or a travel agent to make sure you understand how a fare (and any ticket you may buy) works. In addition, the travel industry is highly competitive and there are many lurks and perks.

The upshot of this is that you should get opinions, quotes and advice from as many airlines and travel agents as possible before you part with your hard-earned cash. The details given in this chapter should be regarded as pointers and are not a substitute for your own careful, up-to-date research.

Getting Around

THE AIRPORT

From the airport you can get to Waikiki by local bus (if your baggage is limited), by airport shuttle services, by taxi or by rental car. A taxi to Waikiki from the airport will cost about $20. The main car rental agencies have booths or courtesy phones in the airport baggage claim area.

The easiest way to drive to Waikiki from the airport is to take Hwy 92, which starts out as Nimitz Hwy and turns into Ala Moana Blvd, leading directly into Waikiki. Although this route hits more local traffic, it's hard to get lost on it.

If you're into life in the fast lane, connect instead with the H-1 freeway heading east.

On the return to the airport from Waikiki, beware of the poorly marked interchange where H-1 and Hwy 78 split; if you're not in the right-hand lane at that point, you could easily end up on Hwy 78. It takes about 20 minutes to get from Waikiki to the airport via H-1 *if* you don't hit traffic.

Bus

Travel time is about an hour between the airport and the far end of Waikiki on city bus Nos 19 and 20; the fare is $1. The bus stops at the roadside median on the second level, in front of the airline counters. There are two stops; it's best to wait for the bus at the first one, which is in front of Lobby 4. Luggage is limited to what you can hold on your lap or store under your seat, the latter space comparable to the space under an airline seat.

Shuttle Bus

The ride between Waikiki and the airport takes about 45 minutes by shuttle bus. These shuttles pick up passengers at the roadside median on the ground level between baggage claim areas E & F. Most charge $6 for adults, $3 for children, with rates including two suitcases and one carry-on bag. Generally, you don't need reserva-

tions from the airport to Waikiki, but you do need to call at least a few hours in advance for the return van to the airport. Two of the larger companies are Airport Express (☎ 949-5249) and Rabi Transportation (☎ 922-4900).

BUS

Oahu's public bus system, which is called TheBus, is extensive and easy to use.

TheBus has about 80 routes, which collectively cover most of Oahu. You can take the bus to watch windsurfers at Kailua or surfers at Sunset Beach, visit Chinatown or the Bishop Museum, snorkel at Hanauma Bay or hike Diamond Head. Some of the island's prime viewpoints are beyond reach, however. For instance, TheBus doesn't go up to Tantalus, on the north side of Honolulu, or stop at the Nuuanu Pali Lookout.

Buses stop only at marked bus stops. Each bus route can have a few different destinations. The destination is written on the front of the bus next to the number.

Buses generally keep the same number when inbound and outbound. For instance, the No 8 bus can take you either into the heart of Waikiki or out away from it towards Ala Moana – so note both the number and the written destination before you jump on.

When in doubt ask the bus driver. They're used to disoriented visitors and most drivers are patient and helpful.

Overall the buses are in excellent condition – if anything, they're a bit too modern, with sealed windows and climate-controlled air-con that can add a chill to the air.

Although TheBus is convenient enough, this isn't Tokyo – if you set your watch by the bus here you'll come up with Hawaiian Time. In addition to not getting hung up on schedules, buses can sometimes bottleneck, with one packed bus after another cruising right by crowded bus stops. Saturday nights between Ala Moana and Waikiki can be a particularly memorable experience.

Still, TheBus usually gets you where you want to go and as long as you don't try to cut anything close or schedule too much in one day it's a great deal.

Bus Fares

The one-way fare for all rides is $1 for adults, 50¢ for children ages six to 18. Children under the age of six ride free. You can use either coins or $1 bills; bus drivers don't make change.

Transfers, which have a time limit stamped on them, are given free when more than one bus is required to get to a destination. If needed, ask for one when you board.

Visitor passes valid for unlimited rides over four consecutive days cost $10 and can be purchased at any of the ubiquitous ABC Discount Stores.

Monthly bus passes valid for unlimited rides in a calendar month cost $25 and can be purchased at satellite city halls, 7-Eleven stores and Foodland and Star supermarkets.

Seniors 65 years and older can buy a $20 bus pass valid for unlimited rides during a two-year period. Senior citizen passes are issued only at TheBus office (☎ 848-4444), 811 Middle St, Honolulu, from 7:30 am to 4 pm Monday to Friday. Bus Nos 1 (Kahili) and 2 (School-Middle) go directly to TheBus office.

Schedules & Information

TheBus has a great telephone service. As long as you know where you are and where you want to go, you can call ☎ 848-5555 anytime between 5:30 am and 10 pm and they'll tell you not only which bus to catch but what time the next one will be there. The same number also has a TDD service for the hearing impaired.

For 24-hour recorded information on getting to major destinations from Waikiki, call ☎ 296-1818 and then enter 8287.

You can get printed timetables for some routes and a handy schematic bus route map free from any satellite city hall, including the one in the Ala Moana Center,

the Waikiki Beach police station and most libraries.

If you're going to be using TheBus extensively it's well worth buying one of the bus guides that are sold in bookstores and convenience stores for around $3. Take time to look a few over. For instance, *Honolulu's Famous TheBus* has actual schedules, but if you're not familiar with the streets a better choice is *Honolulu & Oahu by The Bus*, a fold-out brochure which doesn't have schedules but has maps showing major visitor destinations with bus stops and numbers. Be sure to get the most up-to-date version.

Common Routes

Bus Nos 8, 19, 20 and 58 run between Waikiki and Ala Moana Center, Honolulu's central transfer point. There's usually a bus every 10 minutes or less. From Ala Moana you can connect with a broad network of buses to points around the island.

Bus Nos 2, 19 and 20 will take you between Waikiki and downtown Honolulu.

Bus No 4 runs between Waikiki and the University of Hawaii.

CAR

The minimum age for visitors to drive in Hawaii is 18 years, though car-rental companies usually have higher age restrictions. If you're under age 25 you should call the car rental agencies in advance to check their policies regarding restrictions and surcharges.

You can legally drive in the state as long as you have a valid driver's license issued by a country that is party to the United Nations Conference on Road & Motor Transport – which covers virtually everyone.

However, car-rental companies will generally accept valid foreign driver's licenses only if they're in English. Otherwise most will require renters to show an international driver's license along with their home license.

Gasoline is about 25% more expensive in Honolulu than on the US mainland, with the price for regular unleaded gasoline averaging about $1.70 a gallon.

Road Rules

As with the rest of the USA, driving is on the right-hand side of the road.

Drivers at a red light can turn right after coming to a full stop and yielding to oncoming traffic, unless there's a sign at the intersection prohibiting the turn.

Hawaii requires the use of seat belts for drivers and front-seat passengers. State law also strictly requires the use of child safety seats for children ages three and under, while four-year-olds must either be in a safety seat or secured by a seat belt. Most of the car rental companies rent child safety seats, usually from $3 to $5 a day, but they don't always have them on hand so it's advisable to reserve one in advance.

Speed limits are posted and enforced. If you are stopped for speeding, expect to get a ticket, as the police rarely just give warnings.

Horn honking is considered very rude in Hawaii unless required for safety.

Rental

Car rentals are readily available at the airport and in Waikiki.

With most companies the weekly rate works out significantly cheaper per day than the straight daily rate. The daily rate for a small car such as a Geo Metro or Ford Escort, with unlimited mileage, ranges from around $25 to $45, while typical weekly rates are $150 to $200. You're usually required to keep the car for a minimum of five or six days to get the weekly rate.

Rates vary a bit from company to company and within each company depending on season, time of booking and current promotional fares. If you belong to an automobile club, a frequent-flyer program or a travel club you'll often be eligible for some sort of discount with at least one of the rental agencies.

One thing to note when renting a car is that rates for mid-size and full-size cars are often only a few dollars more per week; because some promotional discounts exclude the economy-size cars, at times the

Circle-Island Route

It's possible to make a nice day excursion circling the island by bus, beginning at the Ala Moana Center. The No 52 Wahiawa-Circle Island bus goes clockwise up Hwy 99 to Haleiwa and along the North Shore. At the Turtle Bay Hilton, on the northern tip of Oahu, it switches signs to No 55 and comes down the windward coast to Kaneohe and down the Pali Hwy back to Ala Moana. The No 55 Kaneohe-Circle Island bus does the same route in reverse. If you were to do it nonstop it would take about four hours and cost just $1.

For a shorter excursion, you can make a loop around southeast Oahu from Waikiki, by taking bus No 58 to Sea Life Park and then No 57 up to Kailua and back into Honolulu.

Because you'll need to change buses, ask for a transfer when you first board. Transfers have time limits and aren't meant to be used as stopovers but you can usually grab a quick break at Ala Moana. Anytime you get off to explore along the route you'll need to pay a new $1 fare when you reboard. ■

lowest rate available may actually be on a larger car.

At any given time any one of the rental companies could be offering the best deal, so you can save money by taking a little time to shop around. Be sure to ask the agent for the cheapest rate as the first quote given is not always the lowest.

It's a good idea to make reservations in advance, and with most companies there's no cancellation penalty if you change your mind. Walking up to the counter without a reservation will not only subject you to higher rates but during busy periods it's not uncommon for cars to be sold out altogether.

Another advantage of advance reservations is that if you have a bottom-line car reserved and there are none in the yard when you show up, the upgrade is free.

On daily rentals, most cars are rented on a 24-hour basis so you could get two days' use by renting at midday and driving around all afternoon, then heading out to explore somewhere else the next morning before the car is due back. Most companies even have an hour's grace period.

Rental rates generally include free unlimited mileage, though if you drop off the car at a different location from where you picked it up there's often a drop-off fee added on.

Having a major credit card greatly simplifies the rental process. Without one some agents simply will not rent vehicles, while others will require prepayment by cash or traveler's checks as well as a deposit, often around $300. Some do an employment verification and credit check, while others don't do background checks but they reserve the right for the station manager to decide whether to rent to you or not. If you intend to rent a car without plastic it's wise to make your plans well in advance, as you may need to submit a written application, a process that can take up to six weeks.

In addition to all rates, the state of Hawaii adds a $2-a-day tax to all car rentals.

Insurance

Collision damage waivers (CDWs) are available from car rental agencies for an additional $12 to $16 a day.

The CDW is not really even insurance (the companies already insure their cars) but rather a guarantee that the rental company won't hold you liable for any damages to their car (though even here there are exclusions). If you decline the CDW you are usually held liable for any damages up to the full value of the car. If damages do occur and you find yourself in a dispute with the rental company, you can call the state Department of Commerce & Consumer Affairs at ☎ 587-1234 and then key in 7222 for recorded information on your legal rights.

If you have collision coverage on your vehicle at home it might cover damages to car rentals in Hawaii. Check with your insurance company before your trip.

Some credit cards, including most 'gold cards' issued by Visa and MasterCard, offer reimbursement coverage for collision damages if you rent the car with that credit card and decline the CDW. If yours doesn't, it may be worth changing to one that does. Be aware that most credit card coverage isn't valid for rentals of more than 15 days or for exotic models, jeeps, 4WD vehicles, vans and motorbikes.

Rental Agencies

The following are international companies operating in Honolulu; their cars can be booked from offices around the world. The phone numbers listed are the Oahu numbers, followed by toll-free numbers in the USA.

Alamo	☎ 833-4585, 800-327-9633
Avis	☎ 834-5536, 800-831-8000
Budget	☎ 537-3600, 800-527-7000
Dollar	☎ 831-2330, 800-367-7006
Hertz	☎ 831-3500, 800-654-3131
National	☎ 831-3800, 800-227-7368

Budget, National, Hertz, Avis and Dollar all have desks at Honolulu International Airport and car lots on the airport grounds. Alamo has its operations about a mile outside the airport, on the corner of Nimitz Hwy and Ohohia St.

All things being equal, try to rent from a company with its lot inside the airport – not only is it more convenient but, more importantly, on the way back all the highway signs lead to the in-airport car returns. Having to run around looking for a car lot outside the airport could cost you valuable time when you're trying to catch a flight.

In addition to their airport operations, most of the international companies have multiple branch locations in Waikiki, many in the lobbies of larger hotels.

Budget gives renters a coupon booklet that allows free admission for one person to many of Oahu's more expensive tourist attractions, including Sea Life Park, Polynesian Cultural Center and Bishop Museum. You don't have to buy one to get one, so for a single traveler it's all free – a particularly good deal if you're renting a car for just a day or two and trying to catch the main sights.

Moped

State law requires mopeds to be ridden by only one person and prohibits their use on sidewalks and on freeways. Renters must be 18 years or older.

Blue Sky Rentals (☎ 947-0101), on the ground floor of Inn on the Park Hotel, 1920 Ala Moana Blvd, is a good Waikiki spot to rent a moped. The rates of $20 from 8 am to 6 pm, $25 for 24 hours or $105 a week, include taxes and insurance.

Mopeds can also be rented at similar rates from Diamond Head Mopeds (☎ 921-2899), which has a location at the corner of Lewers St and Kuhio Ave and another on Kuhio Ave just east of the Royal Garden Hotel.

Parking

Parking can be a challenge in Honolulu's busiest areas.

In Waikiki, most hotels charge $8 to $12 a day for guest parking in their garages. However, if you're willing to go a little out of your way you could save money.

At the west end of Waikiki, there's a public parking lot at the Ala Wai Yacht Harbor, which has free parking up to a maximum of 72 hours. At the east end of Waikiki, the zoo parking lot on Kapahulu Ave has meters that cost just 25¢ an hour with a four-hour parking limit.

In downtown Honolulu, there's metered parking along Punchbowl St and on Halekauwila St opposite the federal building. There are also a limited number of

Driving Times

While your actual driving time may vary depending upon traffic conditions, the average driving times and distances from Waikiki to points of interest around Oahu are as follows:

Arizona Memorial	12 miles	30 minutes
Haleiwa	29 miles	50 minutes
Hanauma Bay	11 miles	25 minutes
Honolulu Airport	9 miles	20 minutes
Kaena Point State Park	43 miles	75 minutes
Kailua	14 miles	25 minutes
Laie	34 miles	60 minutes
Makaha Beach	36 miles	60 minutes
Nuuanu Pali Lookout	11 miles	20 minutes
Sea Life Park	16 miles	35 minutes
Sunset Beach	37 miles	65 minutes
Waimea	34 miles	60 minutes
Waipahu	16 miles	30 minutes

metered spaces in the basement of the state office building on the corner of Beretania and Punchbowl Sts.

Both downtown and the adjacent Chinatown area also have parking garages that charge by the hour.

TAXI

Metered taxis start with a flag-down fee of $2 and then click up in 25¢ increments at a rate of $2 per mile. There's an extra charge of 35¢ for each suitcase or backpack.

Taxis are readily available at the airport and larger hotels, but otherwise generally hard to find. To phone for one, try Sida (☎ 836-0011), Charley's (☎ 955-2211), Americabs (☎ 591-8830) or City Taxi (☎ 524-2121). The latter offers a 10% discount to senior citizens over the age of 60.

BICYCLE

It's possible to bicycle around the greater Honolulu area, but there's a lot of traffic to contend with and roads don't have designated bike lanes. In Waikiki, the best main roads for cyclists are the one-way streets of canalside Ala Wai Blvd and beachside

Kalakaua Ave, both of which have minimal cross-traffic.

The State Department of Transportation has published a new 'Bike Oahu' map with possible routes, divided into those for novice cyclists, those for experienced cyclists and routes that are not bicycle-friendly. The map can usually be found at the HVB visitor information center in Waikiki, or call ☎ 527-5044.

If you want to get out of town and just cycle back one way, a number of public buses have been equipped with racks that can carry two bicycles. To use them, you simply secure your bicycle on the front of the bus, board the bus and pay the regular passenger fare. Because only about one-third of the buses have these cycle racks, its wise to call TheBus (☎ 848-5555) in advance to make sure a rack-equipped bus is scheduled on the route you plan to take.

Planet Surf (☎ 926-2060), 419 Nahua St in Waikiki, rents mountain bikes for $15/65 a day/week and beach cruisers for $13/50.

There are a few other rental places in Waikiki that rent bicycles for around $20 a day, including one next to InterClub Hostel Waikiki, 2413 Kuhio Ave, and Blue Sky Rentals at 1920 Ala Moana Blvd.

The state of Hawaii does not require bicyclists to wear helmets, but some bicycle rental shops, including Planet Surf, provide them free of charge.

The Hawaii Bicycling League (☎ 735-5756), Box 4403, Honolulu, HI 96812, holds bike rides around Oahu nearly every Saturday and Sunday, ranging from 10-mile jaunts to 60-mile treks. Rides are free and open to the public.

WALKING

Because of traffic on the main thorough-fares and the distances between Waikiki and other attractions in Honolulu, walking is generally not the preferred way to get between different parts of the city. There are, however, sections of the city that are quite pleasant for strolling, including Kapi-olani Park, Waikiki Beach, Chinatown and downtown. For information on wooded walks see Hiking in the Things to See & Do chapter.

ORGANIZED TOURS
Bus Tours
Conventional sightseeing tours by van or bus are offered by E Noa Tours (☎ 591-2561), Polynesian Adventure Tours (☎ 833-3000) and Roberts Hawaii (☎ 539-9400).

These companies offer several different tours. Polynesian Adventure Tours, for example, has a half-day Honolulu city tour that includes the main downtown sights, Punchbowl and the Arizona Memorial and another half-day tour of southeast Oahu that stops by Diamond Head, Hanauma Bay, Sandy Beach, Nuuanu Pali Lookout, Queen Emma's Summer Palace and Tantalus; each tour costs $23 for adults, $18 for children.

In addition there are full-day circle-island tours which average $55 and encompass southeast Oahu, the windward coast and the North Shore.

Keep in mind that the big-company bus tours make sightseeing stops but don't allow time for swimming and similar activities. For those who want to get into the water and relax along the way, a good alternative island tour is offered by Alala EcoAdventures. It costs just $22 and is booked through Hostelling International Honolulu (☎ 946-0591).

Waikiki Trolley
The Waikiki Trolley is an open-air trolley-style bus running between Waikiki and Honolulu that's geared for tourists making a beaten path around the main city shopping and sightseeing attractions. It makes 19 stops, including the Honolulu Zoo, Ala Moana Center, Honolulu Academy of Arts, Iolani Palace, Foster Botanic Garden, Chinatown, Bishop Museum, Aloha Tower Marketplace and the Ward Centre. Sightseeing narration is provided en route and passengers can get off at any stop and then pick up the next trolley. Trolleys depart from the Royal Hawaiian Shopping Center in Waikiki every 15 minutes between 8 am and 4:30 pm.

One-day passes cost $17 for adults, $5 for children ages 11 and under, while five-day passes cost $30 for adults, $10 for children. The trolley can be convenient if you're sticking solely to its transcribed route, but it's a pricey alternative to the public bus, which is fairly frequent along most of these routes and offers a four-day pass for only $10.

Guided Walking Tours

There are a handful of educational and cultural groups offering insightful walking tours of the city.

For those who want to delve into local lore, Kapiolani Community College leads downtown walking tours with varied historical themes – from ghosts of old Honolulu to the crime beat of the 1920s. The cost is $5 and advance registration is required. Schedules are available from the Office of Community Services (☎ 734-9245), Kapiolani Community College, 4403 Diamond Head Rd, Honolulu, HI 96816. Honolulu TimeWalks does similar theme walking tours for $8; call (☎ 943-0371) for schedule information.

A couple of organizations offer Chinatown walking tours. It should be noted, however, that Chinatown is a fun place to poke around on your own and it can feel a bit touristy being led around in a group. Still, the guides provide colorful commentary with historical insights and often take you to a few places you're unlikely to walk into otherwise.

The Hawaii Heritage Center (☎ 521-2749) leads walking tours of Chinatown from 9:30 am to noon on Fridays for $4. Meet in front of Ramsay Galleries at 1128 Smith St.

The Chinese Chamber of Commerce (☎ 533-3181) conducts walking tours of Chinatown from 9:30 am to noon on Tuesdays for $5. Meet at the chamber office at 42 N King St.

Tours to the Neighbor Islands

If you want to visit another island but only have a day or two to spare, it might be worth looking into 'overnighters,' which are mini-packaged tours to the Neighbor Islands that include roundtrip airfare, car and hotel. Rates depend on the accommodations you select, with a one-night package typically starting around $125 per person, based on double occupancy. You can add on additional days for an additional fee, usually about $60 per person.

The largest companies specializing in overnighters are Roberts Hawaii (☎ 523-9323 on Oahu, 800-899-9323 from the mainland) and Pleasant Island Holidays (☎ 922-1515).

Cruises   American Hawaii Cruises (☎ 800-765-7000), 2 N Riverside Plaza, Chicago, IL 60606, operates the cruise ship *Independence*, which makes a seven-day tour around Hawaii. The ship leaves Honolulu each Saturday all year round and visits Kauai (Nawiliwili Harbor), Maui (Kahului Harbor) and the Big Island (Hilo and Kona) before returning to Honolulu.

Rates start at $1145 for the cheapest inside cabin and go up to $3195, with the cheapest outside cabin priced at $1345. Fares are per person, based on double occupancy, and there's an additional $85 for port charges.

Although more modest than the modern mammoths that cruise the Caribbean, the *Independence* is a full-fledged cruise ship, 682 feet long, with lavish buffet meals, swimming pools and the like. Each carries a crew of 325 along with 960 passengers.

Things to See & Do

Honolulu has a wide range of things to see and do. The largest concentration of historical and cultural sights are clustered in downtown Honolulu and adjacent Chinatown, which are well suited for getting about on foot.

If you prefer to spend your time in the water, good conditions for swimming, snorkeling, diving, surfing, windsurfing and kayaking are easy to find at Waikiki Beach and elsewhere on the island. To hit the water without getting wet, you can choose from a plethora of cruises and glassbottom boats, and even a submarine.

For land lovers, there's a nice variety of hikes and walks in greater Honolulu, as well as a wide sweep of sporting activities from tennis and jogging to kite flying. If you'd rather see it all from the air, you can go gliding or take a tandem skydive.

HIGHLIGHTS

Vibrant Waikiki Beach is the venue for most tourist activities, with sunbathing, swimming, water sports and people watching among its highlights. At the less-touristed end of Waikiki is Kapiolani Park with its newly renovated aquarium and zoo and its numerous community attractions from concerts to sporting events.

Still, to experience most of what Honolulu has to offer, you'll need to go beyond Waikiki. Don't miss a stroll through downtown Honolulu's historic district, including Iolani Palace, the State Capitol and early mission church sights.

Another delightful place for walking is the adjacent Chinatown area, with its lively markets and inexpensive neighborhood restaurants. While you're there, stroll through Foster Botanic Garden, which has some of the island's loftiest trees and rarest plants.

For a city of its size, Honolulu has some surprisingly good museums. Spending a few hours at the renowned Bishop Museum

Favorite Places

Sunsets All of Waikiki Beach is a fun place to be at sunset, with Kapahulu Groin a particular favorite. A top runner-up is Magic Island, which is adjacent to Ala Moana Beach Park and overlooks the Ala Wai Yacht Harbor.

Picnics Fort DeRussy Beach, at the west end of Waikiki, has arbored picnic shelters with barbecue pits; take a swim while you wait for the grill to fire up. If you just want to spread out a blanket and unpack a picnic basket, Kapiolani Beach Park, at the opposite end of Waikiki, has inviting lawns.

Scenic Views For a panoramic view of Waikiki, take a hike up to Diamond Head summit. For the most spectacular vista of Honolulu, drive up to Puu Ualakaa State Park in the Tantalus area, which has a sweeping view from Diamond Head to Pearl Harbor. ■

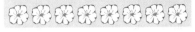

will give you a great introduction to Hawaiian culture. The Honolulu Academy of Arts has a quality fine arts collection, while the more recently established Contemporary Arts Museum displays modern art in a lovely estate setting.

The most scenic drive around Honolulu is the Tantalus-Makiki Drive at the north side of the city. The highlight along this route is the panoramic view of greater Honolulu from Puu Ualakaa State Park.

There are some great hikes just beyond the city center. For a solitary wilderness walk, the hike to Manoa Falls is a good choice. If you want a view and don't mind lots of company, the walk up to the summit of Diamond Head offers a sweeping panorama of Waikiki.

For many people the USS Arizona Memorial at Pearl Harbor is a 'must' and for any visitor it's a moving experience. The other major war memorial of interest is the National Cemetery of the Pacific at Punchbowl.

Beyond Honolulu, a trip around southeast Oahu offers fine scenery and a glimpse of a less-developed side of the island. Don't miss Hanauma Bay for both its striking view and easy-access snorkeling. Also along this route is the quiet walk to Makapuu lighthouse and the variety of marine-animal displays at Sea Life Park.

WAIKIKI (Map 4)

Waikiki, the largest tourist destination in Hawaii, has a long attractive white-sand beach that's lined with high-rise hotels and set against a backdrop of scenic Diamond Head.

Crowded with package tourists from both Japan and North America, Waikiki has 25,000 permanent residents and some 65,000 visitors on any given day, all in an area roughly 1½ miles long and half a mile wide. It boasts 33,000 hotel rooms, 450 restaurants, 350 bars and clubs, and more shops than you'd want to count.

Waikiki has plenty of clichéd activities that can make for good fun, such as the Kodak Hula Show, outrigger canoe rides and sunning on the beach. Like any city scene, the deeper you dig, the more you'll find. You can also join in a Japanese tea ceremony, take a surfing lesson from one of the aging beachboys who used to ride the waves with Duke Kahanamoku or listen to a free Sunday concert by the Royal Hawaiian Band in Kapiolani Park.

While the beaches are packed during the day, most of the action at night is along the streets, where window-shoppers, cruising pedicabs, time-share touts and street-corner prostitutes all go about their business. A variety of live music, from mellow Hawaiian to rock, wafts from streetside clubs and hotel lounges.

Waikiki Beach has wonderful orange sunsets, with the sun dropping down between cruising sailboats. The beach is also quite romantic to stroll along at night, enhanced by both the city skyline and the surf lapping at the shore, and it's dark enough to enjoy the stars.

Orientation

Waikiki is bounded on two sides by the Ala Wai Canal, on another by the ocean and on the fourth by the expansive Kapiolani Park. There are three parallel roads through Waikiki: Kalakaua Ave, the beach road; Kuhio Ave, the main drag for Waikiki's buses; and Ala Wai Blvd, which borders the canal.

City buses are not allowed on Kalakaua Ave and trucks are prohibited at midday. Traffic on this four-lane road is one-way so it's relatively smooth for driving. However, pedestrians need to be cautious as cars tend to zoom by at a fairly fast clip.

Waikiki Walking Tour

It's possible to make an interesting two- to three-hour walking tour of Waikiki by combining a stroll along the beach with a walk along Kalakaua Ave.

You can walk the full length of Waikiki along the sand and the sea wall. Although the beach walk gets crowded at midday, at other times it's usually less packed than the sidewalks along Kalakaua Ave.

A good place to begin the walk is at Kapahulu Groin, near the northern border of Kapiolani Park, where you can observe Waikiki's top boogie-boarding action. As you continue west along the beach you can stop for a swim, watch surfers ride the offshore breaks and take a look at some of the seaside hotels. After you reach the Halekulani Hotel, continue to the US Army Museum at the Fort DeRussy Military Reservation and then head up Beach Walk to Kalakaua Ave, where you'll turn right. On the corner of Lewers St and Kalakaua Rd is the First Hawaiian Bank, the interior of which has notable Hawaiiana murals by the fresco artist Jean Charlot. Pick up a free brochure describing the murals from the bank's information desk.

From Swamp to Resort

Little more than a century ago Waikiki was almost entirely wetlands. It had more than 50 acres of fishponds as well as extensive taro patches and rice paddies. Fed by mountain streams from the upland Manoa and Makiki valleys, Waikiki was one of Oahu's most fertile and productive areas.

By the late 1800s Waikiki's narrow beachfront was lined with private gingerbread-trimmed cottages, built by Honolulu's more well-to-do citizens.

Author Robert Louis Stevenson, who frequented Waikiki in those days, wrote:

HAWAII STATE ARCHIVES

If anyone desires such old-fashioned things as lovely scenery, quiet, pure air, clear sea water, heavenly sunsets hung out before his eyes over the Pacific and the distant hills of Waianae, I recommend him to Waikiki Beach.

Tourism took root in 1901 when the Moana opened its doors as Waikiki's first real hotel. A tram line was constructed to connect Waikiki to downtown Honolulu and city folk crowded aboard for outings to the beach. Tiring quickly of the pesky mosquitoes that thrived in the wetlands, these early beachgoers petitioned to have Waikiki's 'swamps' brought under control.

In 1922 the Ala Wai Canal was dug to divert the streams that flowed into Waikiki. Old Hawaii lost out, as farmers had the water drained out from under them. Coral rubble was used to fill the ponds, creating what was to become Hawaii's most valuable piece of real estate. Water buffaloes were replaced by tourists.

As you continue down Kalakaua Ave, you can take in the historic Royal Hawaiian and Moana hotels, visit the Oceanarium at the Pacific Beach Hotel and take a look at the Damien Museum behind St Augustine's Church. Upon returning to Kapahulu Groin, you can visit the Honolulu Zoo and, if you still have time, stroll around Kapiolani Park and take in the Waikiki Aquarium. All of these sights are described in the sections that follow.

Waikiki Beaches

The two-mile stretch of white sand that runs from the Hilton Hawaiian Village to Kapiolani Park is commonly called Waikiki Beach, although different sections along the way have their own names and characteristics.

In the early morning the beach belongs to walkers and joggers and it's surprisingly quiet. Strolling down the beach towards Diamond Head at sunrise can actually be a meditative experience.

By midmorning it looks like a normal resort beach, with boogie board and surfboard concessionaires setting up shop and catamarans pulling up on the beach offering $15 sails. By noon it is packed and the challenge is to walk down the beach without stepping on anyone.

Waikiki is good for swimming, boogie boarding, surfing, sailing and other beach activities most of the year. Between May

Waikiki's second hotel, the Royal Hawaiian, was built in 1927 and became the crown jewel of the Matson Navigation Company.

The Royal was the land component for cruises on the *Malolo*, one of the premier luxury ships of the day. The $7.5-million ship, built while the $2-million hotel was under construction, carried 650 passengers from San Francisco to Honolulu each fortnight. The Pink Palace, as the Royal Hawaiian was nicknamed, opened with an extravagant $10-a-plate dinner.

Hotel guests ranged from the Rockefellers to Charlie Chaplin, Babe Ruth to royalty. Some guests brought dozens of trunks, their servants and even their Rolls Royces.

The Depression put a damper on things and WWII saw the Royal Hawaiian turned into an R&R center for servicemen.

In 1950, Waikiki had only 1400 hotel rooms. In those days surfers could drive their cars to the beach and park right on the sand. In the '60s tourism took over in earnest. By 1968 Waikiki had some 13,000 hotel rooms and in the following two decades that number more than doubled.

The lack of available land finally halted the boom of new hotels. In a desperate attempt to squeeze in one more high-rise, St Augustine's Catholic Church, standing on the last speck of uncommercialized property along busy Kalakaua Ave, was nearly sold in 1989 to a Tokyo developer for $45 million. It took a community uproar and a petition to the Vatican to nullify the deal. ■

DAVID RUSS

and September, summer swells can make the water a little rough for swimming, but they also make it the best season for surfing. Waikiki beaches simply aren't that good for snorkeling; the best of them is Sans Souci.

There are lifeguards and showers at many places along the beach.

Kahanamoku Beach Fronting the Hilton Hawaiian Village, Kahanamoku Beach is the westernmost section of Waikiki. It was named for Duke Kahanamoku, a surfer and swimmer who won Olympic gold in the 100-meter freestyle in 1912 and went on to become a Hawaiian celebrity.

Kahanamoku Beach is protected by a breakwater at one end and a pier at the other, with a coral reef running between the two. It's a calm swimming area with a sandy bottom that slopes gradually.

Fort DeRussy Beach One of the least crowded Waikiki beaches, Fort DeRussy Beach borders 1800 feet of the Fort DeRussy Military Reservation. Like all beaches in Hawaii, it's public; the federal government provides lifeguards and there are showers and other facilities, including arbored picnic shelters. In addition, you'll find an inviting grassy lawn that gets at least sparse shade from palm trees, providing an alternative to frying on the sand.

The water is usually calm and good for

Borrowed Sands

Most of Waikiki's beautiful white sand is not its own. It is barged in by the ton, much of it from Papohaku Beach on Molokai.

As the beachfront developed, landowners haphazardly constructed sea walls and offshore barriers to protect their property. In the process they blocked the natural forces of sand accretion, and erosion has long been a serious problem at Waikiki.

Sections of the beach are still being replenished with imported sand, although much of it ends up washing into the ocean, where it fills channels and depressions and alters the surf breaks. ■

swimming. When conditions are right, you can windsurf, boogie board and board surf as well. There are two beach huts, open daily, where you can rent windsurfing equipment, boogie boards, kayaks and snorkel sets.

Gray's Beach Gray's Beach, the local name for the beach near the Halekulani Hotel, was named for a boarding house called Gray's-by-the-Sea that stood on the site in the 1920s. On the same stretch of beach was the original Halekulani, a lovely low-rise mansion that was converted into a hotel in the 1930s. In the 1980s, the mansion gave way to the present high-rise hotel.

Because the sea wall in front of the Halekulani was built so close to the waterline, the beach fronting the hotel is often totally submerged.

The section of beach between the Halekulani and the Royal Hawaiian Hotel varies in width from season to season. The waters off the beach are shallow and calm.

Central Waikiki Beach The area from the Royal Hawaiian Hotel to the Waikiki Beach Center is the busiest section of the whole beach and has a nice spread of sand for sunbathing.

Most of the beach has a shallow bottom with a gradual slope. There's pretty good swimming here, but there's also a lot of activity, with catamarans, surfers and plenty of other swimmers in the water. Keep your eyes open.

Offshore are Queen's Surf and Canoe's Surf, Waikiki's best-known surf breaks.

Waikiki Beach Center The area opposite the Hyatt Regency Waikiki is the site of the Waikiki Beach Center. It has restrooms, showers, a police station, surfboard lockers and rental concessions.

The **Wizard Stones of Kapaemahu** – four boulders on the Diamond Head side of the police station – are said to contain the secrets and healing powers of four sorcerers, named Kapaemahu, Kinohi, Kapuni and Kahaloa, who visited from Tahiti in ancient times. Before returning back to Tahiti, they transferred their powers to these stones.

Just west of the stones is a bronze **statue of Duke Kahanamoku** (1890-1968), Hawaii's most decorated athlete, standing with one of his longboards. Considered the 'father of modern surfing,' Duke, who made his home in Waikiki, gave surfing demonstrations on beaches around the world from Sydney, Australia, to Rockaway Beach, New York. Many local surfers took issue with the placement of the statue as Duke is standing with his back to the sea, a position they say he never would have taken in real life. In response the city moved the statue as close to the sidewalk as possible.

Star Beach Boys, a beachside concession stand, rents surfboards and boogie boards by the hour, gives surfing lessons and offers inexpensive outrigger canoe rides.

Kuhio Beach Park Kuhio Beach Park is marked on its east end by Kapahulu Groin, a walled storm drain with a walkway on top that juts out into the ocean from the end of Kapahulu Ave.

A low breakwater sea wall runs about 1300 feet out from Kapahulu Groin, paralleling the beach. This breakwater was built to control sand erosion and in the process two nearly enclosed swimming pools were formed. Local kids walk out on the breakwater, which is called The Wall, but it can be dangerous to the uninitiated due to a slippery surface and breaking surf.

The pool closest to Kapahulu Groin is best for swimming, with the water near the breakwater reaching overhead depths. However, because circulation is limited, the water gets murky with a noticeable film of suntan oil. The 'Watch Out Deep Holes' sign refers to holes in the pool's sandy bottom that can be created by swirling currents. Those who can't swim should be cautious in the deeper areas of the pool as the holes can take waders by surprise.

The park, incidentally, is named after the distinguished Hawaiian statesman Prince Jonah Kuhio Kalanianaole, who maintained his residence on this beach. His house was torn down in 1936, 14 years after his death, in order to expand the beach.

Between the old-timers who gather each afternoon to play chess and cribbage at Kuhio's sidewalk pavilions and the kids boogie boarding off the Groin, this section of the beach has as much local color as tourist influence.

Kapahulu Groin Kapahulu Groin is one of Waikiki's hottest boogie-boarding spots. If the surf's right, you can find a few dozen boogie boarders, mostly teenage boys, riding the waves.

The kids ride straight for the Groin's cement wall and then veer away at the last moment, drawing 'oohs' and 'ahs' from the tourists who gather to watch them.

Kapahulu Groin is also a great place to catch sunsets.

Kapiolani Beach Park Kapiolani Beach Park starts at Kapahulu Groin and runs down to the Natatorium, past Waikiki Aquarium.

Queen's Surf is the name given to the wide midsection of Kapiolani Beach. The stretch in front of the pavilion is a popular beach with the gay community. It's a pretty good area for swimming, with a sandy bottom. The section of beach between Queen's Surf and Kapahulu Groin is shallow and has a lot of broken coral.

Kapiolani Beach Park is a relaxed place with little of the frenzied activity found in front of the central strip of Waikiki hotels. It's a popular weekend picnicking spot for local families who unload the kids to splash in the water as they line up the barbecue grills.

You can layout on a big grassy field that's good for spreading out a beach towel and unpacking a picnic basket. Free parking is available near the beach along Kalakaua Ave. There are restrooms and showers at the Queen's Surf pavilion.

The surfing area offshore is called Public's.

NED FRIARY

Duke Kahanamoku

Natatorium The Natatorium, at the Diamond Head end of Kapiolani Beach, is a 100-meter-long saltwater swimming pool built after WWI as a memorial for soldiers who died in that war. There were once hopes of hosting an Olympics on Oahu, with this pool as the focal point.

The Natatorium, which is on the National Register of Historic Places, is now closed and in disrepair, but the state has tentative plans to restore the facility.

Sans Souci Beach Down by the New Otani Kaimana Beach Hotel, Sans Souci is a nice little sandy beach away from the main tourist scene. It has outdoor showers and a lifeguard station.

Many residents come to Sans Souci for daily swims. A shallow coral reef close to shore makes for calm, protected waters and provides reasonably good snorkeling. More coral can be found by following the Kapua Channel as it cuts through the reef, although beware of currents that can pick up in the channel. Check conditions with the lifeguard before venturing out.

Historic Hotels

Waikiki's two historic hotels, the Royal Hawaiian and the Moana (now the Sheraton Moana Surfrider), both retain their period character and are worth a visit. These beachside hotels, which are on the National Register of Historic Places, are a couple of blocks apart on Kalakaua Ave.

With its pink turrets and Moorish/Spanish architecture, the Royal Hawaiian Hotel is a throwback to the era when Rudolph Valentino was *the* romantic idol and travel to Hawaii was by luxury liner. Inside, the hotel is lovely and airy with high ceilings and chandeliers and everything in rose colors.

The hotel was originally on a 20-acre coconut grove, but over the years the grounds have been chipped away by a huge shopping center on one side and a high-rise mega-hotel on the other. Still, the small garden at the rear is filled with birdsong, a rare sound in most of Waikiki.

The Sheraton Moana Surfrider, which has recently undergone a splendid restoration, has the aura of an old plantation inn. The 2nd floor has a display of memorabilia from the early hotel days, with scripts from 'Hawaii Calls,' woolen bathing suits, period photographs and a short video. At 11 am and 5:15 pm daily there are hour-long historical tours of the hotel that leave from the concierge desk and are free to the public; reservations are not necessary.

Fort DeRussy

Fort DeRussy Military Reservation is a US Army post used mainly as a recreation center for the armed forces. This large chunk of Waikiki real estate was acquired by the US Army a few years after Hawaii was annexed to the USA. Prior to that it was swampy marshland and a favorite duck hunting spot for Hawaiian royalty.

The Hale Koa Hotel on the property is open only to military personnel, but there's public access to the beach and the adjacent military museum. The section of Fort DeRussy between Kalia Rd and Kalakaua Ave has public footpaths that provide a shortcut between the two roads.

US Army Museum of Hawaii Battery Randolph, a reinforced concrete building built in 1911 as a coastal artillery battery, houses the army museum at Fort DeRussy. It once held two 14-inch-diameter disappearing guns that had an 11-mile range and were designed to recoil down into the concrete walls for reloading after each firing. A 55-ton lead counterweight would then return the carriage to position. When the guns were fired, the entire neighborhood shook. To get a sense of how huge these guns were, go up to the roof where you'll see one of the seven-inch replacements – despite being half the size of the original, it still has a formidable presence.

The battery houses a wide collection of weapons, from Hawaiian shark-tooth clubs to WWII tanks, as well as exhibits on military history as it relates to Hawaii told through dioramas, scale models and period photos. There are interesting historic displays on King Kamehameha and Hawaii's role in WWII. There's also a theater with films outlining current-day projects by the Army Corps of Engineers in Hawaii and Micronesia.

The museum is open from 10 am to 4:30 pm daily, except on Mondays, Christmas and New Year's Day. Admission is free.

Kapiolani Park

The nearly 200-acre Kapiolani Park, at the Diamond Head end of Waikiki (see Map 9), was given by King Kalakaua to the people of Honolulu in 1877. Hawaii's first public park, it was dedicated to Kalakaua's wife, Queen Kapiolani.

In its early days horseracing and concerts were the park's biggest attractions. Although the race track is gone, the concerts continue and Kapiolani Park is still the venue for a wide range of community activities.

The park contains the Waikiki Aquarium, the Honolulu Zoo, Kapiolani Beach Park, the Waikiki Shell, the Kodak Hula Show grounds and the Kapiolani Bandstand.

The Royal Hawaiian Band presents free afternoon concerts nearly every Sunday at the Kapiolani Bandstand. Dance competitions, Hawaiian music concerts and other activities occur at the bandstand throughout the year.

The Waikiki Shell is an outdoor amphitheater where symphony, jazz and rock concerts take place. For current information on performances, check the papers or call the Blaisdell Center (☎ 591-2211).

Kapiolani Park also has sports fields, tennis courts, tall banyan trees and expansive lawns that are ideal for kite flying. It's a pleasant park and despite all the activities that go on, it's large enough to also have a lot of quiet space.

Waikiki Aquarium This interesting aquarium (☎ 923-9741), 2777 Kalakaua Ave, dates to 1904 and has recently undergone a $3 million makeover. The aquarium has new interactive displays, a mini-theater and a viewing gallery where visitors can sit and look through a 14-foot glass window at circling reef sharks.

The aquarium is a great place to identify colorful coral and fish you've seen while snorkeling or diving. Tanks re-create various Hawaiian reef habitats, including those of a surge zone, a sheltered reef, a deep reef and an ancient reef.

In addition to Hawaiian marine life, there are various exhibits on other Pacific ecosystems. In 1985 the aquarium was the first to breed the Palauan chambered nautilus in captivity. A few of these sea creatures, with their unique spiral chambered shells, are on display. There are also some giant clams from Palau; less than an inch long when acquired in 1982, they now measure over two feet and rank as the largest in the USA.

The aquarium has a touch tank for children, a mahimahi hatchery, green sea turtles and Hawaiian monk seals. Visitors can watch the monk seals being fed at 2:30 pm Friday to Tuesday, 1:30 pm on Wednesdays and 10 am on Thursdays.

The aquarium is open from 9 am to 5 pm daily, although entry is not allowed after 4:30 pm. Admission is $6 for adults, $4 for senior citizens over 60 and students with ID, $2.50 for children ages 13 to 17, and free for children 12 and under.

Honolulu Zoo The Honolulu Zoo (☎ 971-7171), at the northern end of Kapiolani Park, has undergone extensive renovations that have upgraded it into a respectable city zoo, with some 300 species spread across 42 acres. The highlight is the naturalized African Savanna section, which has lions, cheetahs, white rhinos, giraffes, zebras, hippos and monkeys. There's also an interesting reptile section and a small 'petting zoo' area that allows children to see animals up close.

The zoo's tropical bird section not only covers the usual exotics like toucans and flamingoes, but also displays a number of Hawaiian natives, such as the Hawaiian stilt, the Hawaiian gallinule, the Hawaiian goose *(nene)* and the *apapane*, a bright red forest bird.

In front of the zoo there's a large banyan tree that is home to hundreds of white pigeons – descendants of a small group brought to the zoo in the 1940s.

The zoo is open from 8:30 am to 5:30 pm (no admittance after 4:30 pm) daily except Christmas and New Year's Day. Admission is $6 for adults, $1 for children ages six to 12, free for children under six.

Kodak Hula Show The Kodak Hula Show (☎ 627-3300), off Monsarrat Ave near the Waikiki Shell, is a staged photo opportunity with hula dancers, ti-leaf skirts and ukuleles. The musicians are a group of older ladies who performed at the Royal Hawaiian Hotel in days gone by.

This is the scene in postcards where dancers hold up letters forming the words 'Hawaii' and 'Aloha.' Though the show is quite touristy, it's entertaining if you're in the mood, and it's free.

Kodak has been putting on this show since 1939. The benches are set up stadium-style around a grassy stage area with the sun at your back. The idea is for everyone to shoot a lot of film. It works. Even though Kodak doesn't monopolize the film market anymore, the tradition continues.

Shows are held from 10 to 11:15 am on Tuesdays, Wednesdays and Thursdays. Make sure you're on time because once it starts they only admit people between acts.

Other Waikiki Sights

Oceanarium The Pacific Beach Hotel, at 2490 Kalakaua Ave, houses an impressive three-story 280,000-gallon aquarium that forms the backdrop for two of the hotel's restaurants. Even if you're not dining there, you can view the aquarium quite easily from the lobby. Divers enter the Oceanarium to feed the tropical fish daily at 11:30 am and 12:30, 6:30 and 8:15 pm.

Damien Museum St Augustine's Church, off Kalakaua Ave and Ohua St, is a quiet little sanctuary in the midst of the hotel district. In the rear of the church a second building houses a modest museum honoring Father Damien, famed for his work at the leprosy colony on Molokai. It has a video presentation on the colony, some interesting historical photos and a few of Damien's personal possessions.

As a befitting tribute to Father Damien's life, the building also houses a lunchtime soup kitchen. Museum hours are 9 am to 3 pm Monday to Friday, until noon on Saturdays; entry is free.

Ala Wai Canal Every day at dawn, people jog and power walk along the Ala Wai Canal, which forms the northern boundary of Waikiki. Late in the afternoon outrigger canoe teams can be seen paddling up and down Ala Wai Canal and out to the Ala Wai Yacht Harbor, offering photo opportunities for passersby.

DIAMOND HEAD (Map 9)

Diamond Head is a tuff cone, composed of volcanic ash. Its crater was formed by a violent steam explosion deep beneath the surface long after most of Oahu's volcanic activity had stopped.

As the backdrop to Waikiki, it's one of the best-known landmarks in the Pacific. The summit is 760 feet high.

The Hawaiians called it Leahi and at its summit they built a *luakini heiau*, a type of temple used for human sacrifices. But ever since 1825, when British sailors found calcite crystals sparkling in the sun and mistakenly thought they'd struck it rich, it's been called Diamond Head.

In 1909 the US Army began building Fort Ruger at the edge of the crater. They constructed a network of tunnels and topped the rim with cannon emplacements, bunkers and observation posts. Reinforced during WWII, it's been a silent sentinel whose guns have never fired.

Today there's a Hawaii National Guard base inside the crater as well as Federal Aviation Administration and civil defense facilities. Diamond Head is a state monument with picnic tables, restrooms, a phone and drinking water. The best reason to visit is to hike the trail to the crater rim for the panoramic view. The gates are open daily from 6 am to 6 pm.

Hiking Diamond Head

The trail to Diamond Head summit was built in 1910 to service the military observation stations along the crater rim.

Don't expect a walk in the park, as it's a fairly steep hike with a gain in elevation of 560 feet, but it's only three-quarters of a mile to the top and plenty of people of all ages hike up. It takes about 30 minutes to reach the summit. The trail is open and hot, so you might want to take along something to drink.

As you start up the trail, you can see the summit ahead a bit to the left at about 11 o'clock.

The crater is dry and scrubby with *kiawe*, *koa haole*, grasses and wildflowers. The little yellow-orange flowers along the way are native *ilima*, Oahu's official flower.

About 20 minutes up the trail you enter a long, dark tunnel. Because the tunnel curves you don't see light until you get close to the end. It's a little spooky, but the ceiling is high enough for you to walk through without bumping your head, there is a hand rail and your eyes should adjust enough to make out shadows in the dark. Nevertheless, to prevent accidents, the park advises hikers to tote along a flashlight.

The tunnel itself seems like it should be the climax of this long climb, but on coming out into the light you are immediately faced with a steep 99-step staircase. Persevere! After this there's a shorter tunnel, a narrow spiral staircase inside an unlit bunker and the last of the trail's 271 steps.

From the top there's a fantastic 360° view taking in the southeast coast to Koko Head and Koko Crater and the leeward coast to Barbers Point and the Waianae Mountains. Below is Kapiolani Park and the orange seats of the Waikiki Shell. You can also see the lighthouse, coral reefs, sailboats and sometimes even surfers waiting for waves at Diamond Head Beach.

Watch your footing at the top, as there are some steep drops.

Getting There & Away From Waikiki, bus Nos 22 and 58, which run about twice an hour, stop near Diamond Head. It's about a 15-minute walk from the bus stop to the trailhead, which is above the parking lot. Once you walk through the tunnel you're in the crater.

By car, take Monsarrat Ave (which goes by the zoo) to Diamond Head Rd and then take the right turn after Kapiolani Community College into the crater.

Diamond Head Beach

Diamond Head Beach is popular with both surfers and windsurfers. Conditions at Diamond Head are suitable for intermediate to advanced windsurfers, and when the swells are up it's a great place for wave riding. Even as a spectator sport it's exhilarating.

The beach has showers but no other facilities.

To get there from Waikiki, follow Kalakaua Ave to Diamond Head Rd. There's a parking lot just beyond the lighthouse. Walk east past the end of the lot and you'll find a paved trail down to the beach. By bus, take No 14, which runs about once an hour.

DOWNTOWN HONOLULU (Map 6)

Downtown Honolulu is a hodgepodge of past and present, with both sleek high-rises and stately Victorian-era buildings. Architecturally, the area has some striking juxtapositions – there's a royal palace, a modernistic state capitol, a coral-block New England missionary church and a Spanish-style city hall all within sight of one another.

The downtown area is intriguing to explore. You can take in a Friday noon band concert on the palace lawn, lounge in the open-air courtyard of Hawaii's central library or catch a sweeping view of the city from the top of the Aloha Tower.

Orientation

Because of the heavy traffic and tight parking in downtown Honolulu, during the week it's best to take advantage of the city's excellent public bus system. Lots of city bus routes converge downtown – so many that Hotel St, which begins downtown and crosses Chinatown, is restricted to bus traffic only.

If you're heading to the Iolani Palace area from Waikiki, the frequent bus No 2 is the most convenient. If you're going directly to Aloha Tower or the Hawaii Maritime Center, take bus No 19 or 20 from Waikiki.

Downtown Walking Tour

Downtown Honolulu is ideal for strolling, with its most handsome buildings all within easy walking distance. You could make a quick tour in a couple of hours, or if you're up for more leisurely exploration, it's possible to spend the better part of a day poking around. For information about a guided walking tour, see Organized Tours in the Getting Around chapter.

A good starting place for a walking tour is Iolani Palace, the area's most pivotal spot both historically and geographically. If time permits, joining a guided tour of Iolani Palace offers a glimpse into the royal past. In any case you're free to stroll around the palace grounds. At the back side of the palace, en route to the State Capitol, you'll find a statue of Queen Liliuokalani. You can enter the capitol through the rear, and exit on the Beretania St side, which is opposite the War Memorial.

After turning left up Beretania, you'll pass Washington Place and St Andrew's Cathedral. In the lobby of the state office tower, directly opposite the cathedral, you'll find a tile wall mural depicting Hawaiian royalty. From there, walk down Richards St past No 1 Capitol District; the Bank of America Center, which has a Hawaiiana mural above the entrance; and the attractive YWCA and Hawaiian Electric buildings.

If you care to make the walk longer, turn right on Merchant St to see the historic buildings that house some of Hawaii's largest corporations and the skyscrapers that have sprung up around them.

Otherwise, turn left down Merchant St, where you'll see the old federal building and Aliiolani Hale, before making another left on Mililani St and an immediate right

on S King St, which will bring you to Kawaiahao Church and the Mission Houses Museum. As you make your way back to Iolani Palace, you can visit two more period buildings on Punchbowl St: Honolulu Hale (City Hall) and the state library. More details on these sights and buildings are given in the sections that follow.

Iolani Palace

Iolani Palace is the only royal palace in the USA. It was the official residence of King Kalakaua and Queen Kapiolani from 1882 to 1891 and of Queen Liliuokalani, Kalakaua's sister and successor, for two years after that.

Following the overthrow of the Hawaiian kingdom in 1893, the palace became the capitol – first for the republic, then for the territory and later for the state of Hawaii.

It wasn't until 1969 that the current State Capitol was built and the legislators moved out of their cramped palace quarters. The Senate had been meeting in the palace dining room and the House of Representatives in the throne room. By the time they left, Iolani was in shambles, the grand koa staircase termite-ridden and the Douglas fir floors pitted and gouged.

After extensive renovations topping $7 million, the palace was largely restored to its former glory and opened as a museum in 1978. Visitors must wear booties over their shoes to protect the highly polished wooden floors.

Iolani Palace was modern for its day. Every bedroom had its own full bath with hot and cold water running into copper-lined tubs, a flushing toilet and a bidet. Palace tour guides make the claim that electric lights replaced the palace gas lamps a full four years before the White House in Washington, DC, got electricity.

The **throne room**, decorated in red and gold, features the original thrones of the king and queen, and a *kapu* stick made of the long, spiral ivory tusk of a narwhal. In addition to celebrations full of pomp and pageantry, it was in the throne room that King Kalakaua danced his favorite Western dances – the polka, the waltz and the Virginia reel – into the wee hours of the morning.

Not all the events that took place there were joyous. Two years after she was dethroned, Queen Liliuokalani was brought back to the palace and tried for treason in the throne room. In a move calculated to humiliate the Hawaiian people she spent nine months as a prisoner in Iolani Palace, her former home.

Guided tours of the palace leave every 15 minutes from 9 am to 2:15 pm Wednesday to Saturday and cost $8 for adults, $2 for children ages five to 12. Children under five are not admitted. The tours last 45 minutes. Sometimes you can join up on the spot, but it's advisable to make advance reservations by phoning ☎ 522-0832. The palace is wheelchair accessible.

Palace Grounds Before Iolani Palace was built there was a simpler house on these grounds used by King Kamehameha III, who ruled for 30 years from 1825 to 1854. In ancient times it was the site of a heiau.

The palace ticket window and gift shop are in the former **barracks** of the Royal Household Guards, a building that looks oddly like the uppermost layer of a medieval fort that's been sliced off and plopped on the ground.

The **domed pavilion** on the grounds was originally built for the coronation of King Kalakaua in 1883 and is still used for the inauguration of governors and for concerts by the Royal Hawaiian Band.

The **grassy mound** surrounded by a wrought iron fence was the site of a royal tomb until 1865 when the remains of King Kamehameha II and Queen Kamamalu (who both died of measles in England in 1824) were moved to the Royal Mausoleum in Nuuanu.

The huge **banyan tree** between the palace and the State Capitol is thought to have been planted by Queen Kapiolani.

Hawaii State Library

The central branch of the statewide library system (☎ 586-3500) is on the corner of King and Punchbowl Sts. Located in a beautifully restored historic building, its collection of over half a million titles is the state's best and includes comprehensive Hawaii and Pacific sections.

The library is open from 9 am to 5 pm on Mondays, Fridays and Saturdays; from 9 am to 8 pm on Tuesdays and Thursdays; and from 10 am to 5 pm on Wednesdays.

The **Hawaii State Archives** next door holds official government documents and an extensive photo collection. It's open to the public for research.

Queen Liliuokalani Statue

The statue of Hawaii's last queen stands between the capitol and Iolani Palace. It faces Washington Place, Liliuokalani's home and place of exile for more than 20 years. The bronze statue holds the Hawaii constitution that Queen Liliuokalani wrote in 1893, which scared US businessmen into overthrowing her; *Aloha Oe*, a popular hymn that she composed; and *Kumulipo*, the Hawaiian chant of creation. The statue is often draped with leis of hibiscus or maile.

State Capitol

Hawaii's State Capitol is not your standard gold dome. Constructed in the late 1960s, it was a grandiose attempt at a 'theme' design.

Its two central legislative chambers are cone-shaped to represent volcanoes; the rotunda is open-air to let gentle trade winds blow through; the supporting columns represent palm trees; and the whole structure is encircled by a large pool symbolizing the ocean surrounding Hawaii.

Unfortunately, the building not only symbolizes the elements but has been quite effective in drawing them in. The pool tends to collect brackish water; rain pouring into the rotunda has necessitated the sealing of many of the skylights; and Tadashi Sato's 'Aquarius' floor mosaic, meant to show the changing colors and patterns of Hawaii's seas, got so weathered it had to be reconstructed.

After two decades of trying unsuccessfully to deal with all the problems on a piecemeal basis, the state put the facility through a thorough renovation, just completed in 1997. Visitors are free to walk through the rotunda, from where you can view the two flanking legislative chambers through observation windows.

In front of the capitol is a **statue of Father Damien**, the Belgian priest who volunteered to work among the lepers of Molokai and died of the disease 16 years later at age 49. The stylized sculpture was created by Venezuelan artist Marisol Escubar.

War Memorial

The war memorial is a sculptured eternal torch dedicated to soldiers who died in WWII. It sits between two underground garage entrances on Beretania St, directly opposite the State Capitol.

Washington Place

Washington Place, the governor's official residence, is a large colonial-style building with stately trees, built in 1846 by US sea captain John Dominis. The captain's son John became the governor of Oahu and married the Hawaiian princess who later became Queen Liliuokalani. After the queen was dethroned she lived at Washington Place in exile until her death in 1917.

A plaque near the sidewalk on the left side of Washington Place is inscribed with the words to *Aloha Oe*, the anthem composed by Queen Liliuokalani.

The large tree in front of the house on the right side of the walkway is a *pili* nut tree, recognizable by the buttresslike roots extending from the base of its trunk. In Southeast Asia the nuts of these trees are used to produce oil.

St Andrew's Cathedral

King Kamehameha IV, who reigned from 1855 to 1863, was attracted by the royal trappings of the Church of England and decided to build his own cathedral in the capital. He and his consort Queen Emma founded the Anglican Church of Hawaii in 1858.

The cathedral's cornerstone was finally laid in 1867 by King Kamehameha V. Kamehameha IV had died four years earlier on St Andrew's Day – hence the church's name.

St Andrew's is on the corner of Alakea and Beretania Sts. The church is of French Gothic architecture, shipped in pieces from England. Its most striking feature is the impressive window of hand-blown stained glass that forms the western façade and reaches from the floor to the eaves. In the right section of the glass you can see the Reverend Thomas Staley, the first bishop sent to Hawaii by Queen Victoria, alongside Kamehameha IV and Queen Emma.

No 1 Capitol District

The elegant five-story building on Richards St opposite the State Capitol houses some of the offices of the state legislature.

The building has something of the appearance of a Spanish mission, with courtyards and ceramic tile walls and floors. Built in 1928, it served as the YMCA Armed Services building for more than five decades.

The building is owned by the Hemmeter Corporation, which put the site through a multimillion-dollar renovation and then used it briefly as its corporate headquarters. Chris Hemmeter, incidentally, was the developer behind many of the extravagant 'fantasy hotels' that were constructed on Maui, Kauai and the Big Island in the 1980s.

Fort St Mall

Fort St is a pedestrian shopping mall lined with an ever-growing number of high-rises. While the mall is not interesting in itself, if you're downtown it's a reasonable place to eat – not as good as Chinatown but a few blocks closer.

Hawaii Pacific University, a small but expanding institution, has much of its campus at the north end of the mall.

Cathedral of Our Lady of Peace

The oldest Catholic cathedral in the USA is the Cathedral of Our Lady of Peace, at the

Beretania St end of Fort St Mall. Built of coral blocks in 1843, it's older and more ornate than St Andrew's Cathedral.

Father Damien, who later served Molokai's leprosy colony, was ordained at the cathedral in 1864.

Aliiolani Hale

Aliiolani Hale ('House of Heavenly Kings') was the first major government building constructed by the Hawaiian monarchy. It has housed the Hawaii Supreme Court since its construction in 1874 and was once also home to the state legislature. The building has a distinctive clock tower, graceful stairwells and a stained-glass skylight. It was designed by Australian architect Thomas Rowe to be a royal palace, although it was never used as such.

It was on the steps of Aliiolani Hale, in January 1893, that Sanford Dole proclaimed the establishment of a provisional government and the overthrow of the Hawaiian monarchy.

Kamehameha Statue

A statue of Kamehameha the Great stands in front of Aliiolani Hale opposite Iolani Palace. On June 11, a state holiday honoring Kamehameha, the statue is ceremoniously draped with layer upon layer of 12-foot leis.

The Kamehameha statue was cast in 1880 in Florence, Italy, by American sculptor Thomas Gould. This one is actually a recast as the original statue was lost at sea near the Falkland Islands.

The sunken statue, which was recovered from the ocean floor after the second version was dedicated here in 1883, eventually completed its trip to Hawaii. Rather than exchange the statues, the original was sent to Kohala, the Big Island birthplace of Kamehameha, where it now stands.

Honolulu Hale

City Hall, also known as Honolulu Hale, is largely of Spanish mission design with a tiled roof, decorative balconies, arches and pillars. Built in 1927, it bears the initials of CW Dickey, Honolulu's most famous

architect of the day. The building, which is on the National Register of Historic Places, has frescos by Einar Peterson and an open-air courtyard that's sometimes used for concerts and art exhibits.

Kawaiahao Church

Oahu's oldest church, on the corner of Punchbowl and King Sts, was built on the site where the first missionaries constructed a thatched house of worship shortly after their arrival in 1820. The original church was an impressive structure that measured 54 feet by 22 feet and seated 300 people on lauhala mats.

Still, thatch wasn't quite what the missionaries had in mind, so they designed a more typically New England-style Congregational church with simple Gothic influences.

Built between 1838 and 1842, the church is made of 14,000 hefty coral slabs, many weighing more than 1000 pounds. Hawaiian divers chiseled the huge blocks of coral out of Honolulu's underwater reef.

The clock tower was donated by Kamehameha III and the clock, built in Boston and installed in 1850, still keeps accurate time.

The interior of the church is breezy and cool. The rear seats, marked by *kahili* (feather) staffs and velvet padding, were for royalty and are still reserved for descendants of royalty today. The church is usually open to visitors from 8 am to 4 pm.

The **tomb of King Lunalilo**, the successor to Kamehameha V, is on the church grounds at the main entrance. Lunalilo ruled for only one year before his death in 1874 at the age of 39.

At the rear of the church is a **cemetery** where many of the early missionaries are buried, along with other important Westerners of the day including the infamous Sanford Dole.

Mission Houses Museum

Three of the original buildings of the Sandwich Islands Mission headquarters still stand: the Frame House (built in 1821), the

Chamberlain House (1831) and the Printing Office (1841).

Together they're open to the public as the Mission Houses Museum (☎ 531-0481), 553 S King St. The houses are authentically furnished with handmade quilts on the beds, settees in the parlor and iron pots in the big stone fireplaces.

The coral-block **Chamberlain House** was the early mission storeroom, a necessity as Honolulu had few shops in those days. Upstairs are hoop barrels, wooden crates packed with dishes and a big desk with pigeon-hole dividers and the quill pen Levi Chamberlain used to work on accounts. Levi was the person appointed by the mission to buy, store and dole out supplies to the missionary families who each had an allowance. His account books show that in the late 1800s, 25¢ would buy either one gallon of oil, one penknife or two slates.

The first missionaries packed more than their bags when they left Boston – they actually brought a prefabricated wooden house around the Horn with them! Designed to withstand cold New England winter winds, the small windows instead block out Honolulu's cooling trade winds, keeping the two-story house hot and stuffy. The **Frame House**, as it's now called, is the oldest wooden structure in Hawaii.

The **Printing Office** housed the lead-type press that was used to print the Bible in the Hawaiian language.

The Mission Houses Museum is open from 9 am to 4 pm Tuesday to Saturday. Admission is $5 for adults and $1 for children (under age six free). While you can explore the visitor center and the Chamberlain House on your own, the Printing Office and Frame House can only be seen with a guide. Guided tours are given at 9:30, 10:30 and 11:30 am and at 1, 2 and 3 pm.

Other Historic Buildings

The **Hawaiian Electric Company's** four-story administration building, on the corner of Richards and King Sts, is of Spanish colonial architecture. It has an arched entranceway and ornate period lamps hanging from hand-painted ceilings. The entrance leads into the customer-service departments so it's fine to walk in and take a look.

Diagonally opposite on Merchant St is the **Old Federal Building**, another interesting edifice with Spanish colonial features. Completed in 1922, it holds a post office and customs house.

Also noteworthy is the three-story YWCA at 1040 Richards St. Built in 1927, it's the work of Julia Morgan, the renowned architect who designed William Randolph Hearst's San Simeon estate in California.

The **old Honolulu Police Station** (1931), on the corner of Bethel and Merchant Sts, has beautiful interior ceramic tile work in earthen tones on its counters and walls. It now houses the state departments of housing and finance. Also worth a look is the old **Honolulu Publishing** building across the street.

The four-story **Alexander & Baldwin Building**, on the corner of Bishop and Queen Sts, was built in 1929. Tropical fruit and the Chinese characters for prosperity and long life are carved into the columns at the Bishop St entrance. Inside the portico are interesting ceramic tile murals of Hawaiian fish.

Samuel Alexander and Henry Baldwin, both sons of missionaries, vaulted to prominence in the sugar industry and created one of Hawaii's 'Big Five' controlling corporations. The other four – Theo Davies, Castle & Cooke, Amfac and C Brewer – all have their headquarters within a few blocks of here.

The four-story 60-year-old **Dillingham Building**, on the corner of Bishop and Queen Sts, is of Italian Renaissance-style architecture with arches, marble walls, elaborate elevator doors and an arty brick floor. This old building is mirrored in the reflective glass of the adjacent 30-story Grosvenor Center – a true study in contrasts.

Hawaii Theatre

The neoclassical Hawaii Theatre (☎ 528-0506), 1130 Bethel St, first opened in 1922 with silent films playing to the tunes of a pipe organ. Dubbed the 'Pride of the Pacific,' it ran continuous shows during WWII. The development of mall cinemas in the 1970s was its undoing.

After closing in 1984, the theater's future looked dim, even though it was on the Register of Historic Places. Theater buffs came to the rescue, forming a nonprofit group and purchasing the property from the Bishop Estate. They raised enough money from donations and grants to undertake a $21 million restoration.

The 1400-seat theater has a lovely interior, with trompe-l'oeil mosaics and bas reliefs depicting scenes from Shakespearean plays. It reopened in 1996 for dance, drama and music performances and is now one of the leading entertainment venues in Honolulu.

Honolulu Academy of Arts

The Honolulu Academy of Arts (☎ 532-8701 for 24-hour recorded information), 900 S Beretania St, is an exceptional museum, with permanent Asian, European, American and Pacific art collections of pieces from ancient times to the present.

Just inside the door and to the right is a room with works by Matisse, Cézanne, Gauguin, van Gogh and Picasso, as well as an inviting place to sit and take it all in.

The museum is open and airy and has numerous small galleries around six garden courtyards. The Spanish Court has a small fountain surrounded by Greek and Roman sculptures and Egyptian reliefs dating back to 2500 BC.

There are sculptures and miniatures from India, jades and bronzes from ancient China, Madonna-and-child oils from 14th-century Italy and quality changing exhibits. The Hawaiian section is small but choice, with feather leis, tapa beaters, poi pounders and koa calabashes. The adjacent collection from Papua New Guinea, Micronesia and the South Pacific includes ancestor figures, war clubs and masks.

The museum is open from 10 am to 4:30 pm Tuesday to Saturday and from 1 to 5 pm on Sunday. Admission is $5 for adults, $3 for senior citizens and students, free for children under 12.

The museum is off the tourist track (see Map 5) and seldom crowded. Bus No 2 from Waikiki stops out front; there's metered parking behind the museum.

The on-site **Academy Theatre** (☎ 532-8768) presents more than 400 programs each year, including foreign and independent films, classical music concerts and art lectures. Movies cost $4, while tickets to musical performances vary but are reasonably priced. An events calendar is available at the museum. There is also a gift shop, library and lunch cafe.

Aloha Tower

Built in 1926, the 10-story Aloha Tower at Pier 9, on the edge of the downtown district, is a Honolulu landmark. In its heyday this icon of pre-wartime Hawaii was the city's tallest building; its four-sided clock tower inscribed with the word 'Aloha' greeted all arriving passengers from the mainland.

The tower is now the centerpiece of a new interisland cruise ship terminal and the Aloha Tower Marketplace shopping center, which has nearly 100 kiosks, stores and eateries.

While the Aloha Tower Marketplace is certainly a more commercial endeavor than the old customs facility that previously sat beneath the tower, the new complex has managed to incorporate some of the Hawaiiana character of former days.

Take a look at the interior of the cruise ship terminal, which has full-wall murals depicting Honolulu in the first half of the century. The scenes include hula dancers, Hawaiian kids diving off the pier and mainland passengers disembarking from one of Matson's San Francisco-to-Honolulu ships that docked here during that era.

Be sure to take the elevator up to the Aloha Tower's top-floor observation deck, which offers a sweeping 360° view of Honolulu's big commercial harbor and the downtown area. It's not the most scenic angle on the city, but it's interesting nonetheless. The observation deck is open

Sunday to Thursday from 9 am to 9 pm, on Friday and Saturday from 9 am to 10 pm. There's no admission charge.

Fittingly, some of the shops in the Aloha Tower Marketplace specialize in Hawaiiana items and most of the places to eat have harbor views. For information on stores and restaurants, see the Shopping and Places to Eat chapters.

Getting There & Away The Aloha Tower can be reached by public bus Nos 19 and 20 from Waikiki.

The route is also covered by a private open-sided trolley-style bus marked with the words 'Aloha Tower Marketplace.' The trolley (☎ 528-5700) runs from Waikiki approximately every 20 minutes from 9 am to 10 pm daily and costs $2 each way. Stops include Hilton Hawaiian Village, the Waikiki police station on Kalakaua Ave and the Outrigger Waikiki Surf on Kuhio Ave.

If you're driving, there's parking directly in front of Aloha Tower Marketplace and southeast of the Hawaii Maritime Center at Pier 6. During peak hours on weekdays, both lots charge $1 per 20 minutes; if you have a meal or make a purchase at the marketplace, you can get a validation that reduces the fee to $2 for the first three hours. All day on weekends, and after 4:30 pm on weekdays, there's a flat rate of just $2.

Hawaii Maritime Center
The Hawaii Maritime Center (☎ 536-6373) is at Honolulu Harbor's Pier 7 on the Diamond Head side of the Aloha Tower. The center has a maritime museum; the *Falls of Clyde*, said to be the world's last four-masted, full-rigged ship; and the berth for the double-hulled sailing canoe *Hokulea*.

The 60-foot *Hokulea* was built to resemble the type of ship used by Polynesians in their migrations. It has made a number of voyages from Hawaii to the South Pacific, retracing the routes of the early Polynesian seafarers using age-old means of navigation, most notably wave patterns and the position of the stars. A recent trip took it to

Rarotonga. When in port, the canoe is docked beside the museum.

Permanently on display is the 266-foot iron-hulled *Falls of Clyde*, which was built in Glasgow, Scotland, in 1878. In 1899 Matson Navigation bought the ship and added a deck house, and the *Falls* began carrying sugar and passengers between Hilo and San Francisco. It was later converted into an oil tanker and eventually stripped down to a barge.

After being abandoned in Ketchikan, Alaska, where it was used as a floating oil storage tank, the *Falls* was towed to Seattle. A group of Hawaiians raised funds to rescue the ship in 1963, just before it was scheduled to be sunk to create a breakwater off Vancouver. With the aid of the Bishop Museum, the *Falls* was eventually brought to Honolulu and restored and is now registered as a National Historic Landmark. Visitors can stroll the deck and walk down into the cargo holds.

The main museum has an interesting mishmash of maritime displays and artifacts, including a good whaling-era section and model replicas of ships. There's a reproduction of a Matson liner stateroom and period photos of Waikiki in the days when just the Royal Hawaiian and the Moana Hotel shared the horizon with Diamond Head. Both hotels belonged to Matson, who spearheaded tourism in Hawaii and ironically sold out to the Sheraton in 1959 just before the jet age and statehood launched sleepy tourism into a booming industry.

The museum is off Ala Moana Blvd, about a mile northwest of Ward Warehouse. There's free parking for visitors at signposted spaces on Pier 6, east of the museum and just before the Aloha Tower Marketplace's paid parking lot; guests should register their cars upon entering the museum. For bus information, see the Aloha Tower Marketplace above.

The Hawaii Maritime Center is open from 8:30 am to 5 pm daily. Admission, which includes boarding the *Falls*, is $7.50 for adults, $4.50 for children ages six to 17 and free for kids under six.

CHINATOWN (Map 6)

A visit to Chinatown is a bit like a journey to Asia – although it's predominantly Chinese, it has Vietnamese, Thai and Filipino influences as well.

Busy and colorful Chinatown has a lively market that could be right off a back street in Hong Kong, fire-breathing dragons that coil around the red pillars outside the Bank of Hawaii, and good, cheap ethnic restaurants. You can get a tattoo, consult with a herbalist, munch on moon cakes or slurp a steaming bowl of Vietnamese soup. There are temples, shrines, noodle factories, antique shops and art galleries to explore.

On Chinatown's northern boundary is a former royal estate that now encompasses the city's finest botanical garden, offering a pleasant contrast to the buzz of activity found in the markets and along the busy streets.

For information about a guided walking tour, see Organized Tours in the Getting Around chapter.

Chinatown Walking Tour

Chinatown is one of the most intriguing quarters of the city for sauntering about. This is best done in the daytime, however, not only because that's when the markets and shops are open, but also because Chinatown has seen a rise in nighttime youth gang activity.

While you could start a walking tour at virtually any street corner, a good spot to begin a rough loop route is in front of the Hawaii Theatre on the corner of Bethel and Pauahi Sts.

You could then proceed up Pauahi and make a left on Nuuanu St, which has a handful of historic buildings. Then turn right onto N Hotel St towards the center of Chinatown. In contrast to the creeping gentrification that marks the downtown edge of Chinatown, N Hotel St still bears witness to Honolulu's seamier side. Here you'll find darkened doorways advertising 'video peeps' for 25¢ and topless-dancing nightspots with names like Risqué Theatre and Club Hubba Hubba.

The Big Fire

Chinese immigrants who had worked off their sugar-cane plantation contracts began settling in Chinatown and opening up small businesses here around 1860.

In December 1899 the bubonic plague broke out in the area. The 7000 Chinese, Hawaiians and Japanese who made the crowded neighborhood their home were cordoned off and forbidden to leave.

As more plague cases arose, the Board of Health decided to conduct controlled burns of infected homes. On January 20, 1900, the fire brigade set fire to a building on the corner of Beretania St and Nuuanu Ave. The wind suddenly picked up and the fire spread out of control, racing towards the waterfront. To make matters worse, police guards stationed inside the plague area attempted to stop quarantined residents from fleeing. Nearly 40 acres of Chinatown burned to the ground.

Not everyone thought the fire was accidental. Just the year before, Chinese immigration into Hawaii had been halted by the US annexation of the islands, and Chinatown itself was prime real estate on the edge of the burgeoning downtown district.

Despite the adverse climate the Chinese held their own and a new Chinatown arose from the ashes.

In the 1940s, thousands of American GIs walked the streets of Chinatown before being shipped off to Iwo Jima and Guadalcanal. Many spent their last days of freedom in Chinatown's 'body houses,' pool halls and tattoo parlors. ■

Turn left at Maunakea St and you're in the heart of Chinatown with its herbalists, noodle shops and the bustling Oahu Market. At the intersection of N King and River Sts are some excellent neighborhood restaurants where you could stop for a quick bite. Continue walking northeast along River St, which turns into a pedestrian mall, passes more restaurants and a couple of religious sites and then terminates opposite the entrance of the Foster Botanic Garden.

After touring the gardens and the nearby Kuan Yin Temple, you could re-enter the main Chinatown district by heading back on Maunakea St. At the intersection of Maunakea and N Beretania you'll find rows of small lei shops where lei-makers deftly string flowers and heady fragrances fill the air.

Oahu Market

The focal point of Chinatown is the Oahu Market, on the corner of Kekaulike and N King Sts.

There are stalls jammed with everything a Chinese cook could need: pig heads, ginger root, fresh octopus, quail eggs, slabs of tuna, jasmine rice, long beans and salted jellyfish.

Oahu Market has been an institution since 1904. In 1984, the tenants organized and purchased the market themselves to save it from falling into the hands of developers.

Maunakea St

A Chinatown landmark on the corner of N Hotel and Maunakea Sts is **Wo Fat**, the distinctive pink restaurant with a façade that resembles a Chinese temple. The oldest restaurant in Honolulu, it's been on this site since just after the Chinatown fire of 1900. However, recent renovations have stripped the interior of its once colorful Chinese decor, and now only the exterior is worth a glimpse.

Shung Chong Yuein, 1027 Maunakea St, sells delicious moon cakes, almond cookies and other pastries at bargain prices. This is the place to buy dried and sugared foods – everything from candied ginger and pineapple to candied squash and lotus root. They also sell boiled peanuts, which are quite good if you can resist comparing them to roasted peanuts.

Across the street is **Cindy's Lei Shop**, a friendly place with leis made of maile, lantern ilima and Micronesian ginger in addition to the more common orchids and plumeria. Prices are very reasonable, starting at $3.50 for a lei of tuberose flowers.

Nuuanu Ave

The **Chinatown Police Station**, on the corner of N Hotel St and Nuuanu Ave in the Perry Block Building (c1888), has enough 1920s atmosphere to resemble a set from *The Untouchables*.

On the same side of Nuuanu Ave is the **Pantheon Bar**, now abandoned but noteworthy as the oldest watering hole in Honolulu and a favorite of sailors in days past.

Across the street, **Lai Fong Department Store** sells antiques, knickknacks and old postcards of Hawaii dating back to the first half of the century. Even walking into the store itself is a bit like stepping back into the 1940s. Lai Fong's,

Wo Fat

which has been in the same family for 70 years, also sells Chinese silks and brocades by the yard and makes silk dresses to order.

There are two noteworthy **art galleries** on Nuuanu Ave. At 1164 Nuuanu Ave you'll find the gallery of Pegge Hopper, whose prints of voluptuous Hawaiian women adorn many a wall in the islands, and at 1121 Nuuanu Ave is Abacus Studio, which features the colorful impressionist works of Maui artist Jan Kasprzycki.

Incidentally, the **granite-block sidewalks** along Nuuanu Ave were made from the discarded ballast of ships that brought tea from China in the 1800s.

Chinatown Cultural Plaza

This plaza covers the better part of a block along N Beretania St between Maunakea and River Sts.

The modern complex doesn't have the character of Chinatown's older shops, but inside it's still quintessential Chinatown, with tailors, acupuncturists and calligraphers alongside travel agents, restaurants and a Chinese news press. One of the kiosks inside the Asia Mall section sells nuts, dried fruit and local honey at good prices. There's a post office and restrooms.

At a small courtyard statue of Kuan Yin, elderly Chinese light incense and leave mangoes.

River St Pedestrian Mall

The River St pedestrian mall has covered tables beside Nuuanu Stream, where old men play mahjong and checkers. A statue of Chinese revolutionary leader Sun Yat-sen stands at the end of the pedestrian mall near N Beretania St.

There are eat-in and takeout restaurants along the mall, including Japanese food, Chinese food and the peculiarly named Kent's Drive In, a hole-in-the-wall eatery serving plate lunches on a *pedestrian* walkway!

Taoist Temple

Organized in 1889, the Lum Sai Ho Tong Society was one of more than 100 societies started by Chinese immigrants in Hawaii to

Herbs & Noodles

Chinatown herbalists are both physician and pharmacist, and their shop walls are lined with small wooden drawers containing different herbs. These herbalists will size you up, feel your pulse and ask you to describe your ailments before they decide which drawers to open, mix herbs and flowers and wrap them for you to take home and boil up together. The object is to balance yin and yang forces. You can find herbalists at the Chinese Cultural Plaza and along N King and Maunakea Sts.

There are also half a dozen noodle factories in Chinatown. If you look inside, you'll see clouds of white flour hanging in the air and thin sheets of dough running around rollers and emerging as noodles. One easy-to-find shop is Yat Tung Chow Noodle Factory, 150 N King St, next to Ba Le, which makes nine sizes of noodles, from skinny golden thread to fat udon. ■

NED FRIARY

help preserve their cultural identity. This one was for the Lum clan, which hails from west of the Yellow River. At one time the society had more than 4000 members, and even now there are nearly a thousand Lums in the Honolulu phone book.

The society's Taoist temple on the corner of River and Kukui Sts honors the goddess

Tin Hau, a Lum child who rescued her father from drowning and was later deified as a saint. Many Chinese claim to see her apparition when they travel by boat. The elaborate altar inside the temple is open for viewing when the street-level door is unlocked, which is usually from 8:30 am to 2 pm daily.

Izumo Taisha Shrine

The Izumo Taisha Shrine, across the river from the Taoist temple on Kukui St, is a small wooden Shinto shrine built by Japanese immigrants in 1923. During WWII the property was confiscated by the city of Honolulu and wasn't returned to its congregation until 1962.

The 100-pound sacks of rice that sit near the altar symbolize good health. Ringing the bell at the shrine entrance is an act of purification for those who come to pray.

Foster Botanic Garden

Foster Botanic Garden covers 20 acres at the northern end of Chinatown. The entrance is on Vineyard Blvd, opposite the end of River St. The garden took root in 1850 when German botanist William Hillebrand purchased five acres of land from Queen Kalama and planted the trees that now tower in the center of the property.

Captain Thomas Foster bought the property in 1867 and continued planting the grounds. In the 1930s the tropical garden was bequeathed to the city of Honolulu and it's now a city park.

The garden is laid out in groupings, including sections of palms, orchids, plumeria and poisonous plants.

If you've ever wondered how nutmeg, allspice or cinnamon grow, stroll through the **economic garden**. In this section there's also a black pepper vine that climbs 40 feet up a gold tree, a vanilla vine and other herbs and spices.

The **herb garden** was the site of the first Japanese language school in Oahu. Many Japanese immigrants sent their children there to learn to read Japanese, hoping to maintain their cultural identity and the

option of someday returning to Japan. During the bombing of Pearl Harbor a stray artillery shell exploded into a room full of students. A memorial marks the site.

At the other end of the park the **wild orchid garden** can be a good place for close-up photography. Unfortunately, this side of the garden is skirted by the H-1 Fwy, which detracts from what would otherwise be a peaceful stroll.

Foster Garden holds many extraordinary plants. For instance, the garden's East African *Gigasiphon macrosiphon*, a tree with white flowers that open in the evening, is thought to be extinct in the wild. The tree is so rare that it doesn't have a common name.

The native Hawaiian *loulu* palm, taken long ago from the upper Nuuanu Valley, may also be extinct in the wild. The garden's *chicle* tree, New Zealand *kauri* tree and Egyptian *doum* palm are all thought to be the largest of their kind in the USA. Oddities include the cannonball tree, the sausage tree and the double coconut palm that's capable of producing a 50-pound nut.

Foster Garden is open from 9 am to 4 pm daily. Admission costs $5 for those ages 13 and over, $1 for children. Trees are marked and a corresponding self-guided tour booklet is available at the entrance.

The Friends of Foster Garden provides volunteer guides who lead hourlong walking tours at 1 pm Monday to Friday. Call ☎ 522-7066 for reservations.

Kuan Yin Temple

The Kuan Yin Temple, on Vineyard Blvd near the entrance of Foster Garden, is a bright red Buddhist temple with a green ceramic-tile roof. The ornate interior is richly carved and filled with the sweet pervasive smell of burning incense.

The temple is dedicated to Kuan Yin Bodhisattva, goddess of mercy, whose statue is the largest in the prayer hall. Devotees burn paper 'money' for prosperity and good luck. Offerings of oranges, fresh flowers and vegetarian food are placed at the altar. The pomelo, the large citrus fruit that is sometimes stacked pyramid-style at the altar, is considered a symbol of fertility because of its many seeds.

Honolulu's multiethnic Buddhist community worships at the temple and respectful visitors are welcome.

Getting There & Away

To get to Chinatown by car from Waikiki, take Ala Moana Blvd and turn at Smith St or Bethel St. Or take Beretania St and head makai down Nuuanu Ave or Maunakea St. Hotel St is open to bus traffic only.

Chinatown is full of one-way streets, traffic is tight and it can be difficult to find a parking space. Your best bet for metered parking ($1 an hour, three-hour limit) is the lot off Smith St between Pauahi and Beretania Sts. There are parking garages with comparable rates at the Chinatown Gateway Plaza on Nuuanu Ave and in the Hale Pauahi complex on N Beretania St just west of Maunakea St.

You can avoid parking hassles by taking bus No 2 or 20 from Waikiki; get off on N Hotel St after Maunakea St and you'll be in the heart of Chinatown.

Although walking from the center of downtown Honolulu to central Chinatown takes only about 15 minutes, you can also catch bus No 2, which runs directly between the two areas.

ALA MOANA (Map 5)

Ala Moana means 'Path to the Sea.' Ala Moana Blvd (Hwy 92) connects the Nimitz Hwy and the airport with downtown Honolulu and continues into Waikiki. Ala Moana is also the name of a land area just west of Waikiki, which includes Honolulu's largest beach park and a huge shopping center.

Ala Moana Center

Ala Moana Center is Hawaii's biggest shopping center, with nearly 200 shops. When outer islanders fly to Honolulu to shop they go to Ala Moana. Tourists wanting to spend the day at a mall usually head there too. Ala Moana Center is Honolulu's major bus transfer point and tens of thousands of passengers transit through daily, so even if you weren't planning to go to the center you're likely to end up there!

Ala Moana has a Sears, Liberty House, JC Penney, Longs Drugs, Foodland supermarket and Shirokiya, an authentic Japanese department store with a top-floor Japanese food market.

You'll also find local color at the Crack Seed Center, where you can scoop from jars full of pickled mangoes, rock candy, salty red ginger, dried cuttlefish and banzai mix.

There are airline offices, a couple of banks, a Thomas Cook currency exchange, a travel agency and a good food court with 20 ethnic fast-food stalls.

On the mountain side of the center, near Sears, is a post office open from 8:30 am to 5 pm Monday to Friday, from 8:30 am to 4:15 pm on Saturday. Also at the ground level but at the opposite end of the row is a satellite city hall where you can get bus schedules and county camping permits.

Ala Moana Beach

Ala Moana Beach Park, opposite the Ala Moana Center, is a fine city park with much less hustle and bustle than Waikiki. The park is fronted by a broad golden sand beach that's nearly a mile long and is buffered from the traffic noise of Ala Moana Blvd by a spacious grassy area with shade trees.

This is where Honolulu residents go to jog after work, play volleyball and enjoy weekend picnics. The park has full beach facilities, several softball fields and tennis courts, and free parking. It's a very popular park yet big enough to feel uncrowded.

Ala Moana is generally a safe place to swim and is a good spot for distance swimmers. However, the deep channel that runs the length of the beach can be a hazard at low tide to poor swimmers who don't realize it's there. A former boat channel, it drops off suddenly to overhead depths.

The 43-acre peninsula jutting from the east side of the park is the **Aina Moana State Recreation Area**, otherwise known as Magic Island. During the school year, you can often find high school outrigger canoe teams practicing here in the late afternoon. There's a nice walk around the perimeter of Magic Island and sunsets can be picturesque with sailboats pulling in and out of the adjoining Ala Wai Yacht Harbor. This is also a hot summer surf spot.

UNIVERSITY OF HAWAII (Map 7)

The University of Hawaii (UH) at Manoa, the central campus of the statewide college system, is east of downtown Honolulu and two miles north of Waikiki.

The university has strong programs in astronomy, geophysics, marine sciences and Hawaiian and Pacific studies. The campus attracts students from islands throughout the Pacific.

Manoa Garden restaurant in Hemenway Hall is a student gathering spot. Hemenway Hall and the Campus Center are behind Sinclair Library, which fronts University Ave opposite Burger King and the bus stop.

Two outside walls of the Campus Center have grand Hawaiiana murals, with scenes based on photos from a classic August 1981 *National Geographic* article on Molokai.

East-West Center

At the east side of the University of Hawaii campus is the East-West Center, 1777 East-West Rd, Honolulu, HI 96848, a federally funded educational institution established in 1960 by the US Congress. The center's stated goal is the promotion of mutual understanding among the people of Asia, the Pacific and the USA.

Some 2000 researchers and graduate students work and study at the center, examining development policy, the environment and other Pacific issues.

Changing exhibits on Asian art and culture are displayed on the 1st floor of the East-West Center's **Burns Hall**, on the corner of Dole St and East-West Rd. It's open weekdays from 8 am to 5 pm; admission is free. The center occasionally has

University Information

UH Tours The Information Center (☎ 956-7235) in the Campus Center can provide campus maps and answer questions. Free one-hour walking tours of the campus, emphasizing art, history and architecture, leave from the Campus Center at 2 pm on Monday, Wednesday and Friday; to join one simply arrive 10 minutes before the tour begins.

Newspaper *Ka Leo O Hawaii*, the student newspaper, lists lectures, music performances and other campus happenings. It can be picked up free at the university libraries and other places around campus.

Bulletin Boards Boards in front of Sinclair Library have notices of rooms for rent, cars and surfboards for sale, concerts, and campus activities. Another board with only listings of rooms for rent is at the campus post office, opposite Hemenway Hall.

Attending University You can get information on undergraduate studies at the University of Hawaii from the Admissions & Records Office (☎ 956-8975), Sakamaki Hall, 2530 Dole St, Honolulu, HI 96822, and on graduate studies from the Graduate Division (☎ 956-8544), Spalding Hall, 2540 Maile Way, Honolulu, HI 96822.

The summer session consists primarily of two six-week terms. Tuition is $130 per credit for nonresidents and $75 per credit for residents. For the summer catalog contact the Summer Session (☎ 956-7221), Box 11450, Honolulu, HI 96828. ■

other multicultural programs open to the public, such as music concerts or scholastic seminars. For current happenings call the center at ☎ 944-7111.

Getting There & Away

Parking at UH is a hassle; you're better off arriving by bus and exploring on foot. Bus No 4 runs between UH and Waikiki, bus No 6 between UH and Ala Moana.

UPPER MANOA VALLEY (Map 8)

The Upper Manoa Valley, mauka of the university, ends at forest reserve land in the hills above Honolulu. The road up the valley runs through a well-to-do residential neighborhood before reaching the trailhead to Manoa Falls and the Lyon Arboretum.

Manoa Falls Trail

The trail to Manoa Falls is a beautiful hike, especially for one so close to the city. The trail runs for three-quarters of a mile above a rocky streambed that leads up to the falls. It takes about 30 minutes one way.

Surrounded by lush, damp vegetation and moss-covered stones and tree trunks, you get the feeling you're walking through a thick rainforest a long way from anywhere. The sounds are purely natural: the chirping of birds and the rush of the stream and waterfall.

There are all sorts of trees along the path, including tall *Eucalyptus robusta* with their soft, spongy, reddish bark, flowering orange African tulip trees and other lofty varieties that creak like wooden doors in old houses. Many of them were planted by the Lyon Arboretum, which at one time held a lease on the property.

Wild purple orchids and red ginger grow up near the falls. The area is quiet and peaceful. The falls are steep and drop about 100 feet vertically into a small shallow pool. The pool is not deep enough for swimming, and occasional falling rocks don't make it advisable anyway.

The trail is usually a bit muddy but not too bad if it hasn't been raining lately. Be careful not to trip over exposed tree roots – they're potential ankle breakers, particu-

Na Ala Hele was established in 1988 with the task of documenting public access to trails as part of a movement to preserve Hawaii's natural environment and cultural heritage.

larly if you're moving with any speed. The packed clay can be slippery in some steep places, so take your time, pick up a walking stick and enjoy the trail.

Aihualama Trail

About 75 feet before Manoa Falls an inconspicuous trail starts to the left of the chain-link fence. This is the Aihualama Trail, well worth a little 15-minute side trip. Just a short way up you get a broad view of Manoa Valley.

After about five minutes you'll enter a bamboo forest with some massive old banyan trees. When the wind blows the forest releases eerie crackling sounds. It's enchanted or spooky, depending on your mood.

You can return to the Manoa Falls Trail or go on another mile to Pauoa Flats where the trail connects with the Puu Ohia Trail in the Tantalus area. See the Tantalus & Makiki Heights section for more trail information.

Lyon Arboretum

The Lyon Arboretum, 3860 Manoa Rd, is a great place to go after hiking to Manoa

Falls if you want to identify trees and plants you've seen along the trail.

Dr Harold Lyon, after whom the arboretum is named, is credited with introducing 10,000 exotic trees and plants to Hawaii. Approximately half of these are represented in this 193-acre arboretum, which is part of the University of Hawaii.

This is not a landscaped tropical flower garden but a mature and largely wooded arboretum, where related species are clustered in a seminatural state.

The Hawaiian ethnobotanical garden has mountain apple, breadfruit and taro; ko, the sugar cane brought by early Polynesian settlers; kukui, which is used to produce lantern oil; and ti, used medicinally since ancient times and for moonshine after Westerners arrived.

The arboretum also has herbs and spices and cashew, cacao, papaya, betel nut, macadamia nut, jackfruit and calabash trees, as well as greenhouses and classrooms.

A good choice among the arboretum's many short trails is the 20-minute walk up to **Inspiration Point**, which offers a view of the hills that enclose the valley. En route you'll encounter wonderful scents, inviting stone benches and lots of birdsong. The path loops through ferns, bromeliads and magnolias and passes by tall trees, including a bo tree, a descendant of the tree Gautama Buddha sat under when he received enlightenment.

The arboretum is open from 9 am to 3 pm Monday to Saturday. A $1 donation is appreciated. Free guided tours (☎ 988-7378 for reservations) are given at 1 pm on the first Friday and third Wednesday of each month and at 10 am on the third Saturday of the month.

The reception center has a book and gift shop as well as helpful staff members who can give you a map of the garden and information on the arboretum's organized hikes, children's programs and one-day workshops.

Getting There & Away

From Ala Moana Center take the No 5 Manoa Valley bus to the end of the line at the junction of Manoa Rd and Kumuone St. From there it's a 10-minute walk to the road's end, where the Manoa Falls Trail begins. Lyon Arboretum is at the end of the short drive off to the left just before the trailhead.

To get there by car, simply drive to the end of Manoa Rd. There's room to park at the trailhead, but it's not a very secure place so don't leave anything valuable in the car. Lyon Arboretum has a parking area adjacent to its gardens that's reserved for arboretum visitors only.

TANTALUS & MAKIKI HEIGHTS (Map 8)

Just two miles from downtown Honolulu a narrow switchback road cuts its way up the lush green forest reserve land of Tantalus and the Makiki Valley. The road climbs up almost to the top of 2013-foot Mt Tantalus, with swank mountainside homes tucked in along the way.

Although it's one continuous road, the western side is called Tantalus Drive and the eastern side Round Top Drive. The 8½-mile loop is Honolulu's finest scenic drive, offering great views of the city below.

The route is winding, narrow and steep, but it's a good paved road. Among the profusion of dense tropical growth, bamboo, ginger, elephant-ear taro and fragrant eucalyptus trees are easily identified. Vines climb to the top of telephone poles and twist their way across the wires.

A network of hiking trails runs between Tantalus Drive and Round Top Drive and throughout the forest reserve, with numerous trailheads off both roads. The trails are seldom crowded, which seems amazing considering how accessible they are. Perhaps because the drive itself is so nice, the only walking most people do is between their car and the scenic lookouts.

The Makiki Heights area below the forest reserve is one of the most exclusive residential areas in Honolulu and the site of a museum of contemporary art. There's bus service as far as Makiki Heights, but none around the Tantalus-Round Top loop drive.

Puu Ualakaa State Park

From Puu Ualakaa State Park you can see an incredible panorama of all Honolulu. The park entrance is 2½ miles up Round Top Drive from Makiki St. It's half a mile in to the lookout; bear left when the road forks.

The sweeping view from the lookout extends from Kahala and Diamond Head on the far left, across Waikiki and downtown Honolulu, to the Waianae Range on the far right. To the southeast is the University of Hawaii at Manoa, easily recognizable by its sports stadium; to the southwest you can see clearly into the green mound of Punchbowl Crater; the airport is visible on the edge of the coast and Pearl Harbor beyond that.

Although the best time for photos is usually during the day, this is also a fine place to watch evening settle over the city. Arrive at least 30 minutes before sunset to see the hills before they're in shadow.

The park gates are locked from 6:45 pm (7:45 pm in summer) to 7 am. For night (and anytime) views, there are a couple of scenic roadside pull-offs before the park.

The Contemporary Museum

The Contemporary Museum (☎ 526-0232), 2411 Makiki Heights Drive, is a delightful modern art museum occupying an estate with 3½ acres of wooded gardens.

The estate house was built in 1925 for Mrs Charles Montague Cooke, whose other former home is the present site of the Honolulu Academy of Arts.

You enter the museum through a covered courtyard with bronze gates and an arrangement of parabolic mirrors reflecting the view hundreds of times over.

Inside are galleries featuring quality changing exhibits of paintings, sculpture and other contemporary artwork by both national and international artists. A newer building on the lawn holds the museum's most prized piece, a vivid environmental installation by David Hockney based on his sets for *L'Enfant et les Sortiléges*, Ravel's 1925 opera. There's also a cafe serving lunch and afternoon desserts.

Rolling Sweet Potatoes

In olden times, the slopes of Puu Ualakaa ('Rolling Sweet Potato Hill') were planted with sweet potatoes, which were said to have been dug up and rolled down the hill for easy gathering at harvest time. The hill's other name, 'Round Top,' dates to more recent times. ■

The museum is open from 10 am to 4 pm Tuesday to Saturday, from noon to 4 pm on Sunday. Docent-led tours are conducted at 1 pm, although of course you can explore at other times on your own. Admission is $5 for adults, $3 for students and senior citizens, free to children ages 12 and under. On the third Thursday of the month, admission is free to everyone.

The Contemporary Museum, which is near the intersection of Mott-Smith Drive and Makiki Heights Drive, can be reached on the No 15 bus from downtown Honolulu.

Meditation Center

The Honolulu Siddha Meditation Center, 1925 Makiki St, Honolulu, HI 96822, is operated by followers of Gurumayi Chidvilasananda. It has early morning chanting sessions open to interested visitors.

On Wednesday and Saturday evenings there are programs that include an orientation to the center, a video of Gurumayi, chanting and meditation. Sometimes group meals, hatha yoga sessions and other programs are open to the public as well; for information call ☎ 942-8887.

Makiki Valley Loop Trail

Three of the Tantalus area hiking trails – Maunalaha Trail, Makiki Valley Trail and Kanealole Trail – can be combined to make the Makiki Valley Loop Trail, a popular 2½-mile hike.

The loop goes through a lush and varied tropical forest that begins and ends in

Hawaii's first state nursery and arboretum. In this nursery, hundreds of thousands of trees were grown to replace the sandalwood forests that had been leveled in Makiki Valley and elsewhere in Hawaii in the 1800s.

The **Maunalaha Trail** begins at the restrooms below the parking lot of the Makiki Forest baseyard. It first crosses a bridge, passes taro patches and proceeds to climb the east ridge of Makiki Valley, passing Norfolk pine, bamboo and fragrant allspice and eucalyptus trees. There are some good views along the way.

After three-quarters of a mile you'll come to a four-way junction, where you'll take the left fork and continue on the **Makiki Valley Trail**. The trail goes through small gulches and across gentle streams with patches of ginger. Near the Moleka Stream crossing are mountain apple trees (related to allspice and guava), which flower in the spring and bear fruit in the summer. Edible yellow and strawberry guavas also grow along the trail. There are some fine views of the city below.

The **Kanealole Trail** begins as you cross Kanealole Stream and then follows the stream back to the baseyard, three-quarters of a mile away. The trail leads down through a field of Job's tears; the beadlike bracts of the female flowers of this tall grass are often picked to be strung in leis.

Kanealole Trail is usually muddy, so wear shoes with good traction and pick up a walking stick. Halfway down there's a grove of introduced mahogany.

Getting There & Away To get to the Makiki Forest baseyard, turn left off Makiki St and go half a mile up Makiki Heights Drive. Where the road makes a sharp bend, proceed straight ahead through a green gate into the Makiki Forest Recreation Area and continue until you reach the baseyard. There's a parking lot on the right just before the office.

You can also take the No 15 bus, which runs between downtown and Pacific Heights. Get off near the intersection of Mott-Smith Drive and Makiki Heights Drive and walk down Makiki Heights Drive to the baseyard. It's a milelong walk between the bus stop and the trailhead.

An alternative is to hike just the Makiki Valley Trail, which you can reach by going up Tantalus Drive two miles from its intersection with Makiki Heights Drive. As you come around a sharp curve, look for the wooden post marking the trailhead on the right. You can take this route in as far as you want and backtrack out or link up with other trails along the way.

Puu Ohia Trail

The Puu Ohia Trail, in conjunction with the Pauoa Flats Trail, leads up to a lookout with a view of the Nuuanu reservoir and valley. It's nearly two miles one way and makes a hardy hike.

The trailhead is at the very top of Tantalus Drive, 3.6 miles up on the left from its intersection with Makiki Heights Drive. There's a large turnoff opposite the trailhead where you can park.

The Puu Ohia Trail starts up reinforced log steps and leads past ginger, bamboo groves and lots of eucalyptus, a fast-growing tree that was planted to protect the watershed. About half a mile up, the trail reaches the top of 2013-foot Mt Tantalus (Puu Ohia).

From Mt Tantalus, the trail leads onto a service road. Continue on the road to its end, where there's a Hawaiian Telephone Building. The trail picks up again behind the left side of the building.

Continue down the trail until it leads into the Manoa Cliff Trail, which you'll go left on for a short distance until you come to another intersection where you'll turn right onto the **Pauoa Flats Trail**. The trail leads down into Pauoa Flats and on to the lookout. The flats area can be muddy; be careful not to trip on exposed tree roots.

You'll pass two trailheads before reaching the lookout. The first is **Nuuanu Trail**, on the left, which runs three-quarters of a mile along the western side of Upper Pauoa Valley and offers broad views of Honolulu and the Waianae Mountains.

The second is **Aihualama Trail**, a bit

farther along on the right, which takes you 1¼ miles to Manoa Falls through bamboo groves and huge old banyan trees. If you were to follow this route, you could then hike down the Manoa Falls Trail, a distance of about a mile, to the end of Manoa Rd and from there catch a bus back to town (see the Upper Manoa Valley section).

PEARL HARBOR (Map 2)

On December 7, 1941, more than 350 Japanese planes attacked Pearl Harbor, home of the US Pacific Fleet.

Some 2335 US soldiers were killed during the two-hour attack. Of those, 1177 died in the battleship USS *Arizona* when it took a direct hit and sank in less than nine minutes.

USS Arizona Memorial

Over 1.5 million people 'remember Pearl Harbor' each year by visiting the USS Arizona Memorial run by the National Park Service. It is Hawaii's most visited attraction.

The visitor center includes a museum and theater as well as the offshore memorial at the sunken USS *Arizona*. The park service provides a 75-minute program that includes a 23-minute documentary film on the attack followed by a boat ride out to the memorial and back. Everything is free. The memorial and all facilities are accessible to the disabled.

The 184-foot memorial, built in 1962, sits directly over the *Arizona* without touching it. It contains the *Arizona*'s bell

The Element of Surprise

The attack upon Pearl Harbor, which jolted the USA into WWII, caught the US fleet totally by surprise. There had, however, been warnings, some of which were far from subtle.

At 6:40 am the USS *Ward* spotted a submarine conning tower approaching the entrance of Pearl Harbor. The *Ward* immediately attacked with depth charges and sank what turned out to be one of five midget Japanese submarines launched to penetrate the harbor.

At 7:02 am a radar station on the north shore of Oahu reported planes approaching. Even though they were coming from the wrong direction, they were assumed to be American planes from the mainland.

At 7:55 am Pearl Harbor was hit. Within minutes the USS *Arizona* went down in a fiery inferno, trapping its crew beneath the surface. Twenty other US ships were sunk or damaged, along with 347 aircraft.

It wasn't until 15 minutes after the bombing started that American antiaircraft guns began to shell the Japanese warplanes. The Japanese lost 29 aircraft in the attack. ■

Honolulu Star-Bulletin 1st EXTRA

(Associated Press by Transpacific Telephone)

SAN FRANCISCO, Dec. 7.—President Roosevelt announced this morning that Japanese planes had attacked Manila and Pearl Harbor.

WAR!

OAHU BOMBED BY JAPANESE PLANES

SIX KNOWN DEAD, 21 INJURED, AT EMERGENCY HOSPITAL

and a wall inscribed with the names of those who went down with the ship. The average age of the enlisted men on the *Arizona* was just 19.

From the memorial the battleship can be viewed eight feet below the surface. The ship rests in about 40 feet of water and even now oozes a gallon or two of oil each day. In the rush to recoup from the attack and prepare for war, the navy exercised its option to leave the men in the sunken ship buried at sea. They remain entombed in its hull.

The visitor center (☎ 422-2771; 24-hour recorded information ☎ 422-0561) is open from 7:30 am to 5 pm daily except on Thanksgiving, Christmas and New Year's Day. There's a snack bar and a shop selling souvenirs and books.

Programs run every 15 or 20 minutes from 8 am to 3 pm (from 7:45 am in summer) on a first-come basis. As soon as you arrive, pick up a ticket at the information booth; the number on the ticket corresponds to the time the tour begins. Generally the shortest waits are in the morning; if you arrive before the first crowds you might get in within half an hour, but waits of a couple of hours are not unknown. Summer months are busiest, with an average of 4500 people taking the tour daily, and the allotment of tickets is sometimes gone by 11 am.

Pearl Harbor survivors, who act as volunteer historians, are sometimes available to give talks about the day of the attack.

There's a little open-air museum to keep you occupied while you're waiting. It has interesting photos from both Japanese and US military archives showing Pearl Harbor before, during and after the attack. One photo is of Harvard-educated Admiral Yamamoto, the brilliant military strategist who planned the attack on Pearl Harbor even though he personally opposed going to war with the USA. Rather than relish the victory, Yamamoto stated after the attack that he feared Japan had 'awakened a sleeping giant and filled him with a terrible resolve.'

Bowfin Park

If you have to wait an hour or two for your Arizona Memorial tour to begin, you might want to stroll over to the adjacent Bowfin Park.

The park contains a moored WWII submarine, the USS *Bowfin*, and the Pacific Submarine Museum, which traces the development of submarines from the turn of the century to the nuclear age.

The *Bowfin*, commissioned in May 1943, sank 44 ships in the Pacific before the end of the war. The submarine tour is self-guided, with a hand-held radio receiver that picks up recorded messages as you walk through. Admission is $8 for adults, $3 for children ages four to 12, and includes entry to both the submarine and museum.

There's no charge to enter the park, where you can view missiles and torpedoes spread around the grounds, look through the periscopes or inspect the Japanese *kaiten*, a suicide torpedo.

The kaiten is just what it looks like: a torpedo with a single seat. As the war was closing in on the Japanese homeland, the kaiten was developed in a last-ditch effort to ward off an invasion. It was the marine equivalent of the kamikaze pilot and his plane. A volunteer was placed in the torpedo before it was fired. He then piloted it to its target. At least one US ship, the USS *Mississinewa*, was sunk by a kaiten. It went down off Ulithi Atoll in southwestern Micronesia in November 1944.

The park and museum are open from 8 am to 5 pm daily.

Getting There & Away

The Arizona Memorial visitor center is off Kamehameha Hwy (Hwy 99) on the Pearl Harbor Naval Base just south of Aloha Stadium. If you're coming from Honolulu, take H-1 west to exit 15A (Stadium/Arizona Memorial). Make sure you follow highway signs for the Arizona Memorial, not Pearl Harbor.

The private Arizona Memorial Shuttle Bus (☎ 839-0911) picks up people from Waikiki hotels every 90 minutes between 7 am and 1 pm; the last bus returns at 3:30 pm. The ride takes around 40 minutes and costs $3 each way. Call to make arrangements.

By public transport, take the No 20 airport bus from Waikiki, which takes about 1¼ hours.

There are also private boat cruises to Pearl Harbor leaving from Kewalo Basin for about $25, but they should be avoided as passengers are not allowed to board the memorial.

OTHER ATTRACTIONS
Bishop Museum

The Bishop Museum (☎ 847-3511), 1525 Bernice St (in western Honolulu; see Map 2), is considered by many to be the best Polynesian anthropological museum in the world. It also has Hawaii's only planetarium.

One side of the main gallery, the **Hawaiian Hall**, has three floors covering the cultural history of Hawaii. The 1st floor, dedicated largely to pre-Western-contact Hawaii, has a full-sized pili-grass thatched house and numerous other displays from carved temple images to calabashes and weapons.

One of the museum's most impressive holdings is a **feather cloak** made for Kamehameha I and passed down to subsequent kings. It was created entirely of the yellow feathers of the now-extinct mamo, a predominately black bird with a yellow upper tail. Around 80,000 birds were caught, plucked and released to create this single cloak.

The 2nd floor is dedicated to 19th-century Hawaii and the top floor to the various ethnic groups that comprise present-day Hawaii. Like Hawaii itself, the top floor has a bit of everything, including samurai armor, Portuguese festival costumes, Taoist fortune-telling sticks and Queen Liliuokalani's royal coach.

The **Polynesian Hall** contains masks from Melanesia, stick charts from Micronesia and weapons and musical instruments from Polynesia.

The **Cooke Rotunda** features an exhibit detailing how ancient Pacific navigators were able to journey vast distances, observing the seas and the skies for direction.

The museum also has a **natural history section**; large seashell collections and flora and fauna collections; and the Kahili

The Last Recordings

Bishop Museum is well respected, not only for its collections but for the ethnological research it spearheaded throughout the Pacific. Beginning in the 1920s, supported by mainland philanthropy and Ivy League scholars, the museum organized teams of archaeologists and anthropologists and sent them to record the cultures of the Pacific islands before they were forever lost.

The most renowned of the researchers was Kenneth Emory, who was born in Boston but spent his early years in Hawaii where he became fluent in the Hawaiian language. His knowledge of Hawaiian gave him the linguistic underpinnings to understand all Polynesian dialects. For five decades he sailed schooners and mailboats to the far corners of the Pacific, cranking out film footage of native dancers, recording their songs, measuring their temples (both buildings and skulls!) and transcribing their folklore.

Emory's treatises are the most important (and sometimes the only) anthropological recordings of many Pacific island cultures, from Lanai to Tuamotu. He was affiliated with the museum until his death at age 94 in January 1992. ■

Room, where children can crawl under large turtle shells, try on a hula skirt or play with Hawaiian rhythm instruments.

In the Hawaiian Hall lobby, craftspeople demonstrate Hawaiian quilting, lauhala weaving, lei making and other traditional crafts from 9 am to 2 pm Monday to Friday. A hula show is presented at 1 pm on weekdays.

The Bishop Museum is open from 9 am to 5 pm daily. Admission, which has recently doubled, is now $14.95 for adults, $11.95 for children ages six to 17, and free for children under age six. The admission price includes all exhibits, demonstrations and the planetarium.

Planetarium shows are held at 11 am and 2 pm daily. On Fridays and Saturdays there's also a show at 7 pm, which on clear nights is followed by viewing from the observatory telescope. Reservations are necessary for the evening programs. Admission to the planetarium alone costs $4.50.

The museum shop sells many books on the Pacific not easily found elsewhere as well as quality Hawaiiana gift items. There's also a snack shop that's open until 4 pm.

Getting There & Away From Waikiki or downtown Honolulu, take the No 2 School St bus to Kapalama St, walk towards the ocean and turn right on Bernice St. By car, take Exit 20B off H-1 west, go mauka on Houghtailing St and turn left on Bernice St.

Moanalua Gardens

Moanalua Gardens, a former property of Princess Pauahi Bishop that's now maintained by the Damon Estate, is a large grassy park with grand shade trees. The park is the site of Kamehameha V's gingerbread-trimmed summer cottage, which overlooks a taro pond. Beyond it a Chinese-style hall is fronted by carp ponds and stands of golden-stemmed bamboo. The center of the park has a grassy stage where the Prince Lot Hula Festival is held on the third Saturday in July.

This is not a must-see spot, except during the festival, but it is a pleasant place to stroll if you happen to be passing through western Honolulu (see Map 2). To get there, take the Puuloa Rd/Tripler Hospital exit off Hwy 78 and then make an immediate right-hand turn into the gardens.

Royal Mausoleum State Monument

The Royal Mausoleum contains the remains of Kings Kamehameha II, III, IV and V as well as King David Kalakaua and Queen Liliuokalani, the last reigning monarchs. Missing is Kamehameha I, the last king to be buried in secret in accordance with Hawaii's old religion.

The original mausoleum building, which is usually locked, is now a chapel; the caskets are in nearby crypts. Other gravestones honor Kamehameha I's British confidante John Young and American Charles Reed Bishop, husband of Bernice Pauahi Bishop.

The mausoleum, at 2261 Nuuanu Ave (just before the avenue meets the Pali Hwy – see Map 8), is open from 8 am to 4:30 pm Monday to Friday. There's no admission charge.

Just across Nuuanu Ave from the mausoleum, on Kawananakoa Place, is **Hsu Yin Temple**, a Buddhist temple that's worth a quick look if you're visiting the mausoleum. At the altar are the standard offerings of oranges and burning incense, while prints on the walls depict Buddha's life story.

Punchbowl

Punchbowl (Map 8) is the bowl-shaped remains of a long-extinct volcanic crater. At an elevation of 500 feet it sits a mile north of the downtown district and offers a fine view of the city out to Diamond Head and the Pacific beyond.

Early Hawaiians called the crater Puowaina, the 'hill of human sacrifices.' It's believed there was a heiau at the crater and that the slain bodies of kapu breakers were brought to Punchbowl to be cremated upon the heiau altar.

Today it's the site of the 115-acre National Memorial Cemetery of the

NED FRIARY

NED FRIARY

NED FRIARY

HAWAII VISITORS BUREAU MARKER

DUKE KAHANAMOKU
HAWAII'S FIRST OLYMPIC CHAMPION
1912 GOLD MEDAL FOR SWIMMING

FATHER OF MODERN SURFING
FIRST PERSON INDUCTED INTO BOTH
SWIMMING & SURFING HALLS OF FAME

NED FRIARY

NED FRIARY

Cliché Hawaiiana

A: NED FRIARY

B: NED FRIARY

C: NED FRIARY

D: NED FRIARY

E: NED FRIARY

A: Hula
B: Ukulele
C: Hibiscus

D: Hula
E: Hawaiian quiltwork

A: Plumeria
B: Bird of Paradise

C: Featherwork
D: Lauhala weaver

A: NED FRIARY

D: NED FRIARY

B: GLENDA BENDURE

C: DAVID RUSS

A: Daewonsa Buddhist Temple, Honolulu
B: Interior of Lum Sai Ho Tong Temple

C: Byodo-In Temple, near Kaneohe
D: Kamehameha IV and Queen Emma, St Andrew's Cathedral

Pacific. The remains of Hawaiians sacrificed to appease the gods now share the crater floor with the bodies of more than 25,000 soldiers, more than half of whom were killed in the Pacific during WWII.

The remains of Ernie Pyle, the distinguished war correspondent who covered both world wars and was hit by machine gun fire on Ie Shima during the final days of WWII, lies in section D, grave 109. Five stones to the left, at grave D-1, lies astronaut Ellison Onizuka, the Big Island native who perished in the 1986 Challenger disaster. Their resting places are marked with the same style of flat granite stone that marks each of the cemetery's graves.

A huge memorial at the head of the cemetery has eight marble courts representing different Pacific regions and is inscribed with the names of the 26,289 Americans missing in action from WWII and the Korean War. Two additional half courts have the names of 2489 soldiers missing from the Vietnam War.

For a good view of the city, walk to the lookout 10 minutes south of the memorial.

The cemetery is open from 8 am to 5:30 pm in winter and to 6:30 pm from March through September.

Getting There & Away The entrance into Punchbowl is off Puowaina Drive. There's a marked exit as you start up the Pali Hwy from H-1; watch closely as it comes up quickly! From there, drive slowly and follow the signs as you wind through a series of narrow streets on the short way up to the cemetery.

By bus, take a No 2 from Waikiki to downtown Honolulu and get off at Beretania and Alapai Sts, where you transfer to bus No 15 (which runs hourly on the half hour). Ask the driver where to get off. It's about a 15-minute walk to Punchbowl from the bus stop.

Pali Hwy

The Pali Hwy (Hwy 61) runs north from Honolulu towards Kailua, cutting through the spectacular Koolau Range. It's a scenic little highway, and if it's been raining heavily, every fold and crevice in the mountains will have a lacy waterfall streaming down it.

Many Kailua residents commute to work over the Pali, so Honolulu-bound traffic can be heavy in the morning and outbound traffic heavy in the evening. It's less of a problem for visitors, however, as most daytrippers will be traveling against the traffic. Public buses travel the Pali Hwy, but none stop at the Nuuanu Pali Lookout.

Past the four-mile marker, look up and to the right to see two notches cut about 15 feet deep into the crest of the *pali* (cliff). These notches are thought to have been dug as cannon emplacements by Kamehameha I.

The original route between Honolulu and windward Oahu was via an ancient footpath that wound its way perilously over these cliffs. In 1845 the path was widened into a horse trail and later into a cobblestone carriage road.

In 1898 the Old Pali Hwy (as it's now called) was built following the same route. It was abandoned in the 1950s after tunnels were blasted through the Koolau Range and the present multilane Pali Hwy opened.

You can still drive a loop of the Old Pali Hwy (called Nuuanu Pali Drive) and hike another mile of it from the Nuuanu Pali Lookout.

Queen Emma Summer Palace At the Pali Hwy two-mile marker is the Queen Emma Summer Palace, which belonged to Queen Emma, the consort of Kamehameha IV.

Emma was three-quarters royal Hawaiian and a quarter English, a granddaughter of the captured sailor John Young, who became a friend and adviser of Kamehameha I. The house is also known as Hanaiakamalama, the name of John Young's home in Kawaihae on the Big Island, where he served as governor.

The Youngs left the home to Queen Emma, who often slipped away from her formal downtown home to this cooler retreat. It's a bit like an old Southern plantation house, with a columned porch, high ceilings and louvered windows to catch the breeze.

The home was forgotten after Emma's death in 1885, and was scheduled to be razed in 1915 when the estate was being turned into a public park. The Daughters of Hawaii rescued it and now run it as a museum.

The house has period furniture collected from five of Emma's homes. Some of the more interesting pieces are a cathedral-shaped koa cabinet made in Berlin and filled with a set of china from Queen Victoria; feather cloaks and capes; and Emma's necklace of tiger claws, a gift from the Maharaja of India.

It's open from 9 am to 4 pm daily except holidays. Admission is $4 for adults and $1 for children under age 16.

Nuuanu Pali Drive For a scenic side trip through a shady green forest, turn off the Pali Hwy onto Nuuanu Pali Drive, half a mile past the Queen Emma Summer Palace. The 2½-mile road runs parallel to the Pali Hwy and then comes back out to it before the Nuuanu Pali Lookout, so you don't miss anything by taking this side loop – in fact, quite the opposite.

The drive goes through mature trees that form a canopy overhead, all draped with hanging vines and wound with philodendrons. The lush vegetation includes banyan trees with hanging aerial roots, tropical almond trees, bamboo groves, impatiens, angel trumpets and golden cup, the latter a tall climbing vine with large golden flowers.

Nuuanu Pali Lookout Whatever you do, don't miss the Nuuanu Pali Lookout (Nuuanu Pali State Park) with its broad view of the windward coast from a height of 1200 feet. From the lookout you can see Kaneohe straight ahead, Kailua to the right and Mokolii Island and the coastal fishpond at Kualoa Park to the far left.

This is *windward* Oahu – and the winds that funnel through the pali are so strong

that you can sometimes lean against them. It gets cool enough to appreciate having a jacket.

In 1795 Kamehameha routed Oahu's warriors up the Nuuanu Trail during his invasion of the island. On these steep cliffs Oahu's warriors made their last stand. Hundreds were thrown to their death over the pali as they were overcome by Kamehameha's troops. A hundred years later, during the construction of the Old Pali Hwy, more than 500 skulls were found at the base of the cliffs.

The abandoned Old Pali Hwy winds down from the right of the lookout, ending abruptly at a barrier near the current highway about a mile away. Few people realize the road is here, let alone venture down it. It makes a nice walk and takes about 20 minutes one way. There are good views looking back up at the jagged Koolau Mountains and out across the valley.

As you get back on the highway, it's easy to miss the sign leading you out of the parking lot and instinct could send you in the wrong direction. Go to the left if you're heading towards Kailua, to the right if heading towards Honolulu.

ACTIVITIES
Beaches & Swimming
Oahu boasts more than 50 beach parks, most with restrooms and showers. Twenty-three of them, including Honolulu's Ala Moana and Waikiki beaches, are patrolled by lifeguards.

Overall the Honolulu area beaches have good swimming conditions all year round, although they can be a bit rougher in summer. For specific water conditions, see the individual beach sections.

Swimming Pools The county maintains 18 community swimming pools on Oahu. Pools in the greater Honolulu area are at these locations:

Palolo Valley District Park
    2007 Palolo Ave (☎ 733-7362)

Manoa Valley District Park
    2721 Kaaipu Ave (☎ 988-6868)

Booth District Park
    2331 Kanealii Ave (☎ 522-7037)

McCully District Park
    831 Pumehana St (☎ 973-7268)

Surfing

Oahu has 594 defined surfing sites, nearly twice as many as any of the other Hawaiian islands. In winter, the North Shore gets some of Hawaii's most spectacular surf, with swells reaching 20 to 30 feet. This is the home of the Banzai Pipeline, Sunset Beach and some of the world's top surfing competitions. On the leeward Waianae Coast, Makaha is the top winter surf spot.

The south shore gets its finest surfing waves in summer, with Waikiki and Diamond Head beaches having some of the best breaks.

In Waikiki, surfing lessons can be arranged from beach concession stands like Aloha Beach Services near Duke's Canoe Club, or Star Beach Boys behind the Waikiki police station. The going rate is $25 for a one-hour lesson. The Waikiki concession stands also rent surfboards for around $7 an hour or $25 a day.

Planet Surf (☎ 926-2060), 421 Nahua St in Waikiki, rents surfboards for $17 per 24 hours and longboard tankers for $20 and also sells used surfboards. Local Motion (☎ 955-7873), 1714 Kapiolani Blvd, rents surfboards for $20 the first 24 hours, $15 for additional days, or $75 a week.

If you want to battle the waves on the North Shore, surfboards can be rented from Surf-N-Sea (☎ 637-9887) in Haleiwa at similar rates.

Surf News Network (☎ 596-SURF) has a recorded surf line reporting winds, wave heights and tides; it's updated three times a day. The National Weather Service (☎ 973-4383) also provides surf reports.

H30, a monthly magazine that interviews surfers and reports on surfing events and surf conditions, is free at surf shops around the island.

Bodysurfing & Boogie Boarding

The island's two hottest (and most dangerous) spots for expert bodysurfers are Sandy Beach Park and Makapuu Beach Park in southeast Oahu. Other top shorebreaks are at Makaha on the Waianae Coast, Waimea Bay on the North Shore, and Kalama Beach in Kailua and Pounders in Laie on the windward coast.

The most popular boogie boarding place in Waikiki is at Kapahulu Groin.

You can rent boogie boards from the concession stands on Waikiki Beach, which generally charge about $5 an hour or $8 for two hours. Planet Surf (☎ 926-2060), 421 Nahua St in Waikiki, rents boogie boards from $7.50 a day, $20 a week, and also sells used boards.

Snorkeling

Because of all the activity in the water, Waikiki Beach is not a good place for snorkeling – Sans Souci Beach, on Waikiki's east side, is the best bet as it still has some coral.

However, a short bus ride from Waikiki will take you to scenic Hanauma Bay in southeast Oahu, which has the island's best year-round snorkeling. In summer, you could also go farther afield to Pupukea Beach Park on the North Shore, which has excellent snorkeling when the waters are calm.

Prime Time Sports, a concession stand at Waikiki's Fort DeRussy Beach, rents snorkel sets for $3 an hour, $10 for 24 hours. Planet Surf (☎ 926-2060), 419 Nahua St in Waikiki, rents snorkel sets for $5.50 a day, $15 a week.

Diving

Oahu's best dive sites are outside Waikiki and the central Honolulu area, but you won't necessarily have to go far.

Hanauma Bay in southeast Oahu has calm diving conditions most of the year. There are a number of other popular dive spots between Hanauma Bay and Honolulu that provide good winter diving. Top summer dive spots include the caves and ledges at Three Tables and Shark's Cove on the North Shore and the Makaha Caverns on the Waianae Coast.

Aloha Dive Shop (☎ 395-5922), Koko Marina Shopping Center, Honolulu, HI

96825, has two-tank boat dives off Koko Head for $75. Two-tank introductory dives also cost $75 and PADI certification courses cost $375. They offer free transport from Waikiki hotels.

Other dive shops have comparable rates, including the following five-star PADI operations in the greater Honolulu area:

Breeze Hawaii Diving Adventure,
    3014 Kaimuki Ave, Honolulu, HI 96816
    (☎ 735-1857)

Dan's Dive Shop, 660 Ala Moana Blvd,
    Honolulu, HI 96813 (☎ 536-6181)

Hawaii Dive College, 24 Sand Island Access Rd,
    Honolulu, HI 96819 (☎ 843-2882)

Hawaii Pro-Dive, Waikiki Trade Center,
    2255 Kuhio Ave, M7, Honolulu, HI 96815
    (☎ 922-0895)

South Sea Aquatics, 2155 Kalakaua Ave,
    Honolulu, HI 96815 (☎ 922-0852)

Sunshine Scuba, 642 Cooke St,
    Honolulu, HI 96813 (☎ 593-8865)

Waikiki Diving Center, 1734 Kalakaua Ave,
    Honolulu, HI 96826 (☎ 955-5151)

Windward Dive Center, 789 Kailua Rd,
    Kailua, HI 96734 (☎ 263-2311)

Snuba Snuba Tours of Oahu (☎ 396-6163) offers snuba, a sort of scuba diving for snorkelers, at Hanauma Bay for $85 (a 3½-hour outing, including transport from Waikiki) or at Maunalua Bay in the Hawaii Kai area in conjunction with a boat cruise, kayaking, snorkeling and lunch for $105. There's also a shorter snuba experience available for $50 at Waikiki, swimming directly out from the Outrigger Reef Hotel beach hut, where the snuba outings are booked.

Snuba utilizes long air hoses attached to a tank on an inflatable raft; the diver simply wears a mask and weight belt and can dive down as far as the air hose allows. This is a nice opportunity to get introduced to the underwater world. All programs include elementary dive instruction, such as how to clear your mask of water and equalizing ear pressure, and an instructor is in the water with you during the entire dive.

Windsurfing

Fort DeRussy Beach is Waikiki's main windsurfing spot. Waikiki Pacific Windsurfing (☎ 949-8952), in the concession stand at Fort DeRussy Beach, rents windsurfing equipment for $18 an hour, $30 for two hours; add $10 more for a lesson.

Still, if you want top-rated windsurfing action you're better off heading for Kailua Bay, a 45-minute bus ride from Honolulu. There you'll find good year-round trade winds, and both flat water and wave conditions in different sections of the bay. Windsurfing shops set up vans at Kailua Beach Park on weekdays and Saturday mornings, renting boards and giving lessons. It's a great place for beginners to try the sport.

Naish Hawaii (☎ 262-6068, 800-767-6068) – as in windsurfing champion Robbie Naish – sells and rents equipment. Their shop is at 155A Hamakua Drive, Kailua, HI 96734, but they can deliver equipment to Kailua Beach. Rental rates vary with the board and rig: beginner equipment costs $15 an hour or $30 a full day; intermediate and advanced equipment is $35 a half day, $40 to $45 a full day. Naish gives introductory group lessons for $35 for three hours. For $55 you can get a 1½-hour private lesson that includes an additional 2½ hours of board use.

Kailua Sailboard Company (☎ 262-2555), 130 Kailua Rd, Kailua, HI 96734, rents beginner equipment for $25 a half day, $30 a day or $123 a week; intermediate or advanced equipment costs $29 a half day, $38 a full day. Three-hour beginner's lessons are $39.

Good spots for advanced windsurfers include Diamond Head for speed and jumps and Backyards for North Shore challenges.

Kayaking

An up-and-coming sport in Hawaii is sea kayaking. Busy Waikiki is not the most ideal place for kayaking, but there are kayak rentals available right on the beach. Both Fort DeRussy Beach and

Sans Souci Beach have fewer swimmers and catamarans to share the water with, and make a better bet than the central Waikiki Beach strip.

Prime Time Sports (☎ 949-8952), at Fort DeRussy Beach, and Leahi Beach Services (☎ 922-5665), at the Outrigger Reef hotel, rent one-person kayaks for $10 an hour, two-person kayaks for around $20. Kayak Oahu Adventures (☎ 923-0539), at Sans Souci Beach, rents one/ two-person kayaks for $10/15 an hour, $30/40 a half day.

The most popular place for kayaking in southeast Oahu is lovely Kailua Beach, which has a near-shore island that can be visited by kayakers. Twogood Kayaks Hawaii (☎ 262-5656), at 171 Hamakua Drive in Kailua, has kayak rentals and lessons. One-person kayaks rent for $22 a half day or $28 a full day; two-person kayaks cost $29/39. Kailua Sailboard Company (☎ 262-2555), at 130 Kailua Rd in Kailua, has kayaks at the same rates.

Hiking

The trail that leads three-quarters of a mile from inside the crater of Diamond Head up to its summit is the most popular hike on Oahu. It's easy to reach from Waikiki and ends with a panoramic view of greater Honolulu.

Another nice short hike is the Manoa Falls Trail, just a few miles north of Waikiki, where a peaceful walk through an abandoned arboretum of huge trees leads to a waterfall.

The Tantalus and Makiki Valley area has the most extensive trail network around Honolulu, with fine views of the city and surrounding valleys. Amazingly, although it's just two miles from the city hustle and bustle, this lush forest reserve is unspoiled and offers quiet solitude.

In addition to these more substantial hikes there are shorter walks that can be taken from the Nuuanu Pali Lookout, just north of Honolulu; to the Makapuu lighthouse in southeast Oahu; and along many beaches.

For more details on these hikes, see the respective sections of this chapter.

Guided Hikes Notices of hiking club outings appear in the *Honolulu Star-Bulletin's* Bulletin Board column on weekdays and in the *Honolulu Advertiser's* Calabash column on Sundays.

By joining one of these outings you get to meet and hike with ecology-minded islanders. It may also be a good way to get to the backwoods if you don't have a car, as they often share rides. Wear sturdy shoes and, for the longer hikes, bring lunch and water.

The Sierra Club (☎ 538-6616) leads hikes and other outings on Saturdays and Sundays. These range from easy 1½-mile hikes to strenuous 10-mile treks. Most outings meet at 8 am at the Church of the Crossroads at 2510 Bingham St in Honolulu. The hike fee is $3. For a copy of the latest newsletter, which includes the hike schedule, send $2 to Sierra Club, Box 2577, Honolulu, HI 96803.

The Hawaii Audubon Society (☎ 528-1432) leads bird-watching hikes once or twice a month, usually on weekends. The suggested donation is $2. Binoculars and a copy of *Hawaii's Birds* are recommended. You can get a free brochure in advance that lists birding sites on Oahu by sending a self-addressed stamped envelope to Oahu Birding Guide, Hawaii Audubon Society, 1088 Bishop St, Suite 808, Honolulu, HI 96813.

The Hawaii Nature Center (☎ 955-0100), at the forestry baseyard camp in Makiki, offers guided hikes on most Saturday mornings for $5. Trails range from the easy 2½-mile Makiki Loop Trail to a strenuous six-mile hike up Mt Kaala, Oahu's highest point. Reservations are required.

The Hawaiian Trail & Mountain Club has guided hikes most weekends, although some are for members only. The hike fee is $2. Hikes generally range from three to 12 miles in length and cover the full gamut from novice to advanced in difficulty. For a copy of the hiking schedule, send $1 and a stamped, self-addressed envelope to the club at Box 2238, Honolulu, HI 96804.

For information on walking tours of downtown Honolulu and Chinatown, see Organized Tours in the Getting Around chapter.

Horseback Riding
While there's no horseback riding offered in the Honolulu area, there are a couple of options around the island.

Kualoa Ranch (☎ 237-8515), opposite Kualoa Regional Park on the windward coast, has 40-minute trail rides in Kaaawa Valley for $25 and 1½-hour rides for $40.

The Turtle Bay Hilton (☎ 293-8811) in Kahuku has 45-minute trail rides for $35 and 1½-hour sunset rides for $65.

Hoku Ranch (☎ 622-2100) at Dole Plantation in Wahiawa has 1¼-hour trail rides past pineapple fields for $25, as well as longer rides.

Tennis
Oahu has 175 county tennis courts. If you're staying in Waikiki, the most convenient locations are the 10 lighted courts at Ala Moana Beach Park (☎ 522-7031), the nine unlighted courts at the Diamond Head Tennis Center (☎ 971-7150) at the Diamond Head end of Kapiolani Park, and the four lighted Kapiolani Park courts opposite the Waikiki Aquarium. Court time at these county facilities is free on a first-come first-served basis.

With ground space at a premium, few Waikiki hotels have room for tennis courts. The largest facilities are at the Ilikai Hotel (☎ 944-6300), 1777 Ala Moana Blvd, which has five courts, rentals, lessons and a pro shop. Rates are $5 per hour per person for hotel guests, $7.50 for non-guests, plus a $2 light charge for night play. Racquets rent for $3. It's open daily from 7 am to 10 pm.

The Pacific Beach Hotel (☎ 922-1233) on Kalakaua Ave has two courts open daily from 8 am to 6 pm and charges $5 per hour per person for guests, $8 for non-guests. Racquets can be rented for $4.

Planet Surf (☎ 926-2060), 419 Nahua St, rents tennis racquets for $5 a day, $20 a week.

Golf
Oahu has five 18-hole municipal golf courses:

Ala Wai Golf Course on Kapahulu Ave,
    mauka of the Ala Wai Canal near Waikiki
    (☎ 733-7387)

Ewa Villages Golf Course in Ewa (☎ 681-0220)

Pali Golf Course, 45-050 Kamehameha Hwy,
    Kaneohe (☎ 266-7612)

Ted Makalena Golf Course, Waipio Point
    Access Rd, Waipahu (☎ 675-6052)

West Loch Golf Course, 91-1126 Okupe St,
    Ewa Beach (☎ 675-6076)

Green fees for 18 holes are $40 per person, plus an optional $14 for a gas-powered cart.

The reservation system is the same at all municipal courses: call ☎ 296-2000 and key information into the recorded system as prompted. The earliest bookings are taken just three days in advance for visitors, but one week in advance for resident golfers.

The only municipal course near Waikiki is the Ala Wai Golf Course, which lays claims to being the 'busiest in the world.' Local golfers who may book earlier in the week usually take all the starting times, leaving none for visitors. However, visiting golfers who don't mind a wait may show up at the Ala Wai window and get on the waiting list; as long as the entire golfing party waits at the course, they'll usually get you on before the day is over. If you come without clubs, you can rent them for $20.

At last count, Oahu also had 18 private (and nine military) golf courses, but the number is rising, fueling many a conflict between environmentalists and overseas developers.

Running
Islanders are big on jogging. In fact, it's estimated that Honolulu has more joggers per capita than any other city in the world. Kapiolani Park and Ala Moana Park are

two favorite jogging spots. There's also a 4.8-mile run around Diamond Head crater that's a well-beaten track.

Oahu has more than 75 road races each year, from one-mile fun runs and five-mile jogs to competitive marathons, biathlons and triathlons. For an annual schedule of running events with times, dates and contact addresses, write to the Department of Parks & Recreation, City & County of Honolulu, 650 S King St, Honolulu, HI 96813.

The city's best-known race is the Honolulu Marathon, which in just a few years has mushroomed into one of the largest marathons in the USA. It's held in early December. For information send a stamped, self-addressed envelope to Honolulu Marathon Association, 3435 Waialae Ave, No 208, Honolulu, HI 96816. Those writing from overseas are asked to include two international response postage coupons.

The Department of Parks & Recreation holds a Honolulu Marathon Clinic at 7:30 am most Sundays at the Kapiolani Park Bandstand. It's free and open to everyone from beginners to seasoned marathon runners. Runners join groups of their own speed.

Skydiving & Glider Rides

Skydiving and glider rides are available at the Dillingham Airfield in Mokuleia on the North Shore.

For $225, Skydive Hawaii (☎ 945-0222) will attach you to the hips and shoulders of a skydiver so you can jump together from a plane at 13,000 feet, freefall for a minute and finish off with 10 to 15 minutes of canopy ride. The whole process, including some basic instruction, takes about 1½ hours. Participants must be over 18 years of age and weigh less than 200 pounds. Arrangements can also be made to take up experienced skydivers for solo jumps. They take off daily (weather permitting) from Dillingham Airfield in Mokuleia. Pick-up service is available from Waikiki.

Glider Rides (☎ 677-3404) offers 20-minute glider rides from the west end of Dillingham Airfield. Flights go daily, weather permitting, between 10:30 am and 5 pm. The cost is $100 for one person or $120 for two.

Soar Hawaii (☎ 637-3147), at the same location, has 20-minute glider rides for $120 for either one or two people. For thrill seekers they also offer acrobatic rides with barrel rolls, spirals and stalls.

Cruises

Numerous sunset sails, dinner cruises and party boats leave daily from Kewalo Basin, just west of Ala Moana Park. Rates range from $20 to $100, with dinner cruises averaging about $50. Many provide transport to and from Waikiki and advertise various come-ons and specials; check the free tourist magazines for the latest offers. Some of the vessels, including a few of the 'catamarans,' are large impersonal operations, so you may prefer to go down to the harbor where the boats are docked and check them out for yourself before buying a ticket.

A handful of catamarans depart from Waikiki Beach, including the *Manu Kai* (☎ 946-7490), which docks behind the Duke Kahanamoku statue and charges $10 for one-hour sails, $20 for 1½-hour sunset sails. The green-sailed *Leahi* catamaran (☎ 922-5665), which departs from the beach in front of the Sheraton Waikiki, has one-hour sails for $16 and 1½-hour sunset sails for $24.

Royal Hawaiian Cruises (☎ 848-6360) runs 2½-hour whale-watching cruises from January to April aboard the *Navatek I*, a sleek high-tech catamaran that's designed to minimize rolling. It leaves daily except Mondays at 8:30 am from Pier 6 near the Aloha Tower and costs $39 for adults and $24 for children ages three to 11.

Atlantis Submarines (☎ 973-9811) has a 65-foot, 48-passenger sightseeing submarine that descends 100 feet about a mile off Diamond Head. The tour lasts 1¾ hours, including boat transport to and from the sub. About 45 minutes are spent cruising beneath the surface around a ship and two planes deliberately sunk to create a dive site. Tours leave from Hilton Hawaiian Village on the hour from 7 am to 4 pm daily and cost from $85 for adults, $39 for children 12 and under.

COURSES

Visitors who want to take courses and learn more about Hawaiian culture have a variety of options available.

While short-term visitors can't join a traditional hula *halau* (school), where students commit themselves to the tutelage of their instructor for years as they master the intricacies of the dance, even the casual visitor can learn the basics of hula. The Royal Hawaiian Shopping Center (☎ 922-0588) in Waikiki offers free hula lessons every Monday, Wednesday and Friday from 10 to 11 am. Everyone is welcome to join. The instructors are patient and cater to both visitors who are only there for a short period and Waikiki residents who attend on a more regular basis.

Other free courses offered at the Royal Hawaiian Shopping Center are lei-making lessons, held each Monday and Wednesday from 11 am to noon; coconut-frond weaving, held on Tuesday from noon to 2 pm and Thursday from 9 to 11 am; ukulele lessons, held on Tuesday and Thursday from 10 to 11 am; and Hawaiian quilt making, held on Tuesday and Thursday from 9:30 to 11:30 am.

Campus Leisure Programs (☎ 956-6468), in the University of Hawaii's Hemenway Hall, offers arts & crafts classes to the general public. Most classes, such as beginning and intermediate hula, lei-making, slack-key guitar and ceramics, meet once or twice a week and cost around $50 for a monthlong session. In addition, there are monthlong fitness programs including martial arts, shiatsu massage, tai chi chuan and yoga. Of course, the University of Hawaii also offers a variety of summer session and regular semester courses; for more information see the earlier University of Hawaii section of this chapter.

The *Japanese Cultural Center of Hawaii* (☎ 945-7633), 2454 S Beretania St, offers a wide variety of courses to the general public, such as kanji calligraphy, tea ceremony, haiku and Japanese brush art. However, sessions generally last three months and are intended to be taken on an ongoing basis. Of more interest to visitors are the shorter workshops and one-day lectures on topics such as the significance of Japanese swords, Noh masks and Japanese cooking demonstrations. Registration for the day courses generally cost under $10, while the three-month sessions cost around $100.

Places to Stay

Honolulu has a wide range of accommodations, from inexpensive hostels to high-priced luxury resorts. While more than 90% of Honolulu's visitor accommodations are in Waikiki, there are also a handful of other places scattered around the city.

Except where noted, the rates given are the same for either singles or doubles. Rates given in this book do not include the combined room and sales tax of 10.17%, which is added to the price of all accommodations.

If you're calling from outside Hawaii, add the 808 area code to all numbers. Numbers beginning with 800 are toll free from the US mainland and sometimes from Canada as well.

TYPES OF ACCOMMODATIONS
Hotels
The vast majority of visitors to Honolulu stay in Waikiki hotels.

In many hotels the rooms themselves are the same, with only the views varying; generally the higher the floor, the higher the price, and an ocean view will commonly bump up the bill 50% to 100%. If you're paying extra for a view, you might want to ask to see the room first, as Waikiki certainly doesn't have any truth-in-labeling laws governing when a hotel can call a room 'ocean-view.' While some 'ocean views' are the real thing, others are merely glimpses of the water as seen through a series of high-rises.

Many hotels have different rates for high and low seasons. The high season most commonly applies to the period from December 15 to April 15, but it can vary by hotel a few weeks in either direction. The rest of the year is the low season, though a few hotels switch to high-season rates in mid-summer and one chain, the Outrigger, has introduced a three-tier system with winter, summer and spring/fall rates. During the low season, not only do many

places drop their rates by 10% to 30%, but getting the room of your choice without advance reservations is far easier.

As a consequence of low occupancy rates, hotel discounts have been fairly prolific in recent years. Some hotels offer reduced promotional rates to pick up the slack while a few of the larger chains, such as Outrigger and Hawaiian Pacific Resorts, commonly have deals that throw in a free rental car. Before booking any hotel, it's worth asking if they're currently running any specials – some places actually have room/car packages for less than their published room rates!

Hostels & Ys
There are two Hostelling International (HI) hostels in Honolulu: Hostelling International Waikiki in the center of Waikiki and Hostelling International Honolulu near the University of Hawaii.

In addition to the two HI hostels, there are a number of small businesses providing hostel-like dormitory accommodations around Waikiki. These make finding a cheap place to crash much easier than it has been in days past. Essentially these places occupy older apartment buildings; some have a cluster of units, while others have taken over the whole complex. They all cater to backpackers and draw a fairly international crowd. There are no curfews or other restrictions, except that to avoid taking on local boarders, some 'hostels' require travelers to show a passport or an onward ticket.

Despite the 'hostel' in their names these private businesses are not members of the Hostelling International association and visitors shouldn't expect the usual HI standards.

In addition, there are three budget places run by the YMCA and one by the YWCA. Unlike the hostels, Ys are not geared solely for visitors and they offer simple,

Travel Clubs

Travel clubs can provide handsome discounts on accommodations. Essentially, hotels try to fill last-minute rooms by offering cut rates to members of these clubs. In many cases you aren't allowed to book more than 30 days in advance and rooms are limited during the busiest periods. A few places even black out winter dates altogether.

Some of Hawaii's larger hotel chains – including Aston, Marc Resorts and Outrigger – participate in the two travel clubs listed below. Both clubs allow members to book hotels directly, so they're easier to use than travel clubs that act more like reservation services.

By far the most prominent is the Entertainment program, which produces an annual book to Hawaii listing dozens of hotels that offer members half off their standard published rates. It also has about 50 Oahu restaurants with two-for-one meals (or half off meals for single diners) and numerous coupons for other discounts. The books, which include a membership card, can be ordered by mail (☎ 800-374-4464) for $43. They are also available in Oahu at Borders bookstores and other places (☎ 737-3252 for locations).

Another popular club, Encore (☎ 800-638-0930), offers the same half-off room discounts and a similar list of hotels as the Entertainment program, but the dining benefits are more marginal. Annual membership costs $50.

One important difference between the two clubs is that Entertainment membership is valid for a one-year period beginning and ending December 1 – a problem for travelers who arrive in November and stay into December. Encore, on the other hand, is valid for 12 months from the time you enroll.

Keep in mind that the number of businesses participating in these programs varies significantly with the economy. When hotel occupancy is low, participation booms; when the economy is brisk, more businesses pull out of the clubs or add restrictions.

Certainly these clubs will work out best for those who are in Hawaii for longer periods of time, have flexibility with hotel preferences and dates, and are traveling outside of the peak winter season. ■

inexpensive rooms (private or semiprivate) rather than dormitories. Although none are in Waikiki, the Central Branch YMCA is conveniently located just outside Waikiki near the Ala Moana Center.

B&Bs

B&Bs are heavily restricted on Oahu and are scarce in the Honolulu area. However, there are some B&B-style rooms in private homes that are available through B&B reservation services, mostly in the city outskirts in areas such as Diamond Head and Manoa Valley. Prices are usually $60 to $100, depending on the room. Many require a minimum stay of two or three days. Some of the agencies listed below can also book whole houses, condos and studio cottages as well, although the majority of these will be in the Kailua area, not Honolulu. B&B agencies require at least part of the payment in advance and have cancellation penalties. The following B&B agencies book rooms in Oahu:

Affordable Paradise Bed & Breakfast
   c/o Maria Wilson, 226 Pouli Rd,
   Kailua, HI 96734
   (☎ 261-1693, fax 261-7315)

All Islands Bed & Breakfast
    823 Kainui Drive, Kailua, HI 96734
    (☎ 263-2342, 800-542-0344; fax 263-0308)

Bed & Breakfast Hawaii
    Box 449, Kapaa, HI 96746
    (☎ 822-7771, 800-733-1632; fax 822-2723;
    bandb@aloha.net)

Bed & Breakfast Honolulu
    3242 Kaohinani Drive, Honolulu, HI 96817
    (☎ 595-7533, 800-288-4666; fax 595-2030;
    bnbshi@aloha.net)

Long-Term Housing

Most tourist accommodations in the Waikiki area are in hotels, not condominiums, so the sort of lease-free monthly condo rentals that are readily found in tourist locales elsewhere in Hawaii are not so easily found here.

While most condos are filled with long-term residents, you can look in the classified sections of Honolulu's two daily newspapers to see what's available – just keep in mind that the vacation-rental listings can be meager, particularly in the winter season. If you're willing to sign a lease, the selection will be larger. Expect a modest one-bedroom condo to run about $1000 a month, a studio about $700; Honolulu is one of the most expensive housing markets in the USA.

Finding a condo requires a bit of footwork. If you're willing to live out of a single room, some hotels do rent out rooms on a long-term basis, often with kitchenettes that allow limited meal preparation. A good budget-end hotel to check is the Waikiki Grand, which commonly has rooms for about $220 a week.

Another option to shouldering the entire expense yourself is to share a house or apartment with others. Start by perusing the 'Rentals to Share' listings in the classified ads. Another place to look is at the University of Hawaii; a board listing rooms for rent can be found at the campus post office, opposite Hemenway Theatre. The listings are usually quite extensive, with the majority of rooms being in shared student households that are looking for long-term roommates.

Camping

There are no campgrounds in the Waikiki or central Honolulu area. Sand Island State Recreational Area, which is out by the airport and used mainly by locals, is the closest to the city, but it's directly under flight paths and is not the most secure or pristine of places.

More recommended is Keaiwa Heiau State Recreational Area near Aiea, about 10 miles northwest of central Honolulu. It has a caretaker and a gate that's locked at night for security. This wooded park is named for the ancient medicinal temple on its grounds. The camping area can accommodate 100 campers and most sites have their own picnic table and barbecue grill. If you're camping in winter, make sure your gear is waterproof – while the temperature is usually pleasant, it rains a lot at the park's 880-foot elevation. There are restrooms, showers, a phone and drinking water. The nearest regular bus service is via bus No 11 (Honolulu-Aiea Heights), but it stops about 1¼ miles south of the park.

Camping is free by permit at either state park and is limited to five nights per month at each. As with all Oahu campgrounds, camping is not permitted on Wednesday and Thursday nights. Permit applications must be submitted at least seven days and no more than 30 days before the first camping date. Applications may be made to the Division of State Parks by mail (Box 621, Honolulu, HI 96809), by phone (☎ 587-0300) or in person (1151 Punchbowl St, Room 310) between 8 am and 3:30 pm Monday to Friday.

There are also two other state campgrounds and 13 county campgrounds scattered farther afield around Oahu. For information on the county campgrounds – which also are free and require a permit – contact the Department of Parks & Recreation (☎ 523-4525) on the ground floor of the Municipal Office Building, 650 S King St, Honolulu, HI 96813. The office is open from 7:45 am to 4 pm Monday to Friday. County camping permits may also be obtained at the satellite city hall (☎ 973-2600) at the Ala Moana Center.

If you don't have your own gear, the Bike Shop (☎ 596-0588), at 1149 S King St in Honolulu, rents North Face two-person tents for $15 a day, $35 a weekend or $70 a week.

WHERE TO STAY
Waikiki

Waikiki's main beachfront strip, Kalakaua Ave, is largely lined with high-rise hotels and $150-plus rooms. As is the norm in resort areas, most of these hotels cater to package tourists, driving the prices up for individual travelers.

Better values are generally found at the smaller hostelries on the back streets, with the prices dropping proportionally as you get farther from the beach. There are hotels in the Kuhio Ave area and up near the Ala Wai Canal that are as nice as some of the beachfront hotels but half the price. If you don't mind walking 10 minutes to the beach, you can save yourself a bundle.

Hostels *Hostelling International Waikiki* (☎ 926-8313, fax 946-5904), 2417 Prince Edward St, Honolulu, HI 96815, is a 50-bed hostel on a back street a few short blocks from Waikiki Beach. Dorm beds cost $16. There are also four rooms for couples at $40, with small refrigerators and private bathrooms. For the private rooms, which can be booked for a maximum of five nights, paid reservations or a credit card hold are required. Office hours are from 7 am to 3 am. There's no dormitory lockout or curfew and a group kitchen is accessible throughout the day. Four parking spaces are available at $5 a day. Occasionally you can be lucky as a walk-in, but at busy times reservations are often necessary two to three weeks in advance. There's a maximum stay of two nights and a $3 surcharge if you're not an HI member; HI membership can be purchased on site for $25 for Americans, $18 for foreign visitors. MasterCard and Visa are accepted.

InterClub Hostel Waikiki (☎ 924-2636, fax 922-3993), 2413 Kuhio Ave, Honolulu, HI 96815, is a well-established private hostel. It has about 75 bunk beds, arranged five to seven to a room. To stay at Inter-Club, you officially need a passport and an onward ticket out of Hawaii. There's a lounge and TV room, a pool table, a washer/dryer, lockers and no curfew. Try to get a bed in one of the rear units, as the rooms closest to the heavy traffic on Kuhio Ave can be very noisy. Dorm beds cost $15. The hostel also has some simple private rooms for $45 with linoleum floors, refrigerators, shared balconies and private baths.

Hawaiian Seaside Hostel (☎ 924-3306, fax 923-2110, seaside@powertalk.com), 419 Seaside Ave, Honolulu, HI 96815, occupies a two-story apartment building set back from the street in an alley off Seaside Ave. It's about a 10-minute walk from Waikiki Beach. Small dorm rooms with four bunk beds cost $13 per bed; there are curtains that can be drawn around the bunks for a bit of privacy. There's usually a separate women's dorm, though occasionally they'll put couples in it as well. You can also get semiprivate rooms that have only two people in them for $15 per person. Guests have use of a kitchen after 6:30 pm. There's a courtyard with cable TV and a pool table; limited water-sports equipment can be borrowed for free. About once a week the hostel throws a keg party, with all-you-can-drink beer for $6. Seaside is open 24 hours a day and has no curfew.

A recommendable hostel close to the beach is the *Polynesian Hostel Beachclub* (☎ 922-1340, fax 955-4470), 2584 Lemon Rd, Honolulu, HI 96815. This clean, friendly place occupies a small three-story apartment complex on a side street behind the Queen Kapiolani Hotel. There are a variety of rooms. You can get a bunk bed in a small dorm (four to six people) for $15.50, one of the bedrooms in a two-bedroom apartment for $29/35 for singles/doubles or a fully private studio with a kitchen for $47 a double. Each apartment has its own toilet and shower, but only the studios have private kitchens. There's a common room with a full kitchen, a laundry area and occasional activities such as barbecues and keg parties. Boogie boards and snorkel sets can be borrowed for free. Parking is available for $5.

Not on par but nearby is *Waikiki Beachside Hostel* (☎ 923-9566, fax 923-7525), 2556 Lemon Rd, Suite B101, Honolulu, HI 96815, another small condo complex that's been converted into hostel-style accommodations. Rates range from $16.50 a day or $99 a week for a bunk in a shared room to $65/350 a day/week for a private room.

On the opposite end of Waikiki is *Island Hostel* (☎/fax 942-8748), 1946 Ala Moana Blvd, Honolulu, HI 96815, which has 17 spartan studio rooms in Hawaiian Colony, an unkempt apartment building. The dorm rooms have up to six bunk beds squeezed in, a table, a TV, a small refrigerator and a bathroom; the cost is $15 per bed. Some units are set up as private rooms with a double bed and can be used by couples for $45.

Hotels – budget *Hale Pua Nui* (☎ 923-9693, fax 923-9678), 228 Beach Walk, Honolulu, HI 96815, is an older four-story building with 22 studio apartments. The rooms are not fancy and it's strictly a budget place, but each has the basics: two twin beds, a kitchenette, fan, air-con, TV and phone. The beach is but a five-minute walk away. Rates are $45/57 in the low/high season and there are discounts for stays of a week or more. There's limited on-site parking for $5 a day.

So many retirees return each winter to the 85-room *Royal Grove Hotel* (☎ 923-7691, fax 922-7508), 151 Uluniu Ave, Honolulu, HI 96815, that it's difficult to get a room in high season without advance reservations. In the oldest wing there are small $43 rooms that have no air-con and are streetside and exposed to traffic noise. The main wing has $57 rooms that are a bit worn but adequate with air-con and lanais. Both types of rooms have a double and a twin bed, TV, kitchenette and private bath. This is an older, no-frills hotel, but unlike other places in this category it has a small pool.

A bit spiffier is the *Waikiki Prince Hotel* (☎ 922-1544), 2431 Prince Edward St,

Honolulu, HI 96815, which has 30 units next door to Hostelling International Waikiki. The rooms are straightforward, but the new owner has given them a fresh coat of paint and they all have air-con, TV and private bath. There are small double rooms for $50 and larger rooms with kitchenette for $65. Prices are a couple of dollars cheaper in the low season and the seventh night is free year round. The office is open from 9 am to 6 pm.

Hawaii Polo Inn (☎ 949-0061, 800-669-7719; fax 949-4906), 1696 Ala Moana Blvd, Honolulu, HI 96815, a member of the Colony chain, is at the westernmost end of Waikiki. The 66 motel-style rooms have cinder-block walls and are lined up in rows with their entrances off a long outdoor corridor. The rooms have been renovated, but they're still straightforward. All have small refrigerators, coffeemakers, phones and TVs; some have lanais, although generally the lanai area is at the expense of room space. Rates, which have recently dropped, start at a reasonable $49/65 in the low/high season.

Hotels – middle The *Waikiki Sand Villa Hotel* (☎ 922-4744, 800-247-1903; fax 923-2541) is at 2375 Ala Wai Blvd, Honolulu, HI 96815, on the Ala Wai Canal, a 10-minute walk from Waikiki Beach. The 223 rooms are rather standard tourist class with cable TV, refrigerators, air-con, room safes, bathtubs and small lanais, some with views across the golf course towards Manoa Valley. Ask for one of the corner units, which have the best views. Children under 12 stay free, and many rooms have both a double and a twin bed. Standard rooms, which are on the lower floors, cost $66/77 in the low/high season, while upper floors are about $10 more. There are also poolside studios with kitchenettes that can sleep up to four people for $125/140. A simple continental breakfast is included in the rate, and overall the hotel is a good value for this price range. The hotel can be booked from overseas by calling ☎ 0014-800-127-756 in Australia, 0800-44-0712 in New Zealand and 0031-11-2858 in Japan.

The nearby *Aloha Surf Hotel* (☎ 923-0222, 800-423-4514; fax 924-7160), 444 Kanekapolei St, Honolulu, HI 96815, is another good value mid-range hotel. Its clean compact rooms have air-con, TVs, phones, room safes, desks and complimentary coffee and cost $70/79 in the low/high season. Higher-floor rooms with lanais cost $10 more. There's a swimming pool and a laundry room.

Waikiki Grand (☎ 923-1511, 800-535-0085; fax 923-4708; marc@aloha.net), 134 Kapahulu Ave, Honolulu, HI 96815, is a 173-room hotel opposite the zoo. Although the rooms have been renovated, they are quite small and ordinary. Still they have the standard amenities: TV, phone, air-con, mini refrigerator and coffeemaker. The hotel has a pool. The rack rates listed in the hotel brochure are a pricey $109 for a standard room or $129 for a room with a kitchenette, but the hotel often advertises hefty discounts in the classifieds section of the Honolulu paper. If you contact the front desk directly and ask for the cheapest 'special' rate, you can commonly get a standard room for around $55 – a good value. The hotel is a member of Marc Resorts, so members of some travel clubs, such as Encore and Entertainment, can often get half off the rack rates.

Hotel Honolulu (☎ 926-2766, 800-426-2766; fax 922-3326; hotelhnl@lava.net), 376 Kaiolu St, Honolulu, HI 96815, is Waikiki's only gay hotel. It's a quiet oasis set back from busy Kuhio Ave and the heart of the gay district. The three-story hotel has the character of an unhurried inn, with helpful management, lots of hanging ferns and a peach-colored cockatoo at the front desk. The 19 main units are decorated with flair, each with its own theme ('Samurai,' 'Deco Deco,' 'Norma Jean,' etc), and these are large and comfortable, with lanais, kitchens, ceiling fans and air-con. Studios cost $89 to $99, one-bedroom units $109 to $119. There are also five smaller, non-theme studios in an adjacent building for $75. Coffee is free and there's a sun deck but no pool. While the guests are predominantly gay, straights are also welcome.

An interesting, little-known option is the *Imperial of Waikiki* (☎ 923-1827, 800-347-2582; fax 923-7848), 205 Lewers St, Honolulu, HI 96815, a pleasant all-suite time-share that rents out unfilled rooms on a space-available basis. It's a good value, especially considering it's directly opposite the Halekulani, Waikiki's most exclusive hotel, and just a two-minute walk from the beach. A studio with a double pull-down bed, queen sofa bed, toaster, coffeemaker and refrigerator costs $79 for up to two people. A small one-bedroom suite with a queen bed in the bedroom and a pull-down bed and queen sofa bed in the living room costs $99 for up to four people. There are also two-bedroom units for $169. There's a pool and a 24-hour front desk.

Ocean Resort Hotel Waikiki (☎ 922-3861, 800-367-2317; fax 924-1982), 175 Paoakalani Ave, Honolulu, HI 96815, has 451 rooms. A former Quality Inn, it's a rather ordinary place that hosts a fair number of people on low-end package tours. Still, rooms are air-conditioned and have standard amenities such as TVs, phones and room safes. Nonsmoking rooms are available on request and there's a pool. Standard rooms begin at $98, those with kitchenettes from $135. All are $10 cheaper in the low season.

The *Ilima Hotel* (☎ 923-1877, 800-367-5172; fax 924-8371; ilima@aloha.com), 445 Nohonani St, Honolulu, HI 96815, is a smaller hotel in a less hurried section of Waikiki about a 10-minute walk from the beach. All 99 units are roomy and light with large lanais, two double beds, tasteful rattan furnishings, cable TV with HBO and kitchens with an oven, microwave and full-size refrigerator. The staff is friendly, the lobby has interesting Hawaiiana murals and there's a small heated pool and fitness room. Popular with business travelers and other return visitors, the Ilima offers free local phone calls and free parking, a rarity in Waikiki. Rates vary according to the floor, although the rooms themselves are essentially the same. High-season rates start at $98/103 for singles/doubles in studios on the 4th floor and rise to

$121/127 for studios on the 10th to 16th floors. There are also some one- and two-bedroom suites for $144 and $187 respectively. All rates are $12 less from April to mid-December.

Patrick Winston owns 11 pleasant units in the *Hawaiian King Hotel* (☎ 924-3332, 800-545-1948; hawnking@iav.com), 417 Nohonani St, Suite 409, Honolulu, HI 96815. Each has one bedroom with either a queen or two twin beds, a living room, TV, phone, air-con, ceiling fans, a lanai and a kitchen with a microwave, refrigerator and hot plate. Many also have an oven, some have a washer/dryer and all have thoughtful touches. Although it's an older complex, Patrick has put a lot of money into his units and they have a spiffy decor that's on par with top-end condo hotels. There's a courtyard pool. Rates are $89 to $99 in the low season and $20 more in the high season; ask about discounts. There's a four-day minimum stay. If you show up on a walk-in basis, be sure to ask for Patrick specifically or else the front desk may book you into one of their own rooms, which are of a lower standard.

The Breakers (☎ 923-3181, 800-426-0494; fax 923-7174), 250 Beach Walk, Honolulu, HI 96815, is a low-rise hotel with 64 units surrounding a courtyard pool. The regular rooms, which are quite comfortable, each have a double bed, a single bed and a kitchenette and cost $91 for a ground-floor room without a lanai or $97 for a 2nd-floor unit with a lanai. Large suites have a separate bedroom with a queen bed, a living room that resembles a studio with two twin beds, a full kitchen and a table for four; they cost $130 for two people, $146 for four. Both categories have air-con, TV, desks and phones. Avoid the rooms closest to Saratoga Rd, which has lots of traffic.

The 20-story *Waikiki Resort Hotel* (☎ 922-4911, 800-367-5116; fax 922-9468) is at 2460 Koa Ave, Honolulu, HI 96815. This Korean-owned hotel has a Korean restaurant, a Korean Air office and Korean-language newspapers in the lobby. Not surprisingly, it books heavily with

Traditional Hawaiian quilt

Korean travelers. Its clean, modern rooms have mini refrigerators, TVs, phones, air-con, room safes and lanais. The regular rates begin at $98/108 in the low/high season; a room and car deal is available for an additional $10. Low-season rates become effective on March 1, a month before other hotels.

The 200-room *Holiday Inn Waikiki* (☎ 955-1111, 800-465-4329; fax 947-1799), 1830 Ala Moana Blvd, Honolulu, HI 96815, is a recommendable mid-range hotel at the western end of Waikiki. Rooms are modern and comfortable with either two doubles or one king bed, a desk, room safe, TV, refrigerator, coffeemaker and bathrooms with a tub and hair dryer. Some also have lanais. Rates depend on the floor and range from $100 to $120. There's a pool and sun deck, and the beach is about a 10-minute walk away. Unlike most hotels on busy Ala Moana Blvd, the Holiday Inn is set back from the road, so it tends to be notably quieter.

A member of Hawaiian Pacific Resorts, *Queen Kapiolani Hotel* (☎ 922-1941, 800-367-5004; fax 922-2694), 150 Kapahulu Ave, Honolulu, HI 96815, is a 313-room 19-story hotel at the quieter Diamond Head end of Waikiki. This older hotel has an aging regal theme: chandeliers, high ceilings and faded paintings of Hawaiian royalty. Standard rooms cost $104/116 in the low/high season. However, rooms are anything but standard and vary greatly in size, with some very pleasant and others so small they can barely squeeze a bed in. The simplest way to avoid a closet-size space is to request a room with two twin beds instead of a single queen. Also, be sure to get a room without interconnecting doors, which act like a sound tunnel to the next room. Some of the ocean-view rooms, which cost $25 more, have lanais with fine unobstructed views of Diamond Head.

The *Coconut Plaza Hotel* (☎ 923-8828, 800-882-9696; fax 923-3473), 450 Lewers St, Honolulu, HI 96815, managed by Hawaiiana Resorts, is a quiet 80-room hotel near Ala Wai Blvd. Rooms have contemporary decor and are comfortable enough, but they are on the small side. Most have refrigerators, microwaves, two-burner stoves, TV, air-con and private lanais and cost $110 to $120. There are also a few rooms without cooking facilities for $97 and some larger suites for $155. Ask about promotions as sometimes steeply discounted specials are available. Rates include continental breakfast. There's a coin laundry, a restaurant and some exercise machines on site.

Waikiki Circle Hotel (☎ 923-1571, 800-922-7866; fax 926-8024), 2464 Kalakaua Ave, Honolulu, HI 96815, booked through the Aston chain, is a small hotel with a good central location opposite the beach. It has 104 rooms on 13 floors, all with lanais, two double beds, room safes, phones, TVs and air-con. The hotel is older but has been renovated and the rooms are comfortable. This circular building has a back room on each floor that's called 'city view' and costs $120; while you can't see the ocean, these are farther from the road and quieter. Each floor also has two rooms with partial ocean views for $135 and five rooms with unobstructed ocean views for $145. All rates are 15% cheaper in spring and autumn. Request one of the upper-floor rooms, which have the same rates but better views.

The *Royal Garden at Waikiki* (☎ 943-

0202, 800-367-5666; fax 946-8777), 440 Olohana St, Honolulu, HI 96815, is a midsize hotel with 230 comfortable rooms. The rooms vary in decor but all have air-con, TV, room safes, phones, one queen or two twin beds, bathrooms with tubs, a wet bar with a refrigerator, and a private lanai. Rates begin at $130 for standard rooms, which are on the lower floors. Complimentary continental breakfast is included. The hotel has an elegant marble lobby, two swimming pools and an exercise room. It can be booked toll free from Australia (☎ 0014-800-125-434) and New Zealand (☎ 0800-433-066).

Pacific Monarch (☎ 923-9805, 800-922-7866; fax 924-3220), 142 Uluniu Ave, Honolulu, HI 96815, is a high-rise condominium hotel with 216 units in 34 stories. The studios are roomy, each with a table, desk, double bed, sofa bed, small refrigerator and two-burner hot plate. The one-bedroom units have a small bedroom and a good-size living space with a full kitchen, a dining table for four, a sofa bed and a large lanai. Aston is the rental agent for more than half of the units, with low/high-season rates at $120/140 for a studio and $150/170 for a one-bedroom unit. Up to four people can stay for these rates. Ask about promotions, as this property sometimes has rates as low as $79.

The *New Otani Kaimana Beach Hotel* (☎ 923-1555, 800-356-8264; fax 922-9404; webmaster@kaimana.com), 2863 Kalakaua Ave, Honolulu, HI 96815, is right on Sans Souci Beach on the quieter Diamond Head side of Waikiki. Popular with return visitors, it's a pleasantly low-key place with 125 units. Room rates start at $99; studios with kitchenettes start at $150. All have air-con, TV, refrigerators and lanais.

More expensive but with a similar atmosphere is the other Sans Souci Beach hotel, the *Colony Surf* (☎ 924-3111, 888-924-7873; fax 923-2249), 2895 Kalakaua Ave, Honolulu, HI 96815, which has a condominium wing with spacious 900-sq-foot seaside units that start at $175 for the lower floors and rise to around $250 for the best ocean-view units. It also has a more typical hotel wing with newly renovated rooms, each furnished with two double beds, a kitchenette and a lanai from $150.

Waikiki Sunset (☎ 922-0511, 800-922-7866; fax 923-8580), 229 Paoakalani, Honolulu, HI 96815, is a 425-unit condominium complex handled by Aston. The one-bedroom units each have a large living room with a full kitchen separated by a serving bar, room safe, TV and lanai; lower floors rent for $165/185 in the low/high season. There are also studios that cost $135/155. Ask about special promotions, AAA rates and travel club discounts. If you get a discounted rate on one of the better-furnished units, it's a reasonable value and the location, just north of Kuhio Ave, is convenient for taking the bus.

Hale Koa Hotel (☎ 955-0555, 800-367-6027; fax 800-425-3329), 2055 Kalia Rd, Honolulu, HI 96815, on Fort DeRussy Beach, is reserved for US military personnel, both active and retired, and their families. Rates, which vary by floor and by the guest's rank, begin around $50 a night. This is a 1st-class hotel, with a large swimming pool and an array of activities available for guests.

Outrigger Hotels The *Outrigger*, Box 88559, Honolulu, HI 96830, has bought up and renovated many of Waikiki's middle-range hotels; at last count it had 20. Overall it's a well-run and fairly good-value chain, although there's a wide range in price and quality. At any rate, with one phone call you can check on the availability of 25% of the hotel rooms in Waikiki!

Ask about promotional deals when making reservations – currently these include a 'Free Ride' program, which provides a free Budget rental car when you book at the regular room rate, and a 20% senior citizen discount (25% to AARP members) for all guests that are at least 50 years old. In addition, a handful of Outrigger hotels, including the low-end Coral Seas and the high-end Outrigger Reef, offer 50% discounts to members of the Encore and Entertainment travel clubs.

All Outrigger rooms have air-con, a phone, cable TV and a coffeemaker. Most also have refrigerators and room safes. Nonsmoking rooms are available and children under 18 stay free.

At some Outrigger hotels guests can opt to pay a $3 daily fee that includes free coffee and tea, use of the room safe and unlimited local phone calls.

To book rooms at any Outrigger, you can call ☎ 303-369-7777 or fax 303-369-9403. Outrigger also has the following toll-free numbers: ☎ 800-688-7444 and fax 800-622-4852 from the USA and Canada; ☎ 800-124-171 from Australia; ☎ 0800-440-0852 from New Zealand; ☎ 0130-81-8598 from Germany; ☎ 0800-89-4015 from the UK; ☎ 0031-11-3479 from Japan; and ☎ 800-7322 from Hong Kong. The email address is reservations@outrigger.com.

The 303-room *Outrigger Waikiki Surf* (☎ 923-7671), 2200 Kuhio Ave, is one of Outrigger's better deals in the Kuhio area. Standard hotel rooms, which cost $65 in the spring and fall, $75 in summer and $85 in winter, are small but otherwise quite pleasant; each has a tiny refrigerator, lanai and either one queen or two twin beds. The kitchenette units are a good value; they cost just $5 to $10 more but are roomier and have two double beds, a larger refrigerator and either a two-burner hot plate or a microwave. There are also one-bedroom units for up to four people for $115 year round.

If preparing your own meals is a consideration, the renovated *Outrigger Waikiki Surf East* (☎ 923-7671), at 422 Royal Hawaiian Ave, a block north of the Outrigger Waikiki Surf, has kitchenettes in all its units. Rates for rooms range from $75 in the spring and fall to $95 in winter; one-bedroom units cost from $115 to $125.

The *Outrigger Surf* (☎ 922-5777), 2280 Kuhio Ave, has 251 pleasant rooms, each with a lanai, refrigerator and two-burner stove with small oven. Rates begin at $78 in the spring and fall, $83 in summer and $88 in winter. The higher-floor rooms, which are $5 to $10 more, are less prone to catch the drone of traffic on busy Kuhio Ave. Although it's a couple of blocks inland, the rooms are otherwise on par with many beachside hotels charging nearly twice the price.

Outrigger Malia (☎ 923-7621), 2211 Kuhio Ave, is a 328-room high-rise hotel opposite the Outrigger Waikiki Surf. Rooms are comfortable, each with a room safe, mini refrigerator, tiny one-chair lanai and in most cases two double beds. Some of the rooms are wheelchair accessible. Ask for an upper-floor room on the back side as they're the quietest. These rooms all cost the same: $85 in the spring and fall, $95 in summer and $105 in winter. One-bedroom suites range from $120 to $135. The hotel has a rooftop tennis court and a 24-hour coffee shop.

There are a number of Outrigger hotels closer to the water, including the 109-room *Outrigger Coral Seas* (☎ 923-3881), 250 Lewers St, a small hotel popular with return guests. Although Outrigger gives the property its low-end economy rating, the rooms are adequately furnished with either one queen or two double beds and have a lanai. Regular rooms cost $75 in the spring and fall, $80 in summer and $85 in winter, while kitchenette units are $10 more.

Just a stone's throw from the beach is the 184-room *Outrigger Edgewater* (☎ 922-6424), 2168 Kalia Rd. It's an older property with simple but sufficient rooms, each with a small refrigerator, room safe and either two twins or a queen bed. Rates begin at $78 in the spring and fall, $83 in summer and $88 in winter. Ask for one of the rear rooms as they tend to be quieter.

Outrigger Royal Islander (☎ 922-1961), 2164 Kalia Rd, is a smaller hotel with 100 rooms, a friendly staff and a good location just across from Fort DeRussy Beach. The rooms in this 12-story hotel are on the small side but are pleasant and have all the standard amenities. For ocean views the best rooms are the upper-floor corner ones, all of which end in the numbers 01. The only drawback is that the hotel is on a busy intersection so roadside rooms on the lower floors can be a bit noisy. Rates begin at $75 in the spring and fall, $80 in summer and $90 in winter; add $15 more for the ocean-view rooms.

The 439-room *Outrigger Waikiki Tower* (☎ 922-6424), 200 Lewers St, is a high-rise hotel a few minutes' walk from the beach. The rooms are comfortable with a lanai, room safe, small refrigerator and either two doubles or a king bed. The cheapest rates are for rooms from the 12th floor down, which cost $90 in the spring and fall, $100 in summer and $110 in winter. Rooms on floors 14 and above are essentially the same but cost $10 more. There are also kitchenette rooms with a microwave for an additional $5.

A tad farther from the beach is the nearby *Outrigger Reef Towers* (☎ 924-8844) at 227 Lewers St, which also has rooms that are comfortable and well equipped. The regular rooms begin at $85 in the spring and fall, $90 in summer and $100 in winter, while roomy kitchenette units with microwaves and an extra sofa bed cost $10 more.

Right on the beach, the 885-room *Outrigger Reef Hotel* (☎ 923-3111), 2169 Kalia Rd, has recently undergone a $50 million renovation. As might be expected, the rooms are spiffy, albeit without much character, and have the usual 1st-class amenities. Wheelchair-accessible rooms are available and some floors have been designated for nonsmokers only. Rates, which are the same year round, range from $155 for a non-view room to $320 for an oceanfront room.

Hotels – top end The following hotels all have standard 1st-class amenities and in-house restaurants. All are on the beach or across the street from it and all have swimming pools.

A good-value top-end hotel is the 298-room *Waikiki Parc Hotel* (☎ 921-7272, 800-422-0450; fax 923-1336), 2233 Helumoa Rd, Honolulu, HI 96815, which is across the street from its more upmarket sister, the Halekulani. Rooms are average in size but have nice touches like ceramic-tile floors, shuttered lanai doors, remote-control TV, a room safe and two phones. The hotel has a pleasantly understated elegance. Standard rooms cost $165, while the upper-level ocean-view rooms top out at $250. If you book in the mid-range, request the 8th floor, which has larger lanais. The hotel often runs cheaper promotional rates, including a 'park and sunrise' deal that includes breakfast and free parking for $130 and a senior citizen rate of $100 for those over 55 years of age. Overseas reservation numbers are the same as those listed under the Halekulani Hotel in this section.

The *Pacific Beach Hotel* (☎ 922-1233, 800-367-6060; fax 922-8061), 2490 Kalakaua Ave, Honolulu, HI 96815, is a high-rise hotel with 831 rooms. The accommodations, while not distinguished, are pleasant with comfortable beds, TVs, phones, room safes, half-size refrigerators, lanais and bathrooms with tubs. Nonsmoking rooms are available. There are tennis courts and a fitness center, and the hotel has an impressive three-story aquarium filled with tropical fish. Room rates range from $170 to $280.

The *Hawaiian Regent* (☎ 922-6611, 800-367-5370; fax 921-5255; hwnrgnt@aloha .net), 2552 Kalakaua Ave, Honolulu, HI 96815, is one of Waikiki's largest hotels, with 1346 rooms in a huge mazelike complex. However, rooms are quite ordinary for the money, with rates ranging from $170 to $260.

The 715-room *Hawaiian Waikiki Beach Hotel* (☎ 922-2511, 800-877-7666; fax 923-3656), 2570 Kalakaua Ave, Honolulu, HI 96815, looks almost like a reflection of the bigger Hawaiian Regent across the street, and the rooms are comparable though cheaper. Prices start at $110/130 in the low/high season. The best value is the Mauka Tower, an annex off to the side of the main building, where the rates are at the low end and the rooms are larger and quieter than in the main hotel.

The *Sheraton* pretty much owns a little stretch of the beach, boasting 4400 rooms in its four Waikiki hotels. The toll-free numbers for all of Sheraton's Hawaii hotels are ☎ 800-325-3535 from the USA and Canada and 008-07-3535 from Australia.

The 1150-room *Sheraton Princess Kaiulani* (☎ 922-5811, fax 923-9912), 120 Kaiulani Ave, Honolulu, HI 96815, is the Sheraton's cheapest Waikiki property. One of Waikiki's older hotels, it was built in the 1950s by Matson Navigation to help develop Waikiki into a middle-class destination, and from the outside it looks rather like an apartment complex. However, the interior is more appealing and the rooms are modern. Rates begin at $145. It's in the busy heart of Waikiki across the street from the beach.

The 793-room *Sheraton Moana Surfrider* (☎ 922-3111, fax 923-0308), 2365 Kalakaua Ave, Honolulu, HI 96815, is a special place for those fond of colonial hotels. Built in 1901, the Moana was Hawaii's first beachfront hotel. It's undergone a $50 million historic restoration, authentic right down to the carved columns on the porte-cochère. Despite the fact that modern wings (the 'Surfrider' section) have been attached to the main hotel's flanks, the Moana has survived with much of its original character intact. The lobby is open and airy with high plantation-like ceilings, reading chairs and Hawaiian artwork. The rooms in the original building have been closely restored to their turn-of-the-century appearance. The furnishings are made from a different wood on each floor (koa on the 5th, cherry on the 6th), with TVs and refrigerators hidden behind armoire doors. Rates in the historic wing range from $230 for city views to $350 for ocean views.

The pink Moorish-style *Royal Hawaiian Hotel* (☎ 923-7311, fax 923-8999), 2259 Kalakaua Ave, Honolulu, HI 96815, now a Sheraton property, was Waikiki's first luxury hotel. It's a beautiful building, cool and airy and loaded with charm. The historic section maintains a classic appeal, with some of the rooms having quiet garden views. This section is easier to book too, since most guests prefer the modern high-rise wing with its ocean views. Rates are from $275 in the historic wing, $450 in the high-rise tower.

Sheraton Waikiki (☎ 922-4422, fax 922-9567), 2255 Kalakaua Ave, Honolulu, HI 96815, is an 1850-room mega-hotel that looms over the Royal Hawaiian Hotel. The bustling lobby resembles an exclusive Tokyo shopping center, lined with expensive jewelry stores and boutiques with French names and designer labels. The hotel has central elevators that deposit guests at some of the longest corridors in Hawaii. Rates range from $210 for a city view to $380 for a luxury ocean-view unit.

Hyatt Regency Waikiki (☎ 923-1234, 800-233-1234; fax 923-7839), 2424 Kalakaua Ave, Honolulu, HI 96815, has twin 40-story towers with 1230 rooms. There's a maximum of 18 rooms per floor, so it's quieter and feels more exclusive than other hotels its size. Rooms are nicely decorated in pastels with rattan furnishings and cost from $200 to $345, depending on the view. Between the towers there's a large atrium with cascading waterfalls and orchids, red torch ginger and other tropical vegetation.

The beachfront *Hilton Hawaiian Village* (☎ 949-4321, 800-445-8667; fax 947-7898), 2005 Kalia Rd, Honolulu, HI 96815, is Hawaii's largest hotel, with 2522 rooms. The ultimate in mass tourism, it's practically a package-tour city unto itself – all self-contained for people who never want to leave the hotel grounds. It's quite a busy place, right down to the roped-off lines at the front desk, which resembles an airline check-in counter. The Hilton is on a nice beach, has some good restaurants and offers free entertainment including Friday-night fireworks. The rooms are modern and comfortable with rates starting at $175 for a garden view, $270 for an ocean view.

The *Halekulani Hotel* (☎ 923-2311, 800-367-2343; fax 926-8004), 2199 Kalia Rd, Honolulu, HI 96815, is considered by many to be Waikiki's premier hotel. The 412 rooms, which are pleasantly subdued rather than posh, have large balconies, marble vanities, deep soaking tubs and little touches like bathrobes and fresh flowers. Rooms with garden views cost $295, while those fronting the ocean are

$400. Suites start at $650. The Halekulani can be booked through Utell International and Prima Reservations System: ☎ 800-676-106 in Australia, 0-800-181-535 in England, 05-90-8573 in France and 0-130-844278 in Germany.

Near the Airport

If you have some dire need to be near Honolulu International, there are three hotels outside the airport along a busy highway and beneath flight paths. All provide free 24-hour transport to and from the airport, which is about 10 minutes away.

In addition, for long layovers or midnight flights there are two cheaper places where you can catnap or just take a shower.

The more attractive option is *Sleep & Shower* (☎ 836-3044, fax 834-8985), Terminal Box 42, Honolulu, HI 96819, right in the airport's main terminal between lobbies five and six. It has 17 small private rooms, each with a single bed and its own bathroom and shower. The place is clean and relatively quiet, although there is some vibration from the shuttle bus that runs overhead. Overnight (eight-hour) stays are $30, a two-hour daytime nap and shower costs $17.50; additional hours are $5. Only one person is allowed to stay in each room. If you want to stop by for a shower only, the cost is $7.50, with towels, shampoo and razors provided. It's open 24 hours. Reservations are taken for the overnight stays and MasterCard and Visa are accepted.

Nimitz Shower Tree (☎ 833-1411), 3085 N Nimitz Hwy, occupies a converted warehouse in an industrial area not far from the airport hotels. The facilities are basic: the private 'roomettes' are rows of simple cubicles with platform beds that cost $22 to $30 for an overnight sleep. You can also go there just to take a shower for $7.50. It's open 24 hours and free transport is available – look for the courtesy phone in the baggage claim area.

The renovated *Best Western Plaza Hotel-Honolulu Airport* (☎ 836-3636, 800-528-1234; fax 834-7406), 3253 N Nimitz Hwy, Honolulu, HI 96819, is a comfortable hotel with 268 rooms, each with a king or two double beds, TV and refrigerator. The only drawback is the heavy traffic noise from the nearby highway – ask for a rear room. Rates start at $89 and nonsmoking rooms are available. There's a pool, lounge and hotel restaurant. The Nimitz Mart center, which is within walking distance, has a handful of fast-food places including a Ba Le Vietnamese cafe, a Subway sandwich shop and Domino's pizza.

Holiday Inn-Honolulu Airport (☎ 836-0661, 800-800-3477; fax 833-1738), 3401 N Nimitz Hwy, Honolulu, HI 96819, on the corner of Rodgers Blvd, has 308 rooms and a standard rate of $112. The rooms are a bit tired, but this four-story hotel has typical Holiday Inn amenities, including a lounge, pool and restaurant. Guests have a choice of a king or two double beds; nonsmoking rooms are available. There's commonly a promotional rate, dubbed the 'managers special,' that discounts the standard rate by 20%.

Pacific Marina Inn (☎ 836-1131, fax 833-0851), 2628 Waiwai Loop, Honolulu, HI 96819, is a mile farther east in an industrial area, but on the plus side it has the least traffic noise. This three-decker motel has small, straightforward rooms for $79, but there's usually an 'airport special' for $60; it can be reached on the courtesy phone in the baggage claim area. The rooms have air-con, TVs and phones, and there's a pool on the grounds.

Elsewhere in Honolulu

Hostels & Ys *Hostelling International Honolulu* (☎ 946-0591, fax 946-5904), 2323A Seaview Ave, Honolulu, HI 96822, is a friendly, well-run hostel in a quiet residential neighborhood near the University of Hawaii. There are seven dorms with bunk beds that can accommodate 42 travelers, with men and women in separate dorms. Rates are $12.50 for HI members and $15.50 for nonmembers. There are also two rooms for couples that cost an extra $10. If you're not a member, there's a three-night maximum stay. HI membership is sold on site; the cost is $25 for Ameri-

cans, $18 for foreign visitors. Credit cards are accepted.

Office hours are from 8 am to noon and 4 pm to midnight. Guests must be out of the dorms from noon to 4 pm, although the TV lounge and common-use kitchen are open during the day. There's a laundry room, lockers and bulletin boards with useful information for new arrivals. From Ala Moana, catch bus No 6 or 18 (University or Woodlawn), get off at the corner of University Ave and Metcalf St, and walk one block uphill to Seaview Ave. By car, take Exit 24B off the H-1 Fwy, go mauka on University Ave and turn left at Seaview Ave.

Fernhurst YWCA (☎ 941-2231, fax 949-0266), 1566 Wilder Ave, Honolulu, HI 96822, has rooms for women only in a three-story building about a mile from the university. There are 60 rooms, each intended for two guests, with two single beds, two lockable closets, two dressers and a desk. Two rooms share one bathroom. The cost is $25 per person. If you get a room to yourself, which is easier during the low season, it costs $5 more. Rates include buffet-style breakfast and dinner except on Sundays and holidays; there's a small kitchen facility on each floor.

Payment is required weekly in advance; guests staying more than three days must become Y members ($30 a year). It costs an additional $20 to rent linen or you can bring your own. Although tourists are accepted, most guests are local, as Fernhurst provides transitional housing for women in need. There's a laundry room, TV room and a garden courtyard with a small pool. Fernhurst is at the intersection of Wilder and Punahou on the No 4 and 5 bus lines.

The *Central Branch YMCA* (☎ 941-3344, fax 941-8821), 401 Atkinson Drive, Honolulu, HI 96814, on the east side of the Ala Moana Center, is the most conveniently located of the YMCAs. There are 114 rooms in all. The rooms with shared bath, which are available to men only, are small and simple and resemble those in a student dorm, with a simple desk, a single bed, a lamp, a chair and linoleum floors.

The cost is $29 for a single, or for $40 they'll put in a rollaway bed and two people can share the room. Rooms with private bath, which are a bit nicer but still small and basic, are open to both men and women and cost $36.50/51.50 for singles/doubles. Guests receive YMCA privileges including free use of the sauna, pool, gym and handball courts. There's a coin laundry, a TV lounge and a snack bar. Credit cards are accepted.

The *Nuuanu YMCA* (☎ 536-3556, fax 533-1286), 1441 Pali Hwy, Honolulu, HI 96813, at the intersection of Pali Hwy and Vineyard Ave, has mostly long-term tenants but rents some rooms for $29 a day, $138 a week. Accommodations are for men only. Rooms are small and spartan, with louvered windows, a single bed and a small metal desk and chair. Bathrooms are shared. Guests have access to a TV lounge, the weight room and pool; there's a microwave in the hall but no guest kitchen.

During the school year the *Atherton YMCA* (☎ 946-0253), 1810 University Ave, Honolulu, HI 96822, operates as a dorm for full-time University of Hawaii students only. During summer holidays (mid-May to mid-August) it's usually open on a space-available basis to non-students, although some years it's full with students year round. Rates are $20 per day for a room with a bed, dresser, desk and chair. Reservations are made by application (available by mail) with a $150 security deposit. The Y is directly opposite the university.

Hotels The *Pagoda Hotel* (☎ 941-6611, 800-367-6060; fax 955-5067), 1525 Rycroft St, Honolulu, HI 96814, north of Ala Moana Center, has two sections. There are studios with kitchenettes in the older apartment section, but they can feel a bit too removed from the main hotel – especially if you're checking in at night. The rooms in the hotel itself are nicer and have the usual amenities, including air-con, TV, phone, refrigerator and a central lobby. Both studios and hotel rooms cost $85. There's no extra charge for children under

18 occupying the same room as their parents. There's nothing distinguished about this hotel other than a restaurant with a carp pond, but it is one way to avoid jumping into the Waikiki scene.

The *Executive Centre Hotel* (☎ 539-3000, 800-949-3932; fax 523-1088), 1088 Bishop St, Honolulu, HI 96813, is Honolulu's only downtown hotel. Geared for businesspeople, it comprises 114 suites, each large and very comfortable with modern amenities that include three phones, private voice mail, two TVs, a refrigerator, room safe and whirlpool bath. A continental breakfast, unlimited local phone calls and the morning newspaper are all complimentary. As the hotel is on the upper floors of a high-rise, most of the rooms have fine city views. There's a heated lap pool and a fitness center as well as a business center with desks, computers, secretarial services and laptop rentals. Rates range from $125 for a mountain view to $180 for an executive ocean-view suite, the latter with kitchen facilities and a washer/dryer. There are also cheaper corporate rates and periodic promotional discounts.

Manoa Valley Inn (☎ 947-6019, 800-535-0085; fax 946-6168; marc@aloha.net), 2001 Vancouver Drive, Honolulu, HI 96822, on a quiet side street near the University of Hawaii, is an authentically restored Victorian inn that's on the National Register of Historic Places. All eight rooms are filled with antiques, one with a four-poster bed, another with furnishings that belonged to silent film star Frances Beaumont. There's complimentary evening wine, a common parlor and a billiard room. Rates, which include continental breakfast, are $100 for rooms with a shared bathroom and $140 to $190 for rooms with a private bathroom. The inn is managed by Marc Resorts.

The 1168-room *Ala Moana Hotel* (☎ 955-4811, 800-367-6025; fax 944-2974), 410 Atkinson Drive, Honolulu, HI 96814, looms above the Ala Moana Center, just beyond Waikiki. The rooms, which resemble those of a chain hotel, are standard fare with TV, phones, air-con, small refrigerators and room safes. Rates are $110 for lower-floor city-view rooms and climb to $195 for 'concierge' ocean-view rooms on the 29th to 35th floors. West of Waikiki, the hotel is a popular place for overnighting airline crews.

Kahala Mandarin Oriental (☎ 739-8888, 800-367-2525; fax 739-8800; mohnl@aol .com), 5000 Kahala Ave, Honolulu, HI 96816, is on its own quiet stretch of beach in the exclusive Kahala area east of Diamond Head. This is where the rich and famous go when they want to avoid the Waikiki scene, a 10-minute drive away. The guest list is Hawaii's most regal: Charles and Di, King Juan Carlos and Queen Sofia, and the last six US presidents. Formerly the Kahala Hilton, the 370-room hotel recently reopened after a yearlong closure and a $75 million facelift. Rates start at $260 for garden-view rooms and $360 for rooms on the hotel's enclosed lagoon where dolphins swim just beyond the lanais. The presidential suite tops off at $2970. The hotel can be booked through Mandarin Oriental Hotels worldwide: ☎ 800-653-328 in Australia, 03-3433-3388 in Tokyo, 0800-96-26-67 in the UK and 0590-76-97 in France.

Places to Eat

FOOD

Eating in Honolulu can be a real treat, as the city's ethnic diversity has given rise to hundreds of different cuisines. You can find every kind of Japanese food, an array of regional Chinese cuisines, spicy Korean specialties, native Hawaiian dishes and excellent Thai and Vietnamese food. The ethnic influence is so pervasive that even McDonald's serves up saimin and Portuguese sausage and Woolworth has sushi at the lunch counter.

Generally, the best inexpensive food is found outside Waikiki, where most Honolulu residents live and eat. There are good cheap neighborhood restaurants to explore throughout greater Honolulu – two particularly rewarding locales are the Chinatown and University of Hawaii areas.

Honolulu also has many upscale restaurants run by renowned chefs. While these feature gourmet foods of all types, including traditional continental fare, the most prevalent influence is the increasingly popular style dubbed 'Pacific Rim' or 'Hawaii Regional' cuisine. This type of cooking incorporates fresh island ingredients, borrows liberally from Hawaii's various ethnic groups and is marked by creative combinations such as kiawe-grilled freshwater shrimp with taro chips, wok-charred ahi with island greens, and Peking duck in ginger-lilikoi sauce.

Hawaiian Food

The traditional Hawaiian feast marking special events is the *luau*. Local luaus are still commonplace in modern Hawaii for events such as baby christenings. In spirit, these local luaus are far more authentic than anything you'll see at a hotel, but they're family affairs and the short-stay visitor would be lucky indeed to get an invitation to one.

The main dish at a luau is *kalua pig*, which is roasted in a pitlike earthen oven called an *imu*. The imu is readied for cooking by building a fire and heating rocks in the pit. When the rocks are glowing red, layers of moisture-laden banana trunks and green ti leaves are placed over the stones. A pig that has been slit open is filled with some of the hot rocks and laid on top of the bed. Other foods wrapped in ti and banana leaves are placed around it. It's all covered with more ti leaves and a layer of mats and topped off with dirt to seal in the heat, which then bakes and steams the food. The process takes about four to eight hours depending on the amount of food. Anything cooked in this style is called *kalua*.

Wetland taro is used to make *poi*, a paste pounded from cooked taro corms. Water is added to make it puddinglike and its consistency is measured in one-, two- or three-finger poi – which indicates how many fingers are required to bring it from bowl to mouth. Poi is highly nutritious and easily digestible, but it's a bit of an acquired taste. It is sometimes fermented to give it a zingier flavor.

Laulau is fish, pork and taro wrapped in a ti leaf bundle and steamed. *Lomi* salmon (also sometimes called *lomilomi* salmon) is made by marinating thin slices of raw salmon with diced tomatoes and green onions.

Other Hawaiian foods include baked *ulu* (breadfruit), *limu* (seaweed), *opihi* (the tiny limpet shells that fishers pick off the reef at low tide) and *pipikaula* (beef jerky). *Haupia*, the standard dessert to a Hawaiian meal, is a custard made of coconut cream thickened with cornstarch or arrowroot.

In Hawaiian food preparation, ti leaves are indispensable, functioning like a biodegradable version of both aluminum foil and paper plates: food is wrapped in it, cooked in it and served upon it.

Many visitors taste traditional Hawaiian food only at expensive tourist luaus or by sampling a dollop of poi at one of the more adventurous hotel buffets.

Although Hawaiian food is harder to find than other ethnic foods, the city has a couple of recommendable Hawaiian restaurants: *Ono Hawaiian Food* on Kapahulu Ave at the edge of Waikiki, and *Helena's Hawaiian Foods*, which is across town on the north side of the city but well worth the effort. For good Hawaiian food in a hotel setting in Waikiki, consider the Waikiki Parc Hotel's *Parc Cafe* Hawaiian lunch buffet on Wednesday.

Local Food

The distinct style of food called 'local' usually refers to a fixed plate lunch with 'two scoop rice,' a scoop of macaroni salad and a serving of beef stew, mahimahi or teriyaki chicken, generally scoffed down with chopsticks. A breakfast plate might have Spam, eggs, kimchi and, always, two scoops of rice.

These plate meals are the standard fare in diners and lunch wagons. If it's full of starches, fats and gravies, you're probably eating local.

Snacks *Pupus* is the local term used for all kinds of munchies or hors d'oeuvres. Boiled peanuts, soy-flavored rice crackers called *kaki mochi* and sashimi are common pupus.

Another local favorite is *poke*, which is raw fish marinated in soy sauce, oil, chili peppers, green onions and seaweed. It comes in many varieties – sesame ahi is a particularly delicious one – and makes a nice accompaniment with beer.

Crack Seed Crack seed is a Chinese snack food that can be sweet, sour, salty or some combination of the three. It's often made from dried fruits such as plums and apricots, although more exotic ones include sweet and sour baby cherry seeds, pickled mangoes and *li hing mui*, one of the sour favorites. Crack seed shops commonly sell dried cuttlefish, roasted green peas, candied ginger, beef jerky and rock candy as well.

Fish

Fresh fish is readily available in Honolulu. Seafood is generally expensive at places catering fancy meals to tourists, but it can be quite reasonable at neighborhood restaurants. Some of the most popular locally caught fish include:

Hawaiian Name	Common Name
ahi	yellowfin tuna
aku	skipjack tuna
au	swordfish, marlin
kaku	barracuda
mahimahi	a fish called 'dolphin' (not the mammal)
mano	shark
onaga	red snapper
ono	wahoo
opah	moonfish
opakapaka	pink snapper
papio or ulua	jack fish
uhu	parrotfish
uku	gray snapper

Shave Ice Shave ice is similar to mainland snow cones, only better. The ice is shaved as fine as powdery snow, packed into a paper cone and drenched with sweet fruit-flavored syrups. Many islanders like the ones with ice cream and/or sweet azuki beans at the bottom, while kids usually opt for rainbow shave ice, which has colorful stripes of different syrups.

DRINKS

Nonalcoholic Drinks

Tap water is safe to drink, although some people prefer the taste of bottled water, which is readily available in grocery stores and at the ubiquitous ABC discount stores.

Cans of Hawaiian-made fruit juices such as guava-orange or passion fruit can be found at most stores. If you're touring around and want to toss a couple of drinks in your daypack, the juices make a good alternative to sodas as they don't explode when shaken and they taste good even when they're not chilled.

Alcoholic Drinks

The minimum drinking age in Hawaii is 21. It's illegal to have open containers of alcohol in motor vehicles, and drinking in public parks or on the beaches is also illegal, despite it being fairly common. All grocery stores sell liquor as do most of the smaller food marts.

Tedeschi Vineyards, a winery on Maui, makes a good pineapple wine, grape wine and champagne that can be picked up at wine shops and grocery stores throughout Honolulu.

Honolulu has a microbrewery, Gordon Biersch, at the Aloha Tower Marketplace, which brews good German-style lagers including both light and dark varieties.

And of course, at every beachside bar you can order one of those ubiquitous tropical drinks topped with a fruit garnish and paper umbrella. Three favorites are: piña colada, with rum, pineapple juice and cream of coconut; mai tai, a mix of rum, grenadine and lemon and pineapple juices; and Blue Hawaii, a vodka drink colored with blue curaçao.

WHERE TO EAT
Waikiki

Waikiki has no shortage of places to eat. While the vast majority of the cheaper eateries are easy to pass up, there are some good moderately priced options. Waikiki's top-end restaurants, on the other hand, are some of the island's best.

Budget For inexpensive bakery items try the *Patisserie*, which has a branch at 2330 Kuhio Ave beside the Outrigger West Hotel, and another at 2168 Kalia Rd in the lobby of the Outrigger Edgewater. Both are open from at least 6:30 am to 9 pm daily

and have reasonably priced pastries, croissants, bread and coffee. If you want to eat in, there's a small sit-down area where you can get standard breakfast items, sandwiches and salads.

The *Saigon Cafe*, on the 2nd floor of 1831 Ala Moana Blvd, has cheap Vietnamese food. A filling main dish is the combination rice noodle plate, which has chopped spring rolls, barbecued pork and lettuce over a bed of noodles; it costs $5 at lunch, $6 at dinner. There's also a breakfast special of pancakes and two eggs for $1.95. It's open from 6:30 am to 10 pm daily.

The *New Tokyo Restaurant*, 286 Beach Walk, is a popular local lunch spot with good, cheap Japanese food served in a pleasant setting. At lunch, pork ginger, chicken teriyaki or grilled salmon costs $6 and is accompanied by miso soup, pickles and rice. Dinner is a far more expensive affair, with prices from $19 to $38. Lunch is served from 11:30 am to 2 pm weekdays, dinner from 5:30 to 9:30 pm nightly.

Nearby at 2126 Kalakaua Ave is *Tenteko Mai*, an unpretentious little place with good authentic Japanese ramen for $5.50 to $7.50. It also has tasty gyoza, a grilled garlic-and-pork-filled dumpling, for $3.75 a half dozen. The scene feels like a neighborhood eatery in Tokyo, with seating at stools around a U-shaped bar and fellow diners chatting away in Japanese. It's open from 11 am to midnight daily.

Treats Hula's, 2109 Kuhio Ave, is an open-air deli restaurant and bar in the middle of the gay district. The food is basic sandwich-and-salad fare, but this is a popular gay meeting spot and a place to linger over an espresso or beer. It's open from 10 am to 2 am daily.

Moose McGillycuddy's, 310 Lewers St, has 20 types of omelets for $6.50 each, but a better deal is the early-bird special (7:30 to 8:30 am) of two eggs, bacon and toast for $1.99. The restaurant is popular with the college-age crowd and has an extensive menu of burgers, sandwiches, Mexican food, salads and drinks at moderate prices. It's open for meals from 7:30 am to 10 pm daily, with breakfast served to 11 am. Drinks are half price from 4 to 8 pm and there's music and dancing nightly.

Fatty's Chinese Kitchen, 2345 Kuhio Ave, is a hole-in-the-wall eatery in an alley at the west side of the Miramar hotel. It serves up some of the cheapest food to be found in these parts, with two scoops of rice or chow mein plus one hot entree for only $3. Add $1 for each additional entree. The atmosphere is purely local, with a dozen stools lining a long bar and the cook on the other side chopping away. Fatty's is open from 10:30 am to 10:30 pm daily.

The two *Perry's Smorgy* restaurants, one at the Outrigger Coral Seas Hotel at 250 Lewers St and the other at 2380 Kuhio Ave on the corner of Kane-kapolei St, offer cheap all-you-can-eat buffets. Breakfast (7 to 11 am) includes pancakes, eggs, ham, coffee and fresh pineapple, papaya and melon. It's a tourist crowd and the food is cafeteria quality, but you can't beat the $4.99 price. Lunch, which includes a reasonable fruit and salad bar as well as simple hot dishes like fried chicken, is from 11:30 am to 2:30 pm and costs $5.99. Dinner (5 to 9 pm) adds on a round of beef and turkey and costs $8.99. If it's convenient, opt for the Kuhio Ave location as it has a surprisingly pleasant gardenlike setting.

Eggs 'n Things, at 1911 Kalakaua Ave, is an all-nighter, open daily from 11 pm to 2 pm. It specializes in breakfast fare, with prices starting at $3 for three pancakes with eggs.

Wailana Coffee House at the Outrigger Malia, 2211 Kuhio Ave, is a classic diner that's open 24 hours a day. It serves inexpensive fare from an extensive menu, with food that's a tad better than other similar low-end restaurants.

At the northwest corner of the *International Market Place* there's a food court with about two dozen stalls selling cinnamon buns, shave ice, frozen yogurt, pizza, hot dogs and various plate lunches, including Korean, Chinese,

Breakfast Ideas

Signs draped from buildings advertising breakfast specials for $2 to $4 are commonplace. *Eggs 'n Things, Moose McGillycuddy's* and *Saigon Cafe* all have cheap breakfast specials (for more on these, see the Budget listings).

Food Pantry has a doughnut counter, while the nearby *Patisserie*, 2330 Kuhio Ave, has a full bakery serving pastries and Danish as well as a few inexpensive egg dishes.

Fast-food chains like *McDonald's* and *Burger King* offer their quick, cheap breakfasts from just about every other corner. The free tourist magazines almost always have a *Jack in the Box* coupon good for a breakfast sandwich and coffee for $1.99. If you're really hungry and not too demanding about quality, the $5 all-you-can-eat breakfast buffet at *Perry's Smorgy* is a good deal.

For between $10 and $20 you can try one of the all-you-can-eat breakfast buffets that many of the larger hotels offer, but few are worth the money. A couple of noteworthy exceptions, both with ocean-view dining, are the simple breakfast buffet at the *Shore Bird Broiler* ($7) in the Outrigger Reef Hotel (7:30 to 11 am daily) and the more elaborate spread at *Duke's Canoe Club* ($10) in the Outrigger Waikiki Hotel. (Look for coupons in the free tourist magazines that knock a dollar off all meal prices at the Shore Bird.) If you don't need a water view, the breakfast buffet at the *Parc Cafe* ($11.50) in the Waikiki Parc Hotel is also a good value.

For a romantic beachfront setting right on Sans Souci Beach, at the Diamond Head end of Waikiki, there's *Hau Tree Lanai* at the New Otani Kaimana Beach Hotel. It has pleasant courtyard dining shaded by a sprawling hau tree and a variety of breakfast combinations priced around $10. ■

Mexican and Greek – nothing really notable, but it is cheap.

There's a *Haagen Dazs* ice cream shop on Kalakaua Ave just east of the International Market Place.

Fast-food chains are well represented in Waikiki: there are three *Burger King*, four *McDonald's* and six *Jack in the Box* restaurants, the latter open 24 hours. All three chains usually have discount coupons in the free tourist magazines.

Middle A fun place to eat is the *Shore Bird Beach Broiler* (☎ 922-2887), at the Outrigger Reef Hotel, 2169 Kalia Rd, which has a fine beachfront location and open-air dining. At one end of the dining room there's a big common grill where you cook your own order; mahimahi, sirloin steak or teriyaki chicken costs $13. Meals come with an all-you-can-eat buffet bar that includes salad, chili, rice and fresh fruit. The buffet bar alone costs $8. Dinner is from 4:30 to 10 pm nightly; get seated before 6 pm and you can enjoy the sunset and take advantage of cheaper early-bird prices as well. It's a busy place, so unless you get there early expect to wait for a table – however, this is scarcely a hardship, as you can hang out on the beach in the meantime.

California Pizza Kitchen (☎ 955-5161), at 1910 Ala Moana Blvd on the corner of Ena Rd, serves up a good thin-crust pizza cooked in a wood-fire brick oven. One-person pizzas range from $7 for a traditional tomato and cheese to $10 for more intriguing creations, such as the tandoori chicken pizza, which comes with mango chutney. This trendy mainland-chain restaurant also has a variety of pasta dishes, both traditional and exotic, for $8 to $12 and good green salads, with generous half-order portions for $5. It's open from 11:30 am to 10 pm Monday to Thursday, 11:30 am to 11 pm on Friday and Saturday, and noon to 10 pm on Sunday.

In the same price range is *Chili's* (☎ 922-9697), 2350 Kuhio Ave. This popular Tex-Mex chain restaurant, new to Hawaii, has soft tacos with rice and beans or burgers with fries for around $8, fajitas for $13 and baby back ribs for a few dollars more. It also has decent salads and some low-fat grilled chicken dishes. It's open from 11 am to 11 pm daily.

Pieces of Eight (☎ 923-6646), in the basement of the Outrigger Coral Seas hotel, 250 Lewers St, has a good-value $7.95 early-bird special from 4:30 to 6:30 pm that consists of grilled chicken or beef stir-fry, accompanied by a small salad bar that includes fresh fruit. After 6:30 pm these dishes cost $12 and the salad bar is an additional $3.50, although you can usually find coupons in the free tourist magazines for adding on the salad bar at no cost. It's open from 4:30 to 11 pm daily.

Duke's Canoe Club (☎ 922-2268), at the Outrigger Waikiki on Kalakaua Ave, has a nice waterfront view. The restaurant takes its name from the late surfing king Duke Kahanamoku and the outrigger canoe club that was on the beach here in earlier days. The food has a mass-produced quality, but it is quite reasonable for the money. From 7 to 10:30 am there's a good breakfast buffet with granola, omelets to order and fresh fruit for $10, or you can pay $8 and select from just the cold dishes. At dinner (5 to 10 pm), various fresh fish dishes cost $20, or you can get a smaller portion of the fish-of-the-day for $17. There are also chicken and steak meals from $15. All dinners come with a full salad bar that includes cold pastas, greens, fruit and muffins. There's also a children's menu with burgers, chicken or spaghetti for $5.

Singha Thai (☎ 941-2898), 1910 Ala Moana Blvd, is the place to go on the western side of Waikiki for authentic Thai food in a somewhat upmarket setting. For starters, the grilled beef salad and the hot-and-sour tom yum soup are tasty house specialties. Entrees, such as spicy chicken shiitake-mushroom stir-fry and various curry and noodle dishes, average $13 at dinner, $9 at lunch. Lunch is served from 11 am to 4 pm on weekdays, dinner from 4 to 11 pm nightly. A troupe of Thai dancers performs nightly.

Kyotaru (☎ 924-3663), 2154 Kalakaua

Splurge Sunday Brunches

Waikiki's classiest Sunday brunch buffet is at *Orchid's* (☎ 923-2311) at the Haleku-lani Hotel. The grand spread includes sashimi, sushi, baron of beef or smoked salmon, roast suckling pig, roast turkey, salads, fruits and a rich dessert bar. There's a fine ocean view, orchid sprays on the tables and a soothing flute and harp duo. The buffet costs $32.50 (more on holidays) and lasts from 9:30 am to 2:30 pm. It's best to make advance reservations or you may encounter a long wait.

Another pleasant option is the Royal Hawaiian Hotel's *Surf Room* (☎ 931-7194), which has an alfresco beachside setting and a decent Sunday brunch spread served from 11 am to 2 pm that includes sashimi, poke, a waffle station, baron of beef, salads and desserts. At $31.75 it's nearly as pricy as Orchid's, although it really isn't quite as much of an event if you're up for pampering and indulgence.

A good-value alternative is the Sunday brunch buffet at the *Parc Cafe* (☎ 921-7272) in the Waikiki Parc Hotel, which has eggs Benedict, prime rib, fresh catch of the day and a nice array of salads such as Peking duck, green papaya and mixed greens. Tempting desserts made at the Halekulani's bakery, a frozen yogurt bar and fresh fruit are also included. Sunday brunch is served from 11 am to 2 pm. There's no ocean view and it's certainly not as elaborate as the buffet at its sister hotel, the Halekulani, but the food is of similar high quality and the price is a more affordable $19.50. ■

Ave, is a popular Japanese restaurant that specializes in reasonably priced sushi for both eat-in and takeout. There are dozens of varieties to choose from, including kamigata sushi (Osaka-style), edomae sushi (Tokyo-style) and California-style sushi, including a tasty rolled version with shrimp and avocado. If you order in, you can get various sushi combination meals, with tempura, yakitori or noodles, for $12 to $25. Takeout is available daily from 10 am to 10 pm, the restaurant menu from 11 am to 3 pm and from 5 to 9:30 pm.

A fun place to dine is *Tanaka of Tokyo*, which has branches in the Waikiki Shopping Plaza at 2250 Kalakaua Ave (☎ 922-4702) and King's Village at 131 Kaliulani Ave (☎ 922-4233). Both restaurants have 18 U-shaped teppanyaki tables, each with a central grill that's presided over by a chef who cooks meals to order and serves them with flair to the diners at his table. The meals are set courses that include salad, miso soup, rice, shrimp appetizer and dessert; the price, which is determined by the entree selected, ranges at dinner from under $20 for chicken or fresh salmon to $36 for lobster tail. Lunch is priced from $10 to $15. Look for coupons in the free tourist magazines good for half off one meal when two people are dining together. Both restaurants are open from 11:30 am to 2 pm on weekdays and from 5:30 to 10 pm nightly.

The Honolulu branch of the *Hard Rock Cafe* (☎ 955-7383), 1837 Kapiolani Blvd, is just over the Ala Wai Canal beyond Waikiki. It's enlivened with loud rock music and decorated with old surfboards and a 1959 Cadillac 'woody' wagon hanging precariously over the bar. They serve quarter burgers with fries and a salad for around $8 and other all-American food including barbecued ribs and milkshakes, but it's the atmosphere as much as the food that draws the crowd. It's open daily from 11:30 am to 11 pm (to 11:30 pm on weekends).

The trendiest spot in Waikiki is the new *Planet Hollywood* (☎ 924-7877) at 2155 Kalakaua Ave. This 2nd-floor restaurant has a flashy celluloid motif, with Hollywood memorabilia lining the walls and flicks playing on big-screen TVs. Part of what packs in the crowds is the hope of catching a glimpse of one of the Hollywood stars and restaurant shareholders – Arnold Schwarzenegger and Whoopi Goldberg among them. Sandwiches, burgers and thin-crust pizzas cost around $10, while pastas and fajitas average $13. It's open daily from 11 am to 11:30 pm.

The *Oceanarium Restaurant* (☎ 922-1233) in the Pacific Beach Hotel, 2490 Kalakaua Ave, has standard fare with anything but standard views, as the dining room wraps around an impressive three-story aquarium filled with colorful tropical fish. At breakfast, you can get oatmeal with papaya for $4, waffles or French toast for $7 or a full buffet for $13. At lunch, sandwiches average $8, while dinners begin around $15. The more expensive *Neptune's Garden*, a seafood restaurant in the same hotel, also has views of the aquarium.

Top End *WC Peacock & Co* (☎ 922-2863) in the Sheraton Moana Surfrider may be the only restaurant in Waikiki where you can look out across the lawn to see nothing but sailboats on the ocean and a few swaying coconut palms. If you get the right table, the only 'modern' structure in view is the 90-year-old Moana hotel, which screens out the high-rises along the beach and helps create an aura of timelessness.

While the setting is a gem, the food is not as notable, though it is OK by Waikiki standards. This dinner-only restaurant features a $20 Sunset Special, from 5 to 6 pm daily, which consists of mahimahi and steak or chicken teriyaki, a small but select salad bar, soup and dessert. Meals other than the Sunset Special range from $19 for chicken to $35 for a seafood platter, salad bar included. Be sure to ask for a lanai table.

The *Parc Cafe* (☎ 921-7272), in the Waikiki Parc Hotel, has continental-style dining in a pleasant setting. There are

buffets for each meal, all attractively prepared with quality food on par with Waikiki's most expensive hotels. The daily breakfast buffet, from 6:30 to 10 am, includes breakfast meats, eggs, French toast, fresh fruit and pastries for $11.50. The lunch buffet (11:30 am to 2 pm) costs $16.50 on Wednesday when it features Hawaiian food, $19.50 on Sunday when it begins at 11 am and is called brunch, and $13.50 on other days when it's centered around a sandwich bar and taco station. All the lunch buffets include hot main dishes, salads and desserts. The dinner buffet (5:30 to 9:30 pm) includes catch of the day, prime rib, exotic salads and sumptuous desserts for $16.50 on weekdays and $24.50 on weekends when it adds on sashimi and seafood dishes.

The *Surf Room* (☎ 931-7194) at the Royal Hawaiian Hotel has outdoor beachside dining, although it can be rather crowded and tends to be pricey for what you get. There's a $20 breakfast buffet, a $21.50 lunch buffet and a light lunch menu that's served until 2 pm. The dinner menu changes nightly, with meat and seafood entrees for $25 to $30. It's open daily from 6:30 am to 9:30 pm.

The best place for Chinese fine-dining is the *Golden Dragon* (☎ 946-5336) in the Hilton Hawaiian Village, which has both excellent food and a good ocean view. The varied menu has some expensive specialties, but there are also many dishes, including oyster beef, roast duck and a deliciously crispy lemon chicken, which are priced around $15. It's open for dinner only, from 6 to 9:30 pm Tuesday to Sunday.

For top-quality Japanese food served by kimono-clad waitresses, the place to go is *Kyo-ya* (☎ 947-3911), 2057 Kalakaua Ave. Set lunches of tempura, fried ahi or beef teriyaki cost $13, including pickles, miso soup and rice. At dinner the same meals, with the addition of sashimi and dessert, cost $42. There are also formal kaiseki ryori meals that include numerous courses and are priced from $50 to $100, although for these you'll need to reserve two days in advance. It's open from 11 am to 2 pm Monday to Saturday and from 5:30 to 10 pm nightly.

Michel's (☎ 923-6552) at the Colony Surf hotel, 2895 Kalakaua Ave, has been riding for years on its reputation as Oahu's most romantic restaurant. While the accolades may be overstated, it's certainly pleasant – fine dining with crystal, china and chandeliers, all fronting Sans Souci Beach. The food is traditional French and prices are steep, with Chateaubriand, rack of lamb and fish priced à la carte from \$35 to \$45. Hors d'oeuvres range from \$13 for oysters on the half shell to \$35 for foie gras. It's open for dinner only from 5:30 to 10 pm nightly. When you make reservations be sure to ask for a window table.

La Mer (☎ 923-2311), in the Halekulani Hotel, is regarded by many to be Hawaii's ultimate fine-dining restaurant. It has a neoclassical French menu and a superb 2nd-floor ocean view. The dining is formal and men are required to wear jackets (loaners are available). The four-course fixed-price dinner of the day costs \$85, the six-course version \$105. Otherwise, appetizers such as tartare of ahi with caviar or grilled lobster salad with hearts of palm average \$23, while à la carte entrees range from \$36 to \$43 and include dishes such as squab with foie gras, bouillabaisse and filet mignon. It's open nightly from 6 to 10 pm.

Other quality top-end Waikiki restaurants are *Bali* (☎ 941-2254) at the Hilton Hawaiian Village, for continental cuisine with Hawaiian influences; and *Cascada* (☎ 945-0270) at the Royal Garden at Waikiki hotel, which blends Mediterranean and Pacific Rim cuisine in an intimate European-style setting.

Kapahulu Ave

A nice alternative to dining in Waikiki proper can be found at a run of neighborhood ethnic restaurants on Kapahulu Ave, the road that starts in Waikiki near the zoo and runs up to the H-1 Fwy. The following restaurants are grouped together about a mile up from Kalakaua Ave.

Ono Hawaiian Food (☎ 737-2275), 726 Kapahulu Ave, is *the* place in the greater Waikiki area to get Hawaiian food served Hawaiian-style. It's a simple diner, but people line up to get in. A kalua pig plate costs \$7.10 and a laulau plate \$7.35. Both come with pipikaula, lomi salmon and haupia with rice or poi. It's open from 11 am to 7:30 pm Monday to Saturday.

New Kapahulu Chop Suey (☎ 734-4953), 730 Kapahulu Ave, serves big plates of Chinese food. The combination special lunch plate costs \$4.15, the special dinner \$5, while a score of other dishes are priced under \$6. While it's certainly not gourmet, it's a lot of food for the money. It's open from 11 am to 9 pm daily.

Irifune's (☎ 737-1141), 563 Kapahulu Ave, is a funky little joint decorated with Japanese country kitsch that serves up tasty food that's free of MSG. Alcohol is not served, but you can bring in beer from the nearby liquor store. The gyoza is good at \$3.50, as is the garlic tofu with vegetables at \$8. There are \$9 combination dinners that include tempura and options such as tataki ahi, a delicious fresh tuna that's seared lightly on the outside, sashimi-like inside, and served with a tangy sauce. Lunch specials begin at \$7.50. Although few tourists come up this way, the restaurant is locally popular. You might have to wait 30 minutes to be seated at dinner, but it's well worth it. Irifune's is open from 11:30 am to 1:30 pm Tuesday to Friday and from 5 to 9 pm Tuesday to Sunday.

Keo's (☎ 737-8240), 625 Kapahulu Ave, is widely regarded as Hawaii's top Thai restaurant. It's decorated with Thai art, sprays of orchids and a wall of photos of owner Keo Sananikone posing with celebrity diners, including the likes of Jimmy Carter, Kevin Costner and Keanu Reeves. Prices are surprisingly moderate considering the chic reputation. House specialties include the Evil Jungle Prince (a spicy dish flavored with fresh basil, coconut and red chili) for \$11, and spring roll appetizers and green papaya salad, each \$7. The most expensive items on the menu are seafood dishes for \$15, so it won't break the bank to dine with the stars here. It's open from 5 pm nightly.

Grocery Stores & Markets

The best place to get groceries in Waikiki is the *Food Pantry*, 2370 Kuhio Ave, which is open 24 hours a day. Its prices are higher than those of the chain supermarkets, which are all outside Waikiki, but lower than those of the smaller convenience stores. Food Pantry, like most grocery stores, accepts credit cards.

Beyond Waikiki, the easiest supermarket to get to without a car is *Foodland* at the Ala Moana Center, as virtually all buses stop at the center. If you have a car, within a short drive from Waikiki you'll find a *Times Supermarket* at 3221 Waialae Ave between 5th and 6th Aves; a *Foodland* a few blocks away near the eastern intersection of King and Kapiolani Sts; and a *Star Market* at the intersection of Beretania and King Sts.

At the county-run People's Open Market program, farmers sell local produce for one hour a week at 22 locations around Oahu. Monday and Wednesday are set aside for the greater Honolulu area. Call ☎ 522-7088 for current times and locations or pick up a schedule at any satellite city hall. ■

KC Drive Inn at 1029 Kapahulu Ave, farther up the road near the freeway, features Ono Ono malts (a combination of chocolate and peanut butter that tastes like a liquified Reese's Cup) for $2.95 and waffle dogs (a hot dog wrapped in a waffle) for $1.80, as well as inexpensive plate lunches, burgers and saimin for either eat-in or takeout. It's been a local favorite since the 1930s.

If you're on foot, *Rainbow Drive-In*, at the intersection of Kapahulu and Kanaina Aves, is much closer to central Waikiki, has similar food and just as much of a local following.

For late-nighters, there's also the *Internet Café* (☎ 735-5282), 559 Kapahulu Ave, which offers up coffees, pastries, foccacia sandwiches and Wolfgang Puck's pizzas to munch while surfing the Net on one of their 10 Macs. It's open 24 hours a day; there's free parking across the street.

University Area

There are some excellent restaurants in the area around the University of Hawaii at Manoa. The following listings are all within a 10-minute walk of the three-way intersection of King St, Beretania St and University Ave.

Coffeeline (☎ 947-1615), at the corner of University and Seaview Aves, is a student hangout serving coffees and vegetarian meals. Vegan soup costs $2.50, omelets, sandwiches and salads are around $4 and a few hot dishes such as spinach lasagna cost $5. It's open from 7:30 am to 4 pm Monday to Friday.

Chan's Chinese Restaurant (☎ 949-1188), 2600 S King St, has inexpensive lunchtime dim sum, including some good steamed seafood varieties. Chan's also has noodles, chow mein and other Chinese dishes, mostly in the $6 to $8 range, although there are lunch specials for around $5. It's open from 10:30 am to 10:30 pm daily.

Ezogiku Noodle Cafe, at 1010 University Ave on the corner of Beretania St, dishes up miso ramen for $5.25, gyoza for $3.50, curries, fried rice and cold noodles. While it's nothing memorable, it is on par with similar fast-food noodle shops in Japan. It's open daily from 11 am to 11 pm.

Across the street at 1091 University Ave, a branch of the Vietnamese restaurant *Ba Le* sells good inexpensive French rolls, croissants and sandwiches that range from a tasty vegetarian version for $2 to a roast beef sandwich for $4.

India Bazaar (☎ 949-4840), in a little shopping center at 2320 S King St, is a small cafe selling inexpensive Indian food. There's a vegetarian thali that includes jasmine rice and three vegetable curries for $5.75 and chicken and shrimp thalis for $7.

A: NED FRIARY

B: DAVID RUSS

D: NED FRIARY

C: NED FRIARY

A, B: Chinatown street scenes
C: Interior of Kuan Yin Temple, Chinatown

D: Chinese Lion Dance at the Bishop Museum

A: Manoa Falls
B: Kite Festival, Kapiolani Park

C: Sightseeing on Diamond Head summit
D: View of Honolulu from Round Top Lookout

NED FRIARY

NED FRIARY

NED FRIARY

NED FRIARY

NED FRIARY

On Oahu you're never far from water and you have many options for playing in it.

A: The Shore Bird Broiler, Waikiki
B: Red ginger
C: Pineapple snack shack

D: Jars of crack seed
E: Torch ginger

Side orders of papadams, chapatis, samosas and raita are each under $1. It's open from 11 am to 9 pm Monday to Saturday. In the same complex is a branch of *Kozo Sushi*, a decent local chain that specializes in inexpensive sushi.

Maple Garden (☎ 941-6641), 909 Isenberg St, around the corner from S King St, is a popular local Sichuan restaurant with good food at reasonable prices. Vegetarian entrees, including a delicious eggplant in hot garlic sauce, average $6.50, while most meat dishes are about a dollar more. If you like duck, they do a tasty smoked Sichuan version for $8. At lunch there are various full-plate specials for $5 to $6. It's open from 11 am to 2 pm and from 5:30 to 10 pm daily.

Diem (☎ 941-8657), at 2633 S King St near the corner of University Ave, is a small family-run restaurant serving some of Honolulu's best Vietnamese food. The shrimp rolls ($5.35) make excellent appetizers, while the spicy lemongrass chicken ($6.50) is a recommendable main dish. There are good-value lunch specials served until 4 pm daily that include an entree, salad, rice and appetizer for around $7.50. Diem is open daily from 10 am to 10 pm.

Aloha Poi Bowl (☎ 944-0798), a little local eatery at 2671 S King St, specializes in Hawaiian fare. A meal of lomi salmon, pipikaula, poi and haupia with your choice of kalua pork, laulau or fried fish costs $7. It's open from 11 am to 2 pm and 4 to 8 pm on weekdays (closed for lunch on Tuesday), from 11 am to 9 pm on Saturday and from noon to 7 pm on Sunday.

Chiang Mai (☎ 941-1151), 2239 S King St, serves northern Thai food. Their wonderful sticky rice, which is reminiscent of Japanese omochi, is served in its own little bamboo steamer. The fresh fish green curry, which at $9 is one of the higher priced dishes, is a recommendable house specialty. There are two dozen vegetarian dishes for around $6 and a range of meat dishes for around $7. It's open from 11 am to 2 pm Monday to Friday and from 5:30 to 10 pm nightly. The menu is the same at lunch and dinner.

Yakiniku Camellia (☎ 946-7595), 2494 S Beretania St, has a tasty all-you-can-cook Korean lunch buffet for $12.95 from 11 am to 3 pm. It's good-quality food and if you've worked up an appetite, it's a fine deal. The mainstay is pieces of chicken, pork and beef that you select from a refrigerated cabinet and grill at your table. Accompanying this are 18 marinated and pickled side dishes, miso and seaweed soups, simple fresh vegetable salads and a few fresh fruits. The mung bean and watercress dishes tossed with sesame seeds are sweet and mild. As for the kimchis, generally the redder they are, the hotter they are. Dinner (3 to 10 pm) costs $15.75 and offers essentially the same fare with the addition of sashimi. Everything is authentic; there's even a newspaper vending machine selling the Korean-language daily.

Down to Earth Natural Foods, 2525 S King St, is a large natural foods supermarket with everything from Indian chapatis to local organic produce and a dozen varieties of granola sold in bulk. It's a great place to shop and the healthier yogurts and whole-grain breads that some of Honolulu's more with-it supermarkets sell are substantially cheaper at Down to Earth. It's open from 8 am to 10 pm daily. The store also has a vegetarian deli, for either eat-in or takeout, with a salad bar ($4 a pound), sandwiches, soups and plate lunches.

The hottest new restaurant in town, *Alan Wong's* (☎ 949-2526), 1857 S King St, features upmarket Hawaiian Regional cuisine. Chef Wong, who won accolades at the Big Island's exclusive Mauna Lani Resort before striking out on his own, features a creative menu with an emphasis on fresh local ingredients. Appetizers such as sashimi, tempura ahi or duck salad cost $7 to $12, while entrees average $30 for spicy seafood paella, beef tenderloin with Kona lobster or a delicious ginger-crusted onaga. Each night there's also a five-course 'chef's tasting menu' for $65. This is a high-energy place with a modern minimalist decor and an open kitchen. It's open from 5 to 10 pm nightly and reservations are often essential.

Ala Moana Area

Ala Moana Center This center's food court is a circus, with neon signs, 800 tiny tables crowded together and 25 fast-food stands circling it all. There's something for everyone, from salads to daiquiris, ice cream to pizza, and Chinese, Japanese, Korean, Hawaiian, Filipino, Thai and Mexican specialties.

If you have the munchies, this is a good place to stop when you're between buses. It's like window-shopping – you can walk through, preview the food and select what you want. Called Makai Market, the food court is oceanside on the ground floor. It's open from 9 am to 9 pm Monday to Saturday and from 10 am to 6 pm on Sunday.

Panda Express has good MSG-free Mandarin and Sichuan food, with dishes like spicy chicken, broccoli beef and eggplant with garlic sauce. Combination plates with fried rice or chow mein and two entrees are $4.89, three entrees $5.89. The food is fresh and you can pick what looks best from the steamer trays.

Yummy Korean BBQ is a similar concept with Korean selections that include rice and a number of tasty pickled veggies and kimchis, with plates from $5.50 to $7.

Patti's Chinese Kitchen is a big-volume restaurant with a few dozen dishes to choose from. It costs $4.75 for two selections, $5.75 for three selections, both of which include rice or noodles. If you really want to indulge, you can get a whole roast duck for $11. There's also a limited selection of dim sum and desserts, including almond cookies.

Kitchen Garden specializes in salads such as curried chicken, Thai peanut pasta, fruit, marinated vegetable and just plain green. The salads are fresh and healthy, and most are priced under $5.

Cactus Jack's offers tacos, tostadas or fajitas with rice and beans from $5 to $6. At nearby *Little Cafe Siam* two tasty skewers of chicken satay cost $2.

Also in the Ala Moana Center there's a *Foodland* supermarket that's open from 7 am to 11 pm daily and branches of *McDonald's, Haagen Dazs* and *Dunkin' Donuts*.

Ward Centre Ward Centre, a shopping complex at 1200 Ala Moana Blvd, has a couple of coffee shops and delis, a branch of *Keo's* Thai restaurant and about a dozen other dining spots.

At the top end is the new *A Pacific Cafe Oahu* (☎ 593-0035), a branch of Jean-Marie Josselin's renowned Pacific Rim restaurant on Kauai. The menu features wood-fired goat-cheese pizzas, fresh fish carpaccio and similar appetizers for around $10. Entrees such as blackened ahi with hearts of palm or a rich seafood bouillabaisse average $22. The lunch menu has similar but lighter servings and prices that are about 40% less. On the center's upper level, it's open from 11:30 am to 2 pm Monday to Friday and 5:30 to 9 pm daily.

The food is a bit too Americanized at *Compadres* (☎ 591-8307), but this busy Mexican restaurant still draws a crowd and wins plenty of local awards. Combination plates with rice and beans average $10 to $15. It's on the center's upper level and is open from 11:30 am to 11 pm on weekdays, until 10 pm on Sunday and to midnight on Friday and Saturday.

Scoozee's (☎ 597-1777), on the center's ground level, is a trendy nouveau Italian cafe with good pastas, pizzas and calzones for $10 and sandwiches for a tad less. It's open from 11 am daily, closing at 10 pm Sunday to Thursday and at 11 pm on Friday and Saturday.

Mocha Java/Crepe Fever, also on the ground level, is a popular hangout serving good coffees, crepes, croissants, sandwiches, desserts and other light eats. It's open from 7 am to 9 pm on weekdays, 8 am to 11 pm on Saturday and 8 am to 4 pm on Sunday.

A slightly more expensive espresso bar can be found inside *Borders* bookstore at the opposite end of the complex – it closes 30 minutes before the bookstore, which is open daily from 9 am to at least 11 pm, except on Sunday when it closes at 9 pm.

Ward Warehouse All of the following restaurants are on the upper level of Ward Warehouse, the shopping complex on the corner of Ala Moana Blvd and Ward Ave. There's free garage parking and bus Nos 8, 19 and 20 stop out front. Each restaurant has a view of the harbor, so when making reservations be sure to ask for a window table.

For cheap eats, the *Old Spaghetti Factory* (☎ 591-2513) is the best deal here. This family-style restaurant has an elaborate decor, filled with antiques, heavy woods, Tiffany stained glass – even an old streetcar. At lunch (11:30 am to 2 pm Monday to Friday), you can get spaghetti with tomato sauce for $3.50, with clam sauce for $4.50 or with meatballs for $5.75. All meals come with warm bread and a simple green salad. Meals are about a dollar more at dinner, which is served weekdays from 5 to 10 pm, Saturday from 11:30 am to 10:30 pm and Sunday from 4 to 9:30 pm. It's certainly not gourmet, but the price is right.

Kincaid's Fish, Chop & Steak House (☎ 591-2005) serves good reasonably priced seafood and steaks in a pleasant setting with ocean-view tables. Consequently, it's a favorite lunch spot for downtown businesspeople. Lunch entrees include a spicy Cajun fettuccine for $9, macnut chicken with banana chutney for $10, seared ahi Caesar salad or oven-roasted garlic prawns for $13, and kiawe-grilled salmon for $14. At dinner, fresh fish entrees and steaks are priced from $15 to $20. It's open daily from 11:15 am to 5 pm for lunch and from 5 to 10 pm for dinner.

Dynasty II (☎ 596-0208) is a Chinese restaurant with fine dining and good food. The à la carte menu tends to be expensive, with most entrees priced from $10 to $18. However, they commonly offer a good-value $12.95 dinner special that includes an appetizer, soup, entree with jasmine rice and dessert, each selected from a limited-choice menu. Lunch is from 11 am to 2 pm, dinner from 5:30 to 10 pm.

Stuart Anderson's (☎ 591-9292) is a chain steak house with lunches in the $7 to $9 range and dinners about double that. Lunch is from 11 am to 4 pm

Monday to Saturday, dinner from 4 pm to at least 10 pm Monday to Saturday and noon to 9:30 pm on Sunday.

In addition to the restaurants, there's the ground-floor *Coffee Works*, a little cafe that has coffee, espresso, scones, bagels and muffins. It's open daily from 7 am to 9 pm, except on Sunday when it's open from 8 am to 6 pm.

Restaurant Row

Restaurant Row, a rather sterile complex on the corner of Ala Moana Blvd and Punchbowl St (see Map 6), caters largely to the downtown business crowd. There's a *Burger King*, a bakery with pastries and sandwiches, a pizzeria, an ice cream shop and about a dozen restaurants, including some recommendable ethnic ones.

Jamaican Bar & Grill (☎ 521-5855) offers up authentic Caribbean cuisine including curries and various meat dishes. Spicy jerk chicken, a tasty plum chicken or curried shrimp, each served with rice and beans, mixed vegetables and a corn dumpling, costs around $7 at lunch, $12 at dinner. There are also pork, beef and goat dishes. It's open daily from 11 am to 11 pm, except on Sunday when it's open from 3 to 10 pm.

Island Salsa (☎ 536-4777) takes its name from its salsa table where customers can select from a variety of these fresh-made sauces, ranging from the tame to the fire-eater. While there's no lard or preservatives in the food, in other ways it's near-authentic Mexican fare. Generous burritos, either tofu or the traditional meat variety, cost $7 to $8, while combo plates with black beans and rice cost $11. It's open daily from 11 am to 11 pm, to midnight on weekends.

Payao (☎ 521-3511), a new Thai eatery by the owners of the popular university-area Chiang Mai restaurant, has an extensive menu, with vegetarian offerings for around $6, curries, beef, chicken and noodle dishes for around $8 and seafood dishes for a bit more. It's open from 11 am to 2:30 pm Monday to Saturday and 5 to 10 pm nightly.

Among the top-end places at Restaurant Row are *Ruth's Chris Steak House* (☎ 599-3860), an upmarket mainland chain restaurant offering quality à la carte steaks for around $25, and the popular *Sunset Grill* (☎ 521-4409), which features grilled fresh fish and meats from around $20 at dinner and salads, calamari and sandwiches for half that price at lunch.

Fort St Mall

The Fort St Mall, a pedestrian street on the edge of the downtown district (see Map 6), has a number of cheap restaurants within walking distance of Iolani Palace. It's convenient for downtown workers and sightseers, but certainly not a draw if you're elsewhere around town.

Taco Bell, *McDonald's*, *Burger King*, *KFC*, *Subway Sandwiches* and *Pizza Hut* are all near the intersection of Hotel St and Fort St Mall.

A good local option is *Ba Le*, a branch of the Chinatown restaurant, which has inexpensive Vietnamese sandwiches, shrimp rolls, green papaya salads and French coffees. It's open from 7 am to 7 pm Monday to Friday and from 8:30 am to 4 pm on Saturday.

Adjacent to Ba Le is the *Fort Street Cafe*, a popular student hangout with plate lunches, Vietnamese pho soups and various saimin dishes for around $5. It's open weekdays from 7 am to 7 pm and Saturday from 8:30 am to 4 pm.

For Chinese fast food there's *Mandarin Express*, 50 yards east of the Fort St Mall at 116 S Hotel St. While its Chinese dishes are served from steamer trays, they're usually quite fresh at meal times and you can eat heartily for around $5. It's open from 9 am to 6 pm on weekdays, 10:30 am to 3 pm on Saturday.

Kozo Sushi, at 1150 Bishop St, has good inexpensive sushi for takeout. It's open from 9 am to 5 pm Monday to Thursday, to 5:30 pm on Friday.

Aloha Tower Marketplace

The Food Lanai on the 2nd floor of the Aloha Tower Marketplace (see Map 6) has a pleasant water-view food court and a dozen fast-food stalls.

Wok & Roll has two-item plate lunches of Chinese food served with rice for $5 – General Tso's chicken is a recommendable choice. At *Pacific Vegetarian Cafe*, you can get a variety of salads, a garden burger or falafel sandwich for $5.50. Other stalls sell Japanese, Cajun, Italian and deli fare.

Gordon Biersch Brewery Restaurant (☎ 599-4877), seaside on the marketplace's 1st floor, is one of the most popular places to go in Honolulu for a drink. This small chain microbrewery features its own German-style lagers accompanied by Hawaiian pupus. Salads and sandwiches are available for under $10, while hot dishes average $15. It's open from 11 am to 10 pm daily.

The adjacent *Scott's Seafood Grill and Bar* (☎ 537-6800), also on the waterfront, specializes in fresh seafood. At lunch, various fish preparations, such as blackened ahi or grilled swordfish with asparagus, are priced from $13 to $16, at dinner from $20 to $25. There are also salads and sandwiches at lunch and chicken, steak and lobster options at dinner. It's open from 10:30 am to 10 pm Sunday to Thursday, to 11 pm on Friday and Saturday.

Chinatown

Krung Thai (☎ 599-4803), 1028 Nuuanu Ave, is a good-value, family-run Thai eatery on the edge of Chinatown between the business and red-light districts. Lunch, the only meal served, is geared to the business community's 30-minute lunch breaks, with dishes ready in steamer trays. There are a dozen hot dishes to choose from, including chicken Panang, beef eggplant and vegetarian curry. One item costs $3.79, two items $4.59, and all are served with jasmine rice, brown rice or noodles. It's open from 10:30 am to 2:30 pm Monday to Friday. There are tables in a quiet rear courtyard where you can sit and enjoy your meal.

Ba Le, 150 N King St, bakes crispy French bread and is a good place for a quick inexpensive bite in Chinatown. Baguettes

For Vegetarians

Honolulu doesn't have many purely vegetarian restaurants, but there are a few.

One recommendable eatery is the *Buddhist Vegetarian Restaurant* in Chinatown. Other vegetarian-only choices are the *Pacific Vegetarian Cafe*, a salad and falafel stall at the Aloha Tower Marketplace, and the deli at *Down to Earth Natural Foods* near the University of Hawaii.

In addition, there are numerous restaurants in Honolulu that have extensive vegetarian selections on their menu. For inexpensive vegetarian Indian food there's *India Bazaar* in the university area. Most Thai restaurants, including those listed in this book, have at least a page of vegetarian offerings, as do a number of Chinese and Vietnamese restaurants.

A few places around Honolulu, such as *Kitchen Garden* in the Ala Moana Center, specialize in salads, and numerous restaurants have extensive salad bars.

For a quick snack, Honolulu's ubiquitous *Ba Le* chain makes a tasty vegetarian sandwich of diced Asian vegetables on a crispy baguette roll for a mere $2.

The Vegetarian Society of Hawaii, a nonprofit organization that aims to educate people about the benefits of vegetarianism, sponsors social activities such as lectures, picnics and dining outings. Call ☎ 944-8344 for a recorded message about upcoming events. ■

can be purchased for 40¢ or as sandwiches for $2 vegetarian style, $3 with meat. The vegetarian sandwich is a tangy combo of crunchy carrots, daikon and cilantro. Sweet, strong French coffee with milk costs $1.50 hot or cold. There are also good croissants, shrimp rolls and tapioca puddings. It's open from 5 am to 5 pm daily.

Our favorite Chinatown eatery is the Vietnamese restaurant *To Chau*, 1007 River St, where the specialty is pho, a delicious soup of beef broth with rice noodles and thin slices of beef garnished with cilantro and green onion. It comes with a second plate of fresh basil, mung bean sprouts and slices of hot chili pepper. The cost is $3.70 for a regular bowl and $5 for an extra-large one. The shrimp rolls with a spicy peanut sauce ($2.85) are recommendable, and the restaurant also serves rice and noodle dishes, but just about everybody comes for the soup. To Chau is open from 8 am to 2:30 pm daily. It's so popular that even at 10:30 am you may have to line up outside the door for one of the 16 tables. It's well worth the wait.

Ha Bien (☎ 531-1185), 198 N King St, next door to To Chau, is another popular Vietnamese restaurant with good inexpensive food. Although Ha Bien specializes in noodle and rice dishes, the menu also includes spring rolls, soups and crepes. Most dishes cost from $5 to $6. It's open from 8 am to 4 pm on weekdays, to 3:30 pm on weekends.

Doong Kong Lau (☎ 531-8833), on the River St pedestrian mall, has an extensive menu that includes Chinese standards as well as more exotic preparations of Hakka cuisine, such as their house specialty, salt-baked chicken. Vegetable, poultry and pork dishes cost from $6 to $7, while seafood plates are a few dollars higher. Generous lunch specials are available for $5 to $6. If you order noodles, be sure to request the cake noodles, pressed and cooked to a crisp on the edges. It's open from 9:30 am to 8:30 pm daily.

Immediately west of Doong Kong Lau on the River St mall is the *Buddhist Vegetarian Restaurant* (☎ 532-8218), a pleasant Chinese dining spot that uses tofu and gluten in place of meats. The menu is both imaginative and extensive, and most dishes are priced from $7 to $10. There's also a dim sum service available at lunch. It's open from 10:30 am to 2 pm and 5:30 to 9 pm daily except on Wednesday.

For more upmarket dining there's *Indigo* (☎ 521-2900), 1121 Nuuanu Ave, which has a relaxing setting, an open-air courtyard and contemporary Asian-Pacific cuisine. A special treat here are the creative dim sum appetizers, such as tempura ahi rolls and goat cheese won tons. Dinner features duck, steak and fish dishes for $13 to $17. At lunch you can order soups, salads and sandwiches from $5 to $9. It's open from 11:30 am to 2 pm Tuesday to Friday and from 5:30 to 9:30 pm Tuesday to Saturday. On the Chinatown-downtown border, behind the Hawaii Theatre, Indigo is a popular dinner spot for theatergoers.

Elsewhere in Honolulu

Helena's Hawaiian Foods (☎ 845-8044), 1364 N King St, is a friendly family-run operation that's been serving excellent, inexpensive Hawaiian food since 1946. It's a totally local eatery, with 10 simple Formica-top tables and a mix of vinyl chairs and stools. The restaurant makes a delicious kalua pig; also notable is the pipikaula and fried ahi. There's not a better place anywhere to sample various Hawaiian dishes. Nearly everything on the à la carte menu is under $2 and complete meals with poi (fresh, day-old or sour) or rice are $5 to $7. It's open from 11 am to 7:30 pm Tuesday to Friday only.

El Burrito (☎ 596-8225), at 550 Piikoi St near the Ala Moana Center, could be a neighborhood restaurant on a back street in Mexico City. This hole-in-the-wall has about a dozen tightly squeezed tables and Honolulu's most authentic Mexican food. Two tamales, enchiladas or chile rellenos with rice and beans average $9. It's open from 11 am to 8 pm Monday to Thursday, to 9 pm on Friday and Saturday. Expect lines at dinnertime.

Mekong (☎ 521-2025), 1295 S Beretania St, home to the original Keo's, has a similar menu to that more upmarket spinoff, but in this tiny eatery posters replace the artwork, you bring your own booze and prices are about a third less. The tasty spring rolls come with lettuce, mint leaves and peanut sauce and cost $6, while most beef, chicken and vegetarian dishes are a dollar more. Nothing on the menu is over $10. It's open from 11 am to 2 pm on weekdays and 5 to 9:30 pm nightly. If you're driving, you may want to opt for *Mekong II* (☎ 941-6184), 1726 S King St, which has the same Thai menu and free parking in the rear.

Although it's well off the beaten path, *Hale Vietnam* (☎ 735-7581), at 1140 12th Ave in the Kaimuki area, is a top-notch local favorite with delicious Vietnamese food at moderate prices. A nice starter is the temple rolls ($4.25), a combination of fresh basil, mint, tofu and yam rolled in rice paper. The yellow curries are excellent and cost $9 for vegetarian, beef or chicken varieties. The extensive menu also features pho soups ($5.95) and a good variety of vegetarian and seafood dishes. It's open from 11 am to 9:45 pm daily, except on Sunday when it closes at 9 pm.

For a genteel treat, try the *Contemporary Cafe* (☎ 523-3362) at the Contemporary Museum in Makiki Valley. It has a pleasant lawn setting and creative salads including a smoked mahi Caesar and a tasty Malaysian shrimp salad in gado-gado dressing, each $10.75. Grilled eggplant or a garden burger sandwich cost $8.50, while chicken and fish sandwiches are a dollar more; all sandwiches are served with a side of tabbouleh. Lunch is from 11 am to 2 pm Tuesday to Saturday and from noon to 2 pm on Sunday. Desserts and beverages are available to 3 pm. Reservations are recommended.

The *Garden Cafe* (☎ 532-8734), a courtyard restaurant in the Honolulu Academy of Arts, 900 S Beretania St, offers a refined lunch setting and a chance to support the museum. The menu, which varies daily, includes sandwiches, soups and hot dishes such as quesadillas or fresh fish for $7 to $10. Seatings are at 11:30 am and 1 pm Tuesday to Saturday. Reservations are suggested.

Auntie Pasto's (☎ 523-8855), 1099 S Beretania St, has good Italian food, including a recommendable eggplant parmigiana, at moderate prices. Pasta costs $5.50 with tomato sauce, $8 with pesto or $7 heaped with fresh vegetables in butter and garlic. The Parmesan cheese is freshly grated and the Italian bread is served warm. Dishes and prices are the same at lunch and dinner. Although it's off the tourist track, this popular spot attracts a crowd and you may have to wait for a table – particularly on weekends. It's open from 11 am to 10:30 pm Monday to Friday and from 4 to 10:30 pm on Saturday and Sunday.

Pagoda Floating Restaurant (☎ 941-6611) at the Pagoda Hotel, 1525 Rycroft St, has a serene setting amidst gardens and a carp pond. This is a nice place to start the day and the breakfast menu (6:30 to 10:30 am) is extensive, with many choices for around $5. On weekdays, from 11 am to 2 pm, there's a lunch buffet of Japanese and American dishes for $10, or you can order off the lunch menu for less. There's also a nightly dinner buffet (4:30 to 9:30 pm), which costs $19 and features an array of dishes including prime rib, Alaskan snow crab, sashimi, tempura and salad and dessert bars.

Two good places for sushi are *Yanagi Sushi* (☎ 537-1525), 762 Kapiolani Blvd, open daily from 11 am to 2 pm and from 5:30 pm to 2 am (to 10 pm on Sunday); and *Sada's* (☎ 949-0646), 1240 S King St, open from 11 am to midnight Monday to Saturday, 5 to 11 pm on Sunday.

A trendy restaurant with a loyal following is *3660 On the Rise* (☎ 737-1177), 3660 Waialae Ave, which features 'Euro-Island' cuisine, blending continental and island flavors. A salad of Big Island organic greens costs $5, while starters such as escargot, ahi poke spring rolls or local barbecued prawns cost $9. Main dishes average $20 and include Hawaiian-style seafood steamed in ti leaf, roast duck in mango salsa and a superb black Angus garlic steak. It's closed Monday but otherwise open for dinner from 5:30 to 9 pm, except on Friday and Saturday when it stays open until 10 pm. Reservations are suggested. The restaurant is out of the way, three miles northeast of Waikiki, on Waialae Ave between 12th and 13th Aves.

Roy's (☎ 396-7697), at Hawaii Kai Corporate Plaza on Hwy 72, a few miles west of Hanauma Bay, has some of the best food in Oahu. High-profile owner Roy Yamaguchi is a creative force behind the popularity of Pacific Rim cuisine, which emphasizes fresh local ingredients and blends the lighter aspects of European cooking with Japanese, Thai and Chinese influences. An open kitchen sits in the center of the dining room, where Roy orchestrates an impressive troupe of sous cooks and chefs.

Starters include spring rolls, imu-oven pizzas and a variety of salads for around $7.50. The crispy lemongrass chicken, topped with a delightful Cabernet curry sauce, costs $16 and makes a fine main dish. Most other meat dishes cost around $20, while fresh fish specials average $24. There are more romantic settings in Oahu, but in all other ways Roy's is a top choice for a night out – the food is attractively presented, the service attentive and the servings good-sized. It's open from 5:30 (from 5 pm on weekends) to 10 pm; reservations are advised.

Entertainment

Honolulu has a lively and varied entertainment scene.

The best place to look for up-to-date entertainment listings is in the free *Honolulu Weekly* newspaper, which is readily found around the downtown and university areas. Other sources are the free tourist magazines available around Waikiki and the daily newspapers, in particular the Night Life column in the Thursday edition of the *Honolulu Star-Bulletin*.

For festivals, fairs and sporting events, see the Special Events section in the Facts for the Visitor chapter.

THEATER & MUSIC

Honolulu has a symphony orchestra, an opera company, ballet troupes, chamber orchestras and numerous community theater groups.

The *Blaisdell Center* (☎ 591-2211), at 777 Ward Ave, presents musical concerts, Broadway shows and family events, with such diverse performers as Depeche Mode, Stone Temple Pilots, the Honolulu Symphony, the Ice Capades and the Brothers Cazimero.

The impeccably restored *Hawaii Theatre* (☎ 528-0506), 1130 Bethel St, has become a major venue for dance, music and theater. It hosts a wide range of performances from Russian ballet to contemporary Hawaiian music, modern dance and film festivals.

The *Academy Theatre* (☎ 532-8768) of the Honolulu Academy of Arts, and to a lesser degree the *East-West Center* (☎ 944-7111), adjacent to the University of Hawaii, both present quality multicultural theater and concerts, such as performances of Chinese opera and recitals of Japanese koto music.

The *Waikiki Shell* in Kapiolani Park hosts both classical and contemporary music concerts. For current schedule information, call the Blaisdell Center box office (☎ 591-2211).

There are more than a dozen theater companies on Oahu, performing everything from South Pacific and Broadway musicals to 'Kabuki Mikado,' David Mamet satires and pidgin fairy tales. For a schedule of current theater productions see the entertainment section of the Honolulu newspapers.

HAWAIIAN MUSIC & DANCE

Waikiki's Hawaiian-style entertainment ranges from Polynesian shows with beating drums and hula dancers to mellow duos playing ukulele or slack-key guitar.

The beachside courtyard at *Duke's Canoe Club* (☎ 922-2268), at the Outrigger Waikiki on Kalakaua Ave, is Waikiki's most popular venue for contemporary Hawaiian music. There's entertainment from 4 to 6 pm and 10 pm to midnight daily, with the biggest names – including the likes of Brother Noland, Henry Kapono and Kapena – appearing on weekend afternoons.

At the Sheraton Moana Surfrider's *Banyan Veranda* you can listen to music beneath the same old banyan tree where *Hawaii Calls* broadcast its nationwide radio show for four decades beginning in 1935. Typically, there's harp music from 7 to 11 am, Hawaiian guitar soloists from 2 to 4:30 pm and steel-guitar music with hula dancing from 5 to 8 pm.

An older, genteel crowd gathers daily at the Halekulani hotel's open-air *House Without a Key* restaurant for sunset cocktails, Hawaiian music and hula dancing by a former Miss Hawaii.

Coconuts (☎ 949-3811) at the Ilikai hotel often has Hawaiian contemporary music on weekends, with a $6 cover.

Luaus

The *Royal Hawaiian Hotel* (☎ 923-7311) has a $74 beachside luau from 6 to 8:30 pm on Monday, with an open bar, buffet-style dinner and Polynesian show; the price for children ages 5 to 12 is $48.

Oahu's two main luaus, *Paradise Cove* (☎ 973-5828) and *Germaine's Luau* (☎ 949-6626), are both huge impersonal affairs held nightly out near the Barbers Point area. Both cost around $45, which includes the bus ride from Waikiki hotels (about one hour each way), a buffet dinner, drinks, a Polynesian show and related hoopla. Children pay about half price.

NIGHTCLUBS & DANCING
In Waikiki
Wave Waikiki (☎ 941-0424), 1877 Kala-kaua Ave, emphasizes alternative music and is one of Oahu's hottest dance clubs. Hours are 9 pm to 4 am nightly, the minimum age is 21 and there's no dress code. There's no cover charge before 10 pm; it's $5 after that.

Rendezvous (☎ 942-5282), just around the corner from Wave Waikiki at 478 Ena Rd, plays techno, tribal and alternative music from 9 pm to 7 am most nights. The cover charge is usually $5 for ages 21 and older, $7 for ages 18 to 20.

At *Moose McGillycuddy's* (☎ 923-0751), 310 Lewers St, live bands play rock 'n roll from 9 pm to 1:30 am nightly. There's a $3 cover charge on weekends (free on most weekdays) and you must be at least 21 to get in.

Hard Rock Cafe (☎ 955-7383), 1837 Kapiolani Blvd, commonly has live rock or reggae music on Friday and Saturday from 10 pm to 12:45 am; there's no cover.

Scruples (☎ 923-9530), 2310 Kuhio Ave, is a top-40, dance-music disco open from 8 pm to 4 am nightly. The cover charge is $5 plus a two-drink minimum, $15 for ages 18 to 20.

In addition, a number of the larger Waikiki hotels have nightclubs, some of which double as discos.

Gay Scene Honolulu's spirited gay scene is centered around the Kuhio district in Waikiki, along Kuhio Ave from Kalaimoku to Kaiolu Sts.

Hula's Bar & Lei Stand (☎ 923-0669), 2103 Kuhio Ave, an open-air video dance club with tables under a big banyan tree, is a favorite place to meet, dance and have a few drinks. It's open from 10 am to 2 am daily.

The nearby *Treats Hula's*, a combo deli and bar, is also a popular gay gathering spot that stays open late. There are other gay hangouts as well, although most seem to come and go. To find out about the most happening spots, pick up the magazine *Island Lifestyle*, which is free at Hula's and other gay-oriented businesses.

Comedy The *Comedy Cow* (☎ 926-2269), at Coconuts at the Ilikai hotel, has standup comedians at 8 pm Tuesday to Sunday evenings; there's an additional 10 pm show on Friday and Saturday. The cost is $12 plus a two-drink minimum.

Elsewhere in Honolulu
Anna Bannanas (☎ 946-5190), 2440 S Bere-tania St not far from the university, has blues, Cajun, rock or reggae bands from 9:30 pm to 1:30 am Thursday to Sunday. There's usually a cover charge of $4.

The *Pier Bar* (☎ 536-2166) at the Aloha Tower Marketplace has live music nightly, including top-name contemporary Ha-waiian musicians such as Willie K and Henry Kapono. Also at the Marketplace is the *Gordon Biersch Brewery Restaurant* (☎ 599-4877), a popular microbrewery that has live jazz and similar music on most nights. At both places performance times vary with the night and there's usually no cover.

Rumours (☎ 955-4811) at the Ala Moana Hotel, 410 Atkinson Drive, has dancing to pre-'70s music on Friday and '70s to '90s music on Saturday, with country music, karaoke or ballroom dancing other nights. It's open from 5 pm (9 pm on Saturday) to 3 am except on Monday. The cover is $5; patrons must be at least 21.

CINEMA
Honolulu has numerous movie theaters. Those in Waikiki include the multiscreen *Waikiki Theatres* (☎ 971-5133), on Seaside

Ave near Kalakaua, and *Marina Twins* (☎ 973-5733), 1765 Ala Moana Blvd; both offer a fairly standard Hollywood diet.

The *IMAX Theatre Waikiki* (☎ 923-4629), 325 Seaside Ave, shows a 40-minute movie of Hawaii vistas throughout the day on a 70-foot-wide screen. It costs $7.50 for adults and $5 for children ages three to 11.

Outside of Waikiki the nine-screen multiplex cinema at *Restaurant Row* (☎ 526-4171) offers a wide variety of first-run feature films.

For progressive movies, there's the *Academy Theatre* (☎ 532-8768) at the Honolulu Academy of Arts, which showcases American independent cinema, quality foreign films and avant-garde shorts. Tickets cost $4.

The *Hemenway Theatre* (☎ 956-6468) at the University of Hawaii's Hemenway Hall shows foreign flicks, select mainstream feature films and local surf films. General admission is $3.50.

The *Movie Museum* (☎ 735-8771), 3566 Harding Ave, shows classic oldies for film buffs at 8 pm Thursday to Monday. Tickets are $5.

TEA CEREMONIES

The *Urasenke Foundation of Hawaii*, at 245 Saratoga Rd in Waikiki, has tea-ceremony demonstrations on Wednesday and Friday, bringing rare moments of serenity to busy Saratoga Rd. Students dressed in kimonos perform the ceremony on tatami mats in a formal tea room and for those participating it can be a meditative experience.

It costs $2 to be served green tea and sweets, or you can watch the ceremony for free. Each demonstration lasts about 30 minutes. The first seating is at 10 am, the last at 11:30 am. Although they're not always essential, reservations can be made by calling ☎ 923-3059. Because guests leave their shoes at the door, they are asked to wear socks. The building is diagonally across the street from the Waikiki post office.

In addition, the *Japanese Cultural Center of Hawaii* (☎ 945-7633), 2454 S Beretania

St near the university, periodically welcomes visitors to participate in tea ceremonies performed by students there.

FREE ENTERTAINMENT
Waikiki

A pleasant way to pass the evening is to stroll along Waikiki Beach at sunset and sample the outdoor Hawaiian shows that take place at the beachfront hotels. You can wander past the Sheraton Moana Surfrider where musicians play at the Banyan Veranda, watch bands performing beachside at Duke's Canoe Club, see the poolside performers at the Sheraton Waikiki and so on down the line.

The *Hilton Hawaiian Village*, at the west end of Waikiki, shoots off fireworks from the beach at 7:30 pm on Friday, preceded at 6:15 pm by a torch-lighting ceremony and a hula show at the hotel pool. The show, minus the fireworks, also takes place from 5:45 to 6:45 pm on Saturday. From Sunday to Thursday from 6 pm there's a brief torchlighting ceremony with Hawaiian music. All are free.

The *Royal Hawaiian Shopping Center* on Kalakaua Ave offers a free Polynesian 'mini-show' at the center's Fountain Court-yard from 6:30 to 9 pm on Monday, Wednesday and Friday and 10 to 11:30 am on Tuesday, Thursday and Saturday. If you want to get into the action yourself, the center offers free hula lessons at 10 am on Monday, Wednesday and Friday.

The Royal Hawaiian Band performs from 2 to 3:15 pm most Sundays (except in August) at the Kapiolani Park Bandstand. It's a quintessential Hawaiian scene that caps off with the audience joining hands and singing Queen Liliuokalani's *Aloha Oe* in Hawaiian.

A free hula show is performed at Kuhio Beach Park, near the Duke Kahanamoku statue, late in the afternoon on Saturday, and other hula performances are periodically scheduled there, mostly on weekends; check with the tourist office for current happenings.

For information on the splashy free Kodak Hula Show, which is performed

Tuesday, Wednesday and Thursday mornings at Kapiolani Park, see the Kapiolani Park heading in the Things to See & Do chapter.

Other free things to see and do in Waikiki include the Damien Museum, dedicated to Father Damien; the Oceanarium, a three-story tropical fish tank at the Pacific Beach Hotel; the US Army Museum at Fort DeRussy Beach; and the tour of the historic Sheraton Moana Hotel. All are detailed under Waikiki sights in the Things to See & Do chapter.

Elsewhere in Honolulu

The *Ala Moana Center* has a courtyard area called Centerstage that is the venue for free performances by high school choirs, gospel groups, ballet troupes, local bands and the like. There's something happening almost daily; look for the schedule in Ala Moana's free shopping magazine.

The Royal Hawaiian Band performs from 12:15 to 1:15 pm on Friday (except in August) on the lawn of the Iolani Palace.

The Mayor's Office of Culture and Arts sponsors numerous free performances, exhibits and events, ranging from street musicians in city parks to band concerts in various locales around Honolulu. Call ☎ 523-4674 for current events.

SPECTATOR SPORTS

Some of the most popular spectator sports in Oahu are surfing, boogie boarding and windsurfing contests, all of which can command high purses and bring out scores of onlookers. Top events include the Morey Bodyboards World Championship, which takes place at the North Shore's Banzai Pipeline in January, and the Triple Crown of Surfing, the world's top surfing event,

which takes place at various North Shore locales beginning in late November.

Road races also attract crowds of spectators, especially the Honolulu Marathon, which is held in mid-December and is now the second largest marathon in the USA.

There's a strong local following for the University of Hawaii's basketball and volleyball teams; call ☎ 956-4481 for ticket information, 956-6376 for recorded schedules.

The state has a winter baseball league that plays from October through December and includes players from Japanese, Korean and US minor-league baseball organizations. One of the four teams, the Honolulu Sharks, has its home field at the University of Hawaii's Rainbow Stadium. Ticket information can be obtained by calling ☎ 956-4481; schedules are printed in the sports pages of the Honolulu papers.

Hawaii does not have teams in the national football, baseball or basketball leagues, but Honolulu does host the Pro Bowl, an all-star game of the National Football League held at the Aloha Stadium near the beginning of February. Two other major bowl games hosted at the Aloha Stadium are the Hula Bowl, an all-star East/West college football game held in January, and the Aloha Bowl, a nationally televised collegiate football game held on Christmas Day. For ticket information on all bowl games contact the Aloha Stadium ticket office (☎ 486-9300) as far in advance as possible.

Honolulu also is host to PGA events, including the Hawaiian Open Golf Tournament (☎ 562-1232) at Waialae Country Club in Kahala, held in mid-February, which attracts top golfing pros with its million-dollar purse.

Shopping

Honolulu is a large, cosmopolitan city with plenty of sophisticated shops selling designer clothing, jewelry and the like. Most of the more fashionable shops are either in Waikiki or have branches there.

Of course, Honolulu also has lots of kitsch souvenir shops selling imitation Polynesian stuff, from Filipino shell hangings and carved coconuts to cheap seashell jewelry and wooden tiki statues. Not surprisingly, the largest collection of such shops is in Waikiki.

In addition, Waikiki has no shortage of swimsuit and T-shirt shops or quick-stop convenience marts. The prolific ABC discount stores (33 in Waikiki at last count) are often the cheapest places to buy more mundane items such as macadamia nuts, beach mats, sunblock and other vacation necessities.

WHERE TO SHOP
Shopping Centers

Hawaii's biggest shopping center is the Ala Moana Center, which has nearly 200 stores. The center has a wide range of places to shop from chain department stores such as Sears, Liberty House and JC Penney to fashionable boutiques and specialty shops. Among the brand-name clothing and accessory shops are Guess, Gap, Gucci, Banana Republic, Burberry's, Polo Ralph Lauren, Christian Dior and Emporio Armani. Jewelry shops include Cartier and Tiffany. Danish design is represented at shops featuring Georg Jensen silverwork and Royal Copenhagen porcelain dinnerware.

For Hawaiian influence, the Ala Moana Center has Crazy Shirts, which specializes in T-shirts with island logos; Locals Only and Hawaiian Island Creations, for beachside casual wear; High Performance Kites, for locally produced Molokai kites; and Ala Moana Stamp & Coin, which has an interesting collection of antique Hawaiian stamps and coins.

The two other significant, but much smaller, shopping centers in central Honolulu are the Ward Centre and the adjacent Ward Warehouse, both on Ala Moana Blvd. The larger of the two is the Ward Warehouse, which has about 60 stores, including Birkenstock footwear, a number of boutique clothing shops and a few craft and jewelry shops.

In Waikiki, the biggest shopping center is the Royal Hawaiian Shopping Center, which spans three blocks along Kalakaua Ave. It has a few dozen designer-fashion clothing and jewelry shops as well as numerous gift shops.

The International Market Place, in the center of Waikiki, is an expansive collection of ticky-tacky shops and stalls set beneath a sprawling banyan tree. Although few of the stalls carry high-quality goods, if you're looking for inexpensive jewelry or T-shirts, it's the place to stroll.

The Kahala Mall, on Waialae Ave in Kahala at the east side of Honolulu, is another large shopping center with Liberty House, Waldenbooks, Banana Republic, Tower Records and many other stores and clothing shops.

Aloha Tower Marketplace

The Aloha Tower Marketplace at Honolulu Harbor has about 50 shops, as well as several dozen kiosks, the latter selling Hawaiian-made foods, handicrafts, jewelry, sun hats and various knickknacks.

One of the more interesting stores to browse through is Martin & MacArthur, which specializes in upmarket Hawaiiana products including calabashes, quilts, furniture, dolls and koa woodwork, all at gallery prices. Other stores include Pakipika Trading Company, which has more moderately priced Hawaii products; Island Muu Muu, which sells men's and women's aloha clothing; and Musicland, which often has discounts on Hawaiian-music CDs and cassettes. There are also numerous clothing and gift stores carrying products from the mainland.

Factory Outlets

The Waikele Center and adjacent Waikele Factory Stores in Waipahu, on the western outskirts of Honolulu, is noted for its factory outlet stores offering discounts on name brands. Shops include a clearing-house branch of the New York-based Saks Fifth Avenue, Levi's Outlet, Oshkosh B'Gosh, Bugle Boy, Local Motion, Mikasa, Anne Klein, DKNY, Izod, Guess, Geoffrey Beene, Van Heusen, Nordic Track, Corning Revere and about 40 more.

To get there from Waikiki, take bus No 2 to downtown Honolulu and change to bus No 48. If driving, take H-1 west to Waipahu exit 8B, stay to the right and merge onto Kamehameha Hwy, then turn left onto Lumiaina St. Once you arrive there's a free trolley bus that runs between shops every 15 minutes.

Thrift Shops

The Waikiki Community Center, at 310 Paoakalani Ave in Waikiki, has a small thrift shop open from 10 am to 2 pm Monday to Friday. There's a fairly big turnover of items, including inexpensive aloha clothing.

There's a Goodwill thrift store located at 780 S Beretania St in downtown Honolulu and a Salvation Army thrift store at 322 Summer St near Dole Cannery Square at the west side of Honolulu; both have a fairly good selection of used clothing.

Aloha Flea Market

For local flavor, the Aloha Flea Market, at Aloha Stadium out near Pearl Harbor, has around 1500 vendors who sell a wide variety of items, from beach towels and bananas to old Hawaiian license plates. It's open from 7 am to 3 pm on Wednesday, Saturday and Sunday. A private shuttle bus (☎ 955-4050) to the flea market leaves from Waikiki at 7:30, 9 and 10:30 am at a cost of $6 roundtrip.

Chinatown

Chinatown can be a fun place to do some offbeat shopping. A good spot to start is the Maunakea Marketplace, which has a hodge-podge of shops and stalls in and around it. One of the more interesting ones is Bo Wah's Trading Co, 1149 Maunakea, where you can find everything from inexpensive rice bowls and stacked bamboo steamers to jasmine soap and Oriental cookie molds. At Hip Shing Fat in the Maunakea Market-place you can get your own personalized seal with your name carved in Chinese characters. Nearby shops sell snuff bottles, cloisonne jewelry, strings of freshwater rice pearls and numerous trinkets.

Chinatown is also a good place to look for art and antiques; see the Art and Antiques categories in the What to Buy section that follows. Also see the sidebar Herbs & Noodles in Things to See & Do.

Bookstores

Honolulu has many good bookstores. Borders, which has a branch in the Ward Centre on Ala Moana Blvd and another in the Waikele Center in Waipahu, is a huge, well-stocked bookstore with comprehen-sive sections on Hawaiian history, flora and fauna, island literature and outdoor activi-ties, as well as maps and a superb travel section. Also worth checking out is the University of Hawaii's bookstore (☎ 956-4338), 2465 Campus Rd.

Waldenbooks, another national chain, has shops in Waikiki in the Waikiki Shopping Plaza and the Waikiki Trade Center and in the Kahala area at the Kahala Mall. All have good Hawaiiana and travel sections.

The local chain Honolulu Book Shops, which has a branch on the corner of Bishop and Hotel Sts in downtown Honolulu as well as in the Ala Moana Center, also has a good selection of general, Hawaiiana and travel books.

The Bishop Museum has a collection of general Hawaiiana books as well as more esoteric scholarly works on various aspects of Hawaiian culture.

Rainbow Books & Records, 1010 University Ave, at the corner of Beretania St near the University of Hawaii, is a good place to look for used books of all sorts as well as current travel guides.

For a list of recommended books on Honolulu and Hawaiiana, see Books in the Facts for the Visitor chapter.

WHAT TO BUY
Hawaiiana

The Hula Supply Center, 2346 S King St in Honolulu, sells feather leis, calabash gourds, lava rock castanets, bamboo sticks, hula skirts and the like. Although they're intended for Hawaiian musicians and dancers, some of the items would certainly make interesting souvenirs and prices are reasonable.

Quilts Hawaii, 2338 S King St, just a minute's walk from the Hula Supply Center, has high-quality Hawaiian quilting, including bedcovers, pillows and wall hangings. It

Lauhala basket in the making

also carries other Hawaiian crafts such as hats, koa chests and dolls. Prices are high but reasonable for the quality.

The gift shop in the Bishop Museum, 1525 Bernice St at the west side of Honolulu, has quality Hawaiian gift items, from $2 lauhala bookmarks to Niihau shell leis selling for up to $3000. You'll also find books on the Pacific, tropical-theme calendars, koa-wood items, handmade dolls, Hawaiian musical instruments, bone jewelry, feather leis and more.

For Hawaiian-made crafts in Waikiki, there's the Little Hawaiian Craft Shop in the Royal Hawaiian Shopping Center. It has a full range of items including $4 kukui nut keychains, reasonably priced quilt-pattern kits and expensive high-quality woodwork.

Handicrafts

Hawaii has a lot of fine craftspeople and choice handicrafts can be readily found in Honolulu.

One of the most prized items is native-wood bowls. Woodworkers generally use beautifully grained Hawaiian hardwoods, such as koa and milo, to create calabashes and other bowls. Hawaiian bowls are not decorated or ornate, but rather are shaped to bring out the natural beauty of the wood. The thinner and lighter the bowl, the finer the artistic skill and greater the value. Quality bowls can run anywhere from $100 to a few thousand dollars. If you're curious to see the various grains of different woods, there's a good display (not for sale) of wooden bowls in the hallway lobby of the Outrigger Reef hotel.

Honolulu has some excellent potters, many influenced by Japanese styles and aesthetics. Good raku work in particular can be found in Honolulu shops, and prices are generally reasonable.

Lauhala, the leaves of the pandanus tree, are woven into placemats, hats and baskets – all of which make long-lasting souvenirs.

For general crafts, you'll usually find the best deals at one of the craft shows that periodically take place in city parks (check the newspapers for schedules). Otherwise, there are a number of shops specializing in crafts. One notable one is the Nohea Gallery in the Ward Warehouse on Ala Moana Blvd, which has quality Hawaiian-made fine arts and crafts, including pottery, fiber baskets, blown glass, wood-work and jewelry.

Art

You can buy paintings directly from island painters at the south side of the Honolulu Zoo on Monsarrat Ave in Kapiolani Park. Local artists have been hanging their paint-ings on the zoo fence each weekend for more than 25 years, and the practice has come to be referred to as 'Art in the Park.' The artwork is on display from 9 am to 4 pm on Saturday and Sunday, from 9 am to noon on Tuesday. It's even possible you might find a great deal here, as many of Hawaii's better painters got their start at the fence.

Perhaps the most recognized contempo-rary painter in Honolulu is Pegge Hopper, whose prints of Hawaiian women adorn many a wall in the islands. At her gallery, 1164 Nuuanu Ave in Chinatown, you can buy signed posters for $40 or originals from $10,000.

Across the street at 1121 Nuuanu Ave is Abacus Studio, which features the colorful impressionist works of Maui artist Jan Kasprzycki, another well-known contem-porary painter.

A block to the northwest at 1128 Smith St is Ramsay Galleries, which features finely detailed pen-and-ink drawings of Honolulu by the artist Ramsay and quality changing collections of works by other local artists.

Antiques

A good place to browse for antiques is at Aloha Antiques and the adjacent Mahalo Antique Mall, at 926 and 930 Maunakea St near the waterfront on the west side of Chinatown. At this site about 20 vendors set out their diverse collections, which include jewelry, Art Deco items, Oriental statues, Steuben crystal, Asian ceramics and '50s collectibles. Prices range from $5 for kitsch items to thousands of dollars for rare antiques.

If you're interested in antique furniture and carved Chinese chests, you might also want to check out CS Li Furnishings in the Chinatown Cultural Plaza.

Lai Fong Department Store, at 1118 Nuuanu Ave in Chinatown, sells an eclectic collection of antiques, including Chinese porcelain, knickknacks and old postcards of Hawaii dating back to the first half of the century.

In Waikiki, the three-story Captain Cook's Antiques at 2145 Kuhio Ave has lots of odds and ends, including jewelry, art glass, posters and old paintings.

Bushido, just west of Waikiki at 1684 Kalakaua Ave, specializes in quality Orien-tal antiques including an extensive collec-tion of Japanese swords and Korean ceramics.

Aloha Clothing

Hawaii's island-style clothing is colorful and light, often with prints of tropical flowers. The classiest aloha shirts are of lightweight cotton with subdued colors (like those of reverse fabric prints). For women there's the muumuu, a loose, com-fortable, full-length Hawaiian-style dress.

For new aloha clothing, there are endless shops along the streets in Waikiki. Most department stores also have aloha clothing sections. Liberty House, an upmarket Hawaiian department store, has good quality clothing, including aloha shirts, at moderate prices and sometimes runs good sales. Liberty House has branches at the Waikiki Beachcomber Hotel on Kalakaua Ave, at the Ala Moana Center and at the Kahala Mall.

For antique and used aloha shirts, Bai-ley's Antique Shop, 517 Kapahulu Ave near Waikiki, has the island's widest selec-tion, with prices from $10 to $1000. It's a great place to go and look around – almost like a museum.

Bargain-hunters can sometimes find used aloha shirts and muumuus at Honolulu thrift shops, though most are in small sizes as they are donated after shrinking!

Designer Fashions

There are numerous shops along Kalakaua Ave in Waikiki selling designer clothing, handbags and accessories. The simplest approach is just to stroll the streets and peruse the lobbies of the more expensive hotels. One particularly interesting hotel for this is the Sheraton Waikiki, which has a bustling lobby that resembles an exclusive Tokyo shopping center, lined with expensive jewelry stores and boutiques with French names and fashionable labels.

The Royal Hawaiian Shopping Center in Waikiki also has a good selection of designer fashions, including DKNY, Calvin Klein, Max Mara, Burberrys, Esprit, Giorgio Armani Le Collezioni, Guess, Hermes and Chanel. A good place to begin is the center's McInerny Galleria, which has one of the broadest selections of both European and American designer labels.

Just outside of Waikiki, you'll find a sizable concentration of designer-fashion shops at the Ala Moana Center; for more information see Shopping Centers at the start of this chapter.

Jewelry

There are lots of places specializing in designer jewelry and European watches. Three Ala Moana Center shops – Cartier, Ben Bridge and Dale G Cripps – carry a wide selection of both top-end watches and jewelry. In Waikiki you can find a number of upmarket jewelry stores under one roof at the Royal Hawaiian Shopping Center, while cheaper costume jewelry abounds in the vendor stalls at the nearby International Market Place.

For local-made jewelry, the premium product in Hawaii is the delicate Niihau shell lei. These necklaces are made from tiny shells that wash up on the island of Niihau and are one of the most prized Hawaiiana souvenirs. Elaborate pieces can cost thousands of dollars and are sold at quality jewelry stores around the city.

Music & Instruments

CDs and cassettes of Hawaiian music make good souvenirs.

You'll find excellent collections of both classic and contemporary Hawaiian music at Borders, which has branches at the Ward Centre in Honolulu and at the Waikele Center in Waipahu, and at Tower Records, which has a branch at the International Market Place in Waikiki and another just north of the Ala Moana Center. Both Borders and Tower Records have handy headphone set-ups that allow you to listen to various Hawaiian-music CDs before you buy.

Hula musical instruments such as nose flutes and gourd rattles are uniquely Hawaiian and make interesting gifts. See the Hula Supply Center under Hawaiiana earlier in this chapter.

Kamaka Hawaii, at 550 South St in Honolulu, specializes in hand-crafted ukuleles, priced from $235.

Food

The standard edible souvenir is macadamia nuts, either canned or covered in chocolate. Locally made macadamia nut butters, lilikoi or poha berry preserves and mango chutney all make convenient, compact gift items.

Another popular food item is Kona coffee, which is grown on the cool hillslopes of the Big Island. If you're buying coffee, note that 'Kona blend' is only 10% Kona coffee. If you want the real thing, make sure it says 100%. Prices change with the market, but it is one of the more expensive gourmet coffees, priced from around $10 a pound.

Pineapples are not a great choice in the souvenir department. Not only are they heavy and bulky, but they're likely to be just as cheap at home.

For those who enjoy cooking Japanese food, Hawaii is a good place to pick up ingredients that might be difficult to find back home. Most grocery stores have a wide selection of things like dried seaweed, mochi and ume plums.

If you just want to buy a carton of macadamia nuts or a few bags of Kona coffee, Longs Drugs generally has better prices than places in Waikiki. There's a Longs at the Ala Moana Center.

Flowers

Beautiful, fragrant flower leis are short-lived but delightful to wear. There are numerous lei shops in Honolulu, including at the airport, in Chinatown (where most leis are made) and in some Waikiki hotel lobbies.

Flowers such as orchids, anthuriums and proteas make good gifts if you're flying straight home. Proteas stay fresh for about 10 days and then can be dried.

Foreign visitors should check with their airline in advance, however, as there are usually restrictions against taking agricultural products across international borders.

Excursions

Oahu is not a terribly big island and few places are more than an hour's drive from Honolulu. Consequently, there are lots of options for day outings from the city.

One of the most popular routes is the scenic loop drive around Southeast Oahu that combines the sights along Hwy 72 and the Pali Hwy. In winter, another popular tour is around the North Shore where huge seasonal waves attract some of the world's top surfers, as well as throngs of sightseers – both tourists and locals – who come to watch the action.

SOUTHEAST OAHU

Some of Oahu's finest scenery is along the southeast coast, which curves around the tip of the Koolau Mountains. Hanauma Bay and the island's most famous bodysurfing beaches are all just a 20-minute ride from Waikiki.

East of Diamond Head, H-1 turns into the Kalanianaole Hwy (Hwy 72), following the southeast coast up to Kailua. It passes the exclusive Kahala residential area, a run of shopping centers and suburban housing developments that creep up into the mountain valleys.

The highway rises and falls as it winds its way around the Koko Head area and Makapuu Point, with beautiful coastal views along the way. The area is geologically fascinating, with boldly stratified rock formations, volcanic craters and lava sea cliffs.

Hanauma Bay Beach Park

Hanauma is a wide, sheltered bay of sapphire and turquoise waters set in a rugged volcanic ring. Hanauma, which means 'Curved Bay,' was once a popular fishing spot. It had nearly been fished out when it was designated a marine-life conservation district in 1967. Now that the fish are fed instead of eaten, they swarm in by the thousands.

From the overlook you can peer into crystal waters and view the entire coral reef that stretches across the width of the bay. You can see schools of silver fish, the bright blue flash of parrotfish and perhaps a lone sea turtle. To see an even more colorful scene, put on a mask, jump in and view it from beneath the surface.

The large sandy opening in the middle of the coral, called the **Keyhole**, is where most beginning snorkelers start. Divers and veteran snorkelers go beyond the reef to deeper parts of the bay.

Hanauma seems to get as many people as fish. With more than a million visitors a year, it's often busy and crowded.

While it's for good reason that everyone's there, the heavy use of the bay has taken its toll. The coral on the shallow reef has been damaged by all the action, and the food that snorkelers feed the fish have increased fish populations in Hanauma well beyond what it can naturally support. Fish feeding will be phased out in the next few years, but in the meantime snorkelers shouldn't feed the fish anything but fish food, which can be bought at the beach concession stand.

Hanauma is both a county beach park and a state underwater park. It has a grassy picnic area, lifeguards, showers, restrooms, changing rooms and access for the disabled. The bay is closed on Wednesdays until noon, but is otherwise open daily from 7 am until 6 pm in winter, and until 7 pm in summer. There's a $5 admission fee for non-Hawaii residents and there are plans to add a $1 parking fee for everyone.

The snack bar sells hot dogs, ice cream and soda. Snorkel sets can be rented at the beach concession stand from 8 am to 4:30 pm for $6.

Paths lead along low ledges on both sides of the bay. Be cautious when the sea is rough or the tide is high, as waves can wash over the ledges.

More people drown at Hanauma than at any other beach on Oahu. Although the figure is high largely because there are so many visitors at this beach, people drowning in the Toilet Bowl or being swept off the ledges have accounted for a fair number of deaths over the years.

Toilet Bowl A 15-minute walk out to the point on the left side of the bay brings you to the Toilet Bowl, a small natural pool in the lava rock. The Toilet Bowl is connected to the sea by an underwater channel, which enables water to surge into the bowl and then flush out from beneath.

People going into the pool for the thrill of it can get quite a ride as it flushes down four to five feet almost instantly. However the rock around the bowl is slippery and hard to grip, and getting in is far easier than getting out. It definitely shouldn't be tried alone.

Witches Brew A 10-minute walk along the right side of the bay will take you to a rocky point. The cove at the southern side of the point is Witches Brew, so named for its swirling, turbulent waters. There's a nice view of Koko Crater from there and green sand made of olivine can be found along the way.

Getting There & Away Hanauma Bay is about 10 miles from Waikiki along Hwy 72. There's a large parking lot, although it sometimes fills in the middle of the day and on weekends. Bus No 22, which runs at least once an hour during the day, goes from Waikiki to Hanauma (and on to Sea Life Park).

Koko Head Regional Park

The entire Koko Head area is a county regional park. It includes Hanauma Bay, Koko Head, Halona Blowhole, Sandy Beach and Koko Crater. Koko Crater and Koko Head are both tuff cones created about 10,000 years ago in Oahu's last gasp of volcanic activity.

The area is backed by Hawaii Kai, an expansive development of condos, houses,

shopping centers, a marina and golf course – all meticulously planned and quite sterile in appearance. Koko Marina Shopping Center, on the corner of Lunalilo Home Rd and Hwy 72, has numerous places to eat, both of the fast-food and sit-down variety.

Koko Head Koko Head, not to be confused with Koko Crater, overlooks and forms the southwest side of Hanauma Bay.

When it's open to the public, the one-mile walk up the road to the summit offers fine coastal views that light up nicely at sunset. The road starts near the highway at the Hanauma Bay entrance.

There are two craters atop Koko Head, as well as telecommunications facilities on the 642-foot summit. The Nature Conservancy maintains a preserve in the shallow Ihiihilauakea Crater, the larger of the two. The crater has a unique vernal pool and a rare fern, the *Marsilea villosa*. For information on work parties or weekend excursions to the preserve, call the Nature Conservancy (☎ 537-4508).

Halona Blowhole About half a mile past Hanauma is a lookout with a view of striking coastal rock formations and crashing surf.

Nearly a mile farther is the parking lot for Halona Blowhole. Water surging through a submerged tunnel in the rock spouts up through a hole in the ledge. It's usually preceded by a gushing sound, created by the air that's being forced out by the rushing water.

Down to the right of the parking lot is **Halona Cove**, the beach where the risqué love scene with Burt Lancaster and Deborah Kerr in *From Here to Eternity* was filmed in the 1950s.

Immediately before the blowhole, a small **stone monument** sits atop Halona Point. It was erected by Japanese fishers to honor those lost at sea.

Sandy Beach Sandy Beach is one of the most dangerous beaches on the island if measured in terms of lifeguard rescues and broken necks. It has a punishing shore-break, a powerful backwash and strong rip currents.

Nevertheless, the shorebreak is extremely popular with bodysurfers who know their stuff. It's equally popular with spectators, who gather to watch the bodysurfers being tossed around in the transparent waves.

Sandy Beach is wide and very long and, yes, sandy. It's frequented by sunbathers, young surfers and their admirers. When the swells are big, board surfers hit the left side of the beach.

Not all the action is in the water. The grassy strip on the inland side of the parking lot is used by people looking skyward for their thrills – it's both a hang-glider landing site and a popular locale for kite flying.

Koko Crater According to Hawaiian legend, Koko Crater is the imprint left by the vagina of Pele's sister Kapo, which was sent here from the Big Island to lure the pig-god Kamapuaa away from Pele.

Inside the crater there's a simple dryland botanic garden of plumeria trees, cacti and other dryland plants that the county is in the process of reviving. To get there, take Kealahou St off Hwy 72 opposite the north-ern end of Sandy Beach. Just over half a mile in, turn left at the road to Koko Crater Stables (no trail rides) and continue a third of a mile to the garden, which is free and open daily from 9 am to 4 pm.

Makapuu

About a mile north of Sandy Beach, the 647-foot Makapuu Point and its coastal **lighthouse** mark the easternmost point of Oahu. The mile-long service road to the lighthouse has recently been deeded by the federal government to Hawaii, thus opening this site to the public. The gate into the service road is locked to keep out private vehicles but you can park off the highway just beyond the gate and walk in from there. There are fine coastal views along the way and at the lighthouse lookout.

Back on the highway, about a third of a

mile farther along, there's a scenic roadside lookout with a view down onto Makapuu Beach, with its aqua waters outlined by white sand and black lava. It's an even more spectacular sight when hang gliders are taking off from the cliffs, Oahu's top hang-gliding spot.

From the lookout you can see two off-shore islands, the larger of which is **Manana**, otherwise known as Rabbit Island. This aging volcanic crater is popu-lated by feral rabbits and burrowing wedge-tailed shearwaters. They coexist so closely that the birds and rabbits sometimes even share the same burrows.

Makapuu Beach Makapuu Beach is one of Oahu's top winter bodysurfing spots, with waves reaching 12 feet and higher. It also has the island's best shorebreak. As with Sandy Beach, Makapuu is strictly the domain of experienced bodysurfers who can handle rough water conditions and dan-gerous currents. Surfboards are prohibited.

In summer, when the wave action disap-pears, the waters can be calm and good for swimming.

The beach is opposite Sea Life Park in a pretty setting, with cliffs in the background and a glimpse of the lighthouse.

Sea Life Park Sea Life Park (☎ 259-7933) is Hawaii's only marine park. Its 300,000-gallon aquarium has eagle rays, hammer-head sharks and thousands of reef fish. A spiral ramp circles the 18-foot-deep aquar-ium, allowing you to view the fish from dif-ferent depths.

In outdoor amphitheaters, jumping dol-phins, waddling penguins and a false killer whale perform the standard marine-life park tricks. There are pools of California sea lions, harbor seals, sea turtles and rare Hawaiian monk seals.

The park's little **Whaling Museum** dis-plays the skeleton of a 38-foot sperm whale that was washed up off Barbers Point in 1980 as well as harpoons, other whaling paraphernalia and a fine collection of whaling-era scrimshaw.

Sea Life Park is open daily from 9:30 am

to 5 pm, with the last series of shows beginning at 3:15 pm.

Admission is $19.95 for adults, $9.95 for children ages four to 12, and free for children under four. You can visit the whaling museum and the park cafeteria without paying admission.

Public bus Nos 22, 57 (Kailua/Sea Life Park) and 58 (Hawaii Kai/Sea Life Park) stop at the park. There's also a free shuttle bus (☎ 955-3474) from Waikiki six times a day.

Waimanalo

Waimanalo Bay has the longest continuous stretch of beach on Oahu: 5½ miles of white sand running north from Makapuu Point to Wailea Point. A long coral reef about a mile out breaks up the biggest waves, protecting much of the shore.

Waimanalo has three beach parks: Waimanalo Beach Park, an in-town beach with attractive soft white sands and water that is good for swimming; Waimanalo Bay Beach Park, a mile to the north, which is popular with board surfers and bodysurfers as it has the area's biggest waves; and Bellows Field Beach Park, which is more secluded in a natural setting backed by ironwood trees, and whose small shorebreak waves are good for beginner surfers and bodysurfers. The first two are county beach parks with full facilities, while the latter fronts Bellows Air Force Base and is open to civilian beachgoers only from noon on Friday until 8 am on Monday.

Waimanalo has a scenic setting, with the scalloped hills of the lower Koolau Range rising up inland of the shore. You should be cautious with your belongings, however, as Waimanalo isn't highly regarded for safety.

Bus No 57, which connects Kailua with Sea Life Park, services Waimanalo.

WINDWARD COAST

Windward Oahu, the island's eastern side, follows the Koolau Range along its entire length. The mountains looming inland are lovely, with scalloped folds and deep valleys. In places they come so near to the shore that they almost seem to crowd the highway into the ocean.

As the windward coast is exposed to the northeast trade winds, it's a popular area for anything that requires a sail – from windsurfing to yachting.

There are some nice swimming beaches on the windward coast – notably Kailua, Kualoa and Malaekahana – although many other sections of the coast are too silted for swimming.

Most of the offshore islets that you'll see along the way have been set aside as bird sanctuaries, providing vital habitat for ground-nesting seabirds.

Two highways cut through the Koolau Range to the windward coast: the Pali Hwy (Hwy 61) goes straight into Kailua and the Likelike Hwy (Hwy 63) runs directly into Kaneohe. If you're heading both to and from windward Oahu through the Koolau Range, take the Pali Hwy up from Honolulu and the Likelike Hwy back to the city, which will allow you to enjoy the fine scenery on both routes. (See the Pali Highway section in the Things to See & Do chapter for details on that drive.)

Kailua

Kailua is the third-largest city in Oahu, with a population of 38,000. In ancient times it was a place of legends, including a giant who was turned into a mountain ridge. Kailua was also home to numerous Oahuan chiefs.

But that's all history. Kailua today is an ordinary middle-class community that might be overlooked by visitors if not for Kailua Beach, one of the island's prettiest strands and Oahu's prime windsurfing spot.

Ulupo Heiau Ulupo Heiau is a large open platform temple, made of stones piled 30 feet high and 140 feet long. Its construction is attributed to *menehunes*, the little people that legends say created much of Hawaii's stonework, finishing each project in one night. Fittingly, Ulupo means 'night inspiration.'

In front of the heiau, which is thought to have been a luakini type where human sacrifices took place, is an artist's rendition of how the site probably looked in the 18th century before Westerners arrived. If you walk out across the top of the heiau you get a view of Kawainui Swamp, one of Hawaii's largest habitats for endangered waterbirds.

Ulupo Heiau is one mile south of Kailua Rd. Coming up the Pali Hwy from Honolulu, take Uluoa St, the first left after passing the Hwy 72 junction. Then turn right on Manu Aloha St and right again onto Manuoo St. The heiau is behind the YMCA.

Kailua Beach Kailua Beach Park, at the southeastern end of Kailua Bay, has a long, broad, white-sand beach with bright turquoise waters. The park is popular for long walks, family outings and a range of water activities.

Onshore trade winds are predominant and windsurfers can sail every month of the year. In different spots around the bay there are different water conditions, some good for jumps and wave surfing, others for flatwater sails. Some windsurfing companies, including Naish Hawaii and Kailua Sailboard, give lessons and rent boards at the beach park on weekdays and Saturday mornings.

Kailua Beach has a gently sloping sandy bottom with waters that are generally calm. Swimming is good year round. The park has restrooms, showers, lifeguards, a snack shop and large grassy expanses partly shaded with ironwood trees.

The island offshore, **Popoia Island** (or Flat Island), is a bird sanctuary where landings are allowed and is a popular destination for kayakers.

To get to Kailua Beach Park, take bus No 56 or 57 from Ala Moana Center and transfer to bus No 70 in Kailua. If you have your own transport, simply stay on Kailua Rd, which begins at the end of the Pali Hwy (Hwy 61) and continues as the main road through town, ending at the beach.

Places to Eat Kailua has many fast-food eateries, such as *Pizza Hut*, *Burger King*

and *McDonald's*, all near the central intersection of Kailua and Kuulei Rds.

Nearby is a family-run Mexican restaurant, *El Charro Avitia*, 14 Oneawa St, with combination plates for around $10, slightly less at lunch. *Assaggio*, 354 Uluniu St, serves good, moderately priced Italian food in a somewhat upmarket setting with lunchtime sandwiches for around $6, hot dishes a few dollars more.

Kaneohe

Kaneohe, with a population of 36,000, is Oahu's fourth largest town.

Kaneohe Bay, which stretches from Mokapu Peninsula all the way up to Kualoa Point, seven miles north, is the state's largest bay and reef-sheltered lagoon. Although inshore it's largely silted and not good for swimming, the near-constant trade winds that sweep across the bay are ideal for sailing.

Kaneohe Marine Corps Air Station occupies the whole of Mokapu Peninsula. H-3, the new cross-island freeway that runs north from Pearl Harbor, terminates at its gate.

Kaneohe is connected to Honolulu by bus Nos 55 and 65 and to Kailua by bus No 56. If you're continuing north from Kaneohe along the windward coast, take bus No 55, which goes up to the Turtle Bay Hilton in Kahuku.

Hoomaluhia Park The county's newest and largest botanic garden is Hoomaluhia, a 400-acre park in the uplands of Kaneohe. The park is planted with groups of trees and shrubs from tropical regions around the world.

It's a peaceful, lush green setting, with a stunning pali backdrop. Hoomaluhia is not a landscaped flower garden, but more of a natural preserve. A network of trails winds through the park and up to a 32-acre lake (no swimming allowed).

The visitor center (☎ 233-7323) has displays on flora and fauna, Hawaiian ethnobotany and on the history of the park, which was originally built by the US Army Corps of Engineers as flood protection for the valley below.

The park is at the end of Luluku Rd, which starts 2¼ miles down Kamehameha Hwy from the Pali Hwy. There's no bus service into the park, which is 1½ miles up Luluku Rd from the highway.

The park is open from 9 am to 4 pm daily. Admission is free and there are guided hikes on weekends.

Valley of the Temples & Byodo-In The Valley of the Temples is an interdenominational cemetery just off the Kahekili Hwy, 1½ miles north of Haiku Rd. The main attraction is Byodo-In, the 'Temple of Equality,' which is a replica of the 900-year-old temple of the same name in Uji, Japan. This one was dedicated in 1968 to commemorate the 100th anniversary of Japanese immigration to Hawaii.

Byodo-In sits against the Koolau Range; the rich red of the temple against the verdant fluted cliffs is strikingly picturesque.

The temple is meant to symbolize the mythical phoenix. Inside the main hall is a large gold-lacquered Buddha sitting on a lotus. Wild peacocks roam the grounds and hang their tail feathers over the upper-temple railings. A three-ton brass bell beside the temple's carp pond is said to bring tranquility and good fortune to those who ring it.

It's all very Japanese, right down to the gift shop selling sake cups, daruma dolls and happy Buddhas. Admission to the temple is $2 for adults, $1 for children under 12. It's open from 8:30 am to 4:30 pm daily.

Heeia State Park Heeia State Park is on Kealohi Point, just off Kamehameha Hwy, and is primarily visited for its coastal views, that of Heeia Fishpond to the south and Heeia-Kea Harbor to the north.

Stone-walled fishponds, used to raise mullet and other fish for royalty, were once common along the coast throughout Hawaii. The ancient **Heeia Fishpond** is an impressive example that remains largely intact despite the invasive mangrove that grows along its walls and takes root between the rocks.

Places to Eat The Windward City Shopping Center, on Kamehameha Hwy (Hwy 83), has a number of standard fast-food restaurants as well as a *Kozo Sushi*, part of a local fast-food chain specializing in good inexpensive sushi. *Chao Phya Thai Restaurant* in the same center is a family-run restaurant serving good Thai food in the $6 to $8 range.

A little farther north is the Windward Mall, at Kamehameha Hwy and Haiku Rd, a large mall with a food court that's lined with stalls selling deli items and Japanese, Chinese, Mexican and Korean foods.

Waiahole & Waikane

Waiahole and Waikane mark the beginning of rural Oahu. The area is home to family-run nurseries and small farms growing coconuts, bananas, papayas and lemons.

Large tracts of Waikane Valley were taken over by the military during WWII for training and target practice, a use that continued up until the 1960s. The government now claims the land has so much live ordnance it can't be returned to the families it was leased from. This is a source of ongoing contention with local residents who are angry that much of the inner valley remains off-limits.

Kualoa Regional Park

This 153-acre county park on Kualoa Point is a nice beach park in a scenic setting. The mountains looming precipitously across the road are, appropriately enough, called Paliku, meaning 'vertical cliff.' When the mist settles it looks like a scene from a Chinese watercolor.

The main island offshore is **Mokolii**, which in Hawaiian legend is said to be the tail of a nasty lizard that was slain by a god and thrown into the ocean.

Apua Pond, a three-acre brackish salt marsh on the point, is a nesting area for the endangered Hawaiian stilt. If you walk down the beach beyond the park you'll see a bit of **Molii Fishpond**, whose rock walls are covered with mangrove and pickleweed.

The park has a long thin strip of beach with shallow waters and safe swimming.

There are camping areas, picnic tables, restrooms, showers and a lifeguard.

Kualoa used to be one of the most sacred places on Oahu. When a chief stood on the point, passing canoes lowered their sails in respect. It was at Kualoa that the double-hulled canoe *Hokulea* landed in 1987, following a two-year rediscovery voyage through Polynesia that retraced the ancient migration routes.

Crouching Lion

In the Kaaawa area, the road hugs the coast and the pali moves right on in, with barely enough space to squeeze a few houses between the base of the cliffs and the road.

The crouching lion is a rock formation at the back of the restaurant of the same name, which comes up shortly after the 27-mile marker.

In Hawaiian legend the rock is said to be a demigod from Tahiti who was cemented to the mountain during a jealous struggle between Pele, the volcano goddess, and her sister Hiiaka. When he tried to free himself by pulling into a crouching position, he was turned to stone.

To find him, stand at the Crouching Lion Inn sign with your back to the ocean and look straight up to the left of the coconut tree. The figure, which resembles a lion, is on a cliff in the background.

Continuing north, just past the inn on the right, you get a glimpse of **Huilua Fishpond** on the coast.

Kahana

In old Hawaii the islands were divided into *ahupuaa* – pie-shaped land divisions reaching from the mountains to the sea that provided everything the early Hawaiians needed for subsistence. Kahana Valley, four miles long and two miles wide, is the only publicly owned ahupuaa in Hawaii.

In pre-contact times, rainy Kahana Valley was planted with wetland taro and the overgrown remnants of more than 130 terraces and irrigation canals have been identified.

In the early 1900s, the area was planted with sugar cane, which was hauled north to the Kahuku Mill via a small railroad. During WWII, the upper part of Kahana Valley was taken over by the military and used for training in jungle warfare. In 1965 the state purchased Kahana Valley from a private owner in order to preserve it from development.

Kahana Valley State Park One mile north of the Crouching Lion Inn is the entrance to Kahana Valley State Park.

When the state purchased Kahana it also acquired tenants, many of whom had been living in the valley for a long time. Rather than evict a struggling rural population, the state created a plan which allows the 140 residents to stay on the land. The concept is to eventually incorporate the families into a 'living park,' with the residents acting as interpretive guides.

The development of the park has been a slow process. A simple orientation center inside the park entrance has been opened, but activities are largely limited to schoolchildren and local groups. The center can, however, provide information on a 1¼-mile loop trail that begins nearby.

Sacred Falls State Park

Sacred Falls is a 1374-acre state park with a two-mile trail leading up the narrow Kaliuwaa Valley, which folds deeply into magical-looking mountains. The park is north of the 23-mile marker.

The trail follows Kaluanui Stream through a narrow canyon and leads to an 80-foot waterfall beneath high, rocky cliffs. The falls are nice though not spectacular and there are lots of mosquitoes.

The hike is of moderate difficulty and takes about 1½ hours. There are a couple of stream crossings on the way that have slippery rocks and, more importantly, are subject to flash flooding. Even when it's sunny on the valley floor, a quick rain storm in the mountains can wash down suddenly, so be sure to head for higher ground if the stream waters start to rise.

The trail is closed when the weather is sufficiently bad or the water level is high. Decisions are made daily and posted at the park or you can call the state parks office at ☎ 587-0300 and find out the status for that day.

Thefts from rental cars left in the parking lot are notorious here so you shouldn't leave anything valuable in your car.

Laie

In ancient times Laie was thought to have been the site of a *puuhonua* – a place where kapu (taboo) breakers and fallen warriors could seek refuge.

Today it's the center of the Mormon community in Hawaii, which in 1919 constructed a stately **temple**, a smaller version of the one in Salt Lake City.

Nearby is the Hawaii branch of **Brigham Young University**, with scholarship programs bringing in students from islands throughout the Pacific.

Laie Shopping Center, about half a mile north of the Polynesian Cultural Center, has restaurants and a supermarket.

Polynesian Cultural Center The Polynesian Cultural Center (PCC) is a 'nonprofit' organization belonging to the Mormon Church. The center draws about 900,000 tourists a year, more than any other attraction on Oahu with the exception of the USS Arizona Memorial.

The park has seven theme villages representing Samoa, New Zealand, Fiji, Tahiti, Tonga, the Marquesas and Hawaii. Each has authentic-looking huts and ceremonial houses which hold weavings, tapa cloth and other handicrafts. People of Polynesian descent in native garb demonstrate crafts, dances and games. There's also a re-creation of an old mission house and a missionary chapel representative of those found throughout Polynesia in the mid-1800s.

Most of the people working here are Pacific Island students at the nearby Brigham Young University, who earn their college expenses in this way while providing PCC with a source of inexpensive labor.

PCC (☎ 293-3333) is open daily except Sundays from 12:30 to 9:45 pm, but most activities cease by 6 pm. Although it can be interesting, PCC is also very touristy and hard to recommend at an admission price of $27 for adults and $16 for children ages five to 11.

The 'Admission-Buffet-Show' ticket, which costs $44 for adults and $27 for children, adds on an uninspired buffet dinner and an evening Polynesian show. This song-and-dance show, which runs from 8 to 9:30 pm, is partly authentic and partly flash – much like an enthusiastic college production with elaborate sets and costumes.

Laie Beaches The 1½ miles of beach fronting the town of Laie between Malaekahana State Recreation Area and Laie Point is used by surfers, bodysurfers and windsurfers.

Half a mile south of the main entrance to PCC, **Pounders** is an excellent bodysurfing beach, but the shorebreak, as the name of the beach implies, can be brutal and there's a strong winter current. The area around the old landing is usually the calmest. Summer swimming is generally good and the beach is sandy.

From **Laie Point** there's a good view of the mountains to the south and of tiny offshore islands. The island to the left with the hole in it is Kukuihoolua, otherwise known as Puka Rock.

To get to Laie Point, head makai on Anemoku St, opposite the Laie Shopping Center, then turn right on Naupaka St and go straight to the end.

Malaekahana State Recreation Area

Malaekahana Beach stretches between Makahoa Point to the north and Kalanai Point to the south. The long narrow sandy beach is backed by ironwoods. Swimming is good year round, although there are occasionally strong currents in winter. This popular family beach is also good for many other water activities, including bodysurfing, board surfing and windsurfing.

Kalanai Point, the main section of the state park, is less than a mile north of Laie and has picnic tables, camping, restrooms and showers.

Mokuauia (Goat Island), a state bird sanctuary just offshore, has a nice sandy cove with good swimming and snorkeling. It's possible to wade over to the island – best when the tide is low and the water's calm, although you should first ask the lifeguard about water conditions and the advisability of crossing. Be careful of the shallow coral and sea urchins.

You can also snorkel across to Goat Island and off its beaches. Beware of a rip current that's sometimes present off the windward end of the island where the water is deeper.

Kahuku

Kahuku is a former sugar town with little wooden cane houses lining the road. The mill in the center of town belonged to the Kahuku Plantation, which produced sugar here from 1890 until it closed in 1971.

A fledgling shopping center has been set up inside Kahuku's old sugar mill, with small shops ringing the old machinery. The mill's enormous gears, flywheels and pipes have been painted in bright colors to help visitors visualize how a sugar mill works. The steam systems are red, the cane-juice systems light green, hydraulic systems dark

blue and so forth. It looks like something out of *Modern Times* – you can almost imagine Charlie Chaplin caught up in the giant gears.

The center has not been wildly successful, but it does have a food mart, a gas station, a bank, a lunch-plate eatery and a few other shops.

By far the best place to eat in these parts is at *Giovanni's Aloha Shrimp*, a food van that specializes in fresh local shrimp and parks along the highway just south of the mill.

Kaihalulu Beach Kaihalulu is a beautiful curved white-sand beach fronted by ironwoods. Although a shoreline lava shelf and rocky bottom make the beach poor for swimming, it's good for beachcombing and you can walk east about a mile to Kahuku Point. Local fishers cast thrownets from the shore and pole fish from the point.

To get there turn into the Turtle Bay Hilton and just before the guard booth turn right into an unmarked parking lot, where there are free spaces for beachgoers. It's a five-minute walk out to the beach. There are no facilities.

CENTRAL OAHU

Central Oahu is the saddle between the Waianae Mountains on the west and the Koolau Mountains on the east.

Three routes lead north from Honolulu to Wahiawa, the town smack in the middle of Oahu. The freeway, H-2, is the fastest route and Hwy 750, the farthest west, is the most scenic. The least interesting option is Hwy 99, which catches local traffic as it runs through Mililani, a modern, nondescript residential community.

Hawaii's Plantation Village

A visit to Hawaii's Plantation Village (☎ 677-0110) in Waipahu provides a glimpse of plantation life and a deeper understanding of Hawaii's multiethnic heritage.

The site encompasses 30 homes and buildings set up to replicate a plantation village of the early 1900s. The cookhouse was originally on this site and the shrine was moved here, but the other structures have been newly built to authentically duplicate the architecture of the time.

The houses are set up with period furnishings that portray the lifestyles of the different ethnic groups – Hawaiian, Japanese, Okinawan, Chinese, Korean, Portuguese, Puerto Rican and Filipino – that worked Hawaii's sugar plantations.

The setting is particularly evocative as Waipahu was one of Oahu's last plantation towns, and its sugar mill, which operated until 1995, still looms on a knoll directly above the site.

There's also a small museum detailing the history of the workers. Artifacts, including a Korean flute, straw slippers and various tools, are accompanied by insightful, interpretive write-ups.

A community-based production, it's open from 9 am to 4 pm Monday to Saturday, with one-hour guided tours given on the hour from 9 am. Admission costs $5 for adults, $3 for children five to 17 and for seniors.

To get there, take exit 7 off H-1, turn south at the end of the off ramp onto Paiwa St, then turn right onto Waipahu St and continue past the mill. The distance from H-1 is about 1½ miles.

Highway 750

Highway 750 (Kunia Rd) adds a few miles to the drive through central Oahu, but if you have the time it's worth it. To get there, follow H-1 to the Kunia/Hwy 750 exit, three miles west of where H-1 and H-2 divide.

After you turn up Hwy 750, you enter plantation lands. This route runs along the foothills of the Waianae Range and the countryside is solidly agricultural from here to Schofield Barracks.

Up the road 2½ miles, you'll come to a strip of corn fields planted by the Garst Seed Co. Three generations of corn are grown here each year, which makes it possible to develop hybrids of corn seed at triple the rate it would take on the mainland.

Farther north is one of the most scenic pineapple fields in Hawaii. There are no buildings and no development – just red earth carpeted with long green strips of pineapples stretching to the edge of the mountains.

Kunia Kunia, a little town in the midst of the pineapple fields, is home to the field workers employed by Del Monte. If you want to see what a plantation town looks like, turn west off Hwy 750 onto Kunia Drive, which makes a 1¼-mile loop through the town.

Rows of grey-green wooden houses with corrugated tin roofs stand on low stilts. People take pride in their little yards, with bougainvillea and other flowers adding a splash of brightness despite the red wash of dust that blows in from the surrounding pineapple fields.

Kunia Drive intersects the highway at about 5½ miles north of the intersection of Hwy 750 and H-1 (there's a store and post office near the turn-off) and again at the six-mile marker.

Kolekole Pass Kolekole is the gap in the Waianae Mountains that Japanese fighter planes flew through on their way to bomb Pearl Harbor. The flight scene was recreated here 30 years later for the shooting of the film *Tora, Tora, Tora*.

The Kolekole Pass, at an elevation of 1724 feet, sits above Schofield Barracks on military property. It can be visited as long as the base isn't on some sort of military alert.

Access is through Foote Gate, on Hwy 750, a third of a mile south of its intersection with Hwy 99. After entering the gate, take the first left onto Road A, then the first right onto Lyman Rd. The drive is 5¼ miles up past the barracks, golf course and bayonet assault course. The parking lot is opposite the hilltop with the big white cross that's visible from miles away.

The five-minute walk to the top of the pass ends at a clearing with a view straight down to the Waianae Coast. The large, ribbed stone that sits atop the ridge here is said to be the embodiment of a woman named Kolekole who took the form of this stone, thus becoming the perpetual guardian of the pass.

Along the side of the stone are a series of ridges, one of them draining down from a bowl-like depression on the top. Shaped perfectly for a guillotine, the depression has given rise to a more recent 'legend' that Kolekole served as a sacrificial stone for the beheading of defeated chiefs and warriors.

Just west of the pass the road continues through a Navy base down to the Waianae Coast, but there's no public access as the base is a stockyard for nuclear weapons.

Wahiawa to the North Shore

If you want to go through Wahiawa to visit the botanic garden and royal birthstones, take Kamehameha Hwy (which is called Hwy 80 as it goes through town, although it's Hwy 99 before and after Wahiawa). To make the bypass around Wahiawa, stick with Hwy 99.

From Wahiawa, Hwy 99 leads through pineapple country down to the North Shore. About two miles northwest of Wahiawa, you can see Kolekole Pass on your left; look for the white cross, which is on the north side of the pass.

Wahiawa Botanic Garden The Wahiawa Botanic Garden, 1396 California Ave, is a mile east of the Kamehameha Hwy. What started out in the 1920s as a site for forestry experiments by the Hawaii Sugar Planters' Association is now a 27-acre city park with grand old trees around a wooded ravine.

The park is a nice shady place to take a stroll. Interesting 60-year-old exotics such as cinnamon, chicle and allspice are grouped in one area. Tree ferns, loulu palms and other Hawaiian natives are in another. The trees are identified by markers and the air is thick with birdsong.

The garden is open from 9 am to 4 pm daily. Admission to the park is free, as is a brochure describing some of the trees.

Royal Birthstones Kukaniloko, a group of royal birthstones where queens gave birth, is just north of Wahiawa. The stones

are thought to date back to the 12th century. It was said that if a woman lay properly against the stones while giving birth, her child would be blessed by the gods, and indeed, many of Oahu's great chiefs were born at this site.

These stones are one of only two documented birthstone sites in Hawaii (the other's in Kauai). Many of the petroglyphs on the stones are of recent origin, but the eroded circular patterns are original.

To get to them, go three-quarters of a mile north on Kamehameha Hwy from its intersection with California Ave. Turn left onto the red dirt road directly opposite Whitmore Ave. The stones are a quarter of a mile down through a pineapple field, amongst a stand of eucalyptus and coconut trees.

Pineapple Sites Del Monte maintains a little pineapple demonstration garden in a triangle at the intersection of Hwys 99 and 80.

Smooth cayenne, the commercial variety of pineapple grown in Hawaii, is shown in various growth stages. Each plant produces just two pineapples. The first takes nearly two years to reach maturity, the second about one year more. Other commercial varieties grown in Australia, the Philippines and Brazil are on display, as well as many varieties of purely decorative bromeliads. You can pull off to the side of the road and walk through on your own at any time.

On Hwy 99, less than a mile north of Del Monte's garden, is the Dole Pineapple Pavilion, a gift and refreshment shop that sits amid Dole's expansive pineapple fields. If you didn't stop at the first garden in back of the Dole pavilion, here you'll find a less mature but similar pineapple demonstration patch.

NORTH SHORE

Oahu's North Shore is synonymous with surfing and prime winter waves. Sunset Beach, the Banzai Pipeline and Waimea Bay are among the world's top surf spots and draw some of the best international surfers.

Other North Shore surf breaks may be

less well known but with names like Himalayas and Avalanche, they're not exactly for neophytes.

Waikiki surfers started taking on North Shore waves in the late 1950s and big-time surf competitions followed a few years later. These days the height of the activity is in November and December when three world-class surf competitions, known as the Triple Crown, take place.

With the exception of Haleiwa Beach Park, North Shore beaches are notorious for treacherous winter swimming conditions. There are powerful currents along the entire shore. If it doesn't look as calm as a lake, it's probably not safe for swimming or snorkeling.

Bus No 52 serves the entire North Shore, connecting Honolulu with Haleiwa, Waimea and all of the area's beach parks.

Haleiwa

Haleiwa is the gateway to the North Shore and the main town catering to the multitude of daytrippers who make the circle-island ride.

The 2500 townspeople are a multiethnic mix of families who have lived in Haleiwa for generations and more recently arrived surfers, artists and New Age folks.

Haleiwa has a picturesque boat harbor, bounded on both sides by beach parks. **Haleiwa Alii Beach Park**, on the south side, is the site of several surfing tournaments and a favorite spot for younger surfers. To the north is **Haleiwa Beach Park**, which is protected by a shallow shoal and breakwater and thus has the North Shore's safest year-round swimming.

Chief among the town's sights is **Matsumoto's**, a tin-roofed general store that's an institution in these parts for its shave ice – a local version of the syrup-drenched snow cone.

Opposite Matsumoto's is **Liliuokalani Protestant Church**, named for Queen Liliuokalani, who spent summers in Haleiwa. Of the most interest is the unusual seven-dial clock which the queen presented to the church in 1892. The clock shows the hour, day, month and year as well as the phases of the moon. The queen's 12-letter name replaces the numerals on the clock face.

Places to Eat Haleiwa has numerous places to eat along its main road, including *Cafe Haleiwa*, a surfers' haunt with good inexpensive breakfasts and lunches, and *Kua Aina*, popular for its burgers and fish sandwiches. Closer to the harbor are a couple of more upscale restaurants, *Chart House* and *Jameson's by the Sea*, which specialize in seafood.

Waimea

Waimea Valley was heavily settled prior to Western contact. The lowlands were terraced in taro, the valley walls dotted with house sites and the ridges topped with heiaus. Just about every crop grown in Hawaii thrived in the valley, including a rare pink taro fancied by the alii.

Waimea River, now blocked at the beach, originally opened into the bay and was a passage for canoes traveling upstream to the villages. The sport of surfing was immensely popular here centuries ago, with the early Hawaiians taking to Waimea's huge waves on their long boards.

A devastating flood in 1894, largely the consequence of deforestation by surrounding plantations, permanently altered Waimea's shore and resulted in the abandonment of the valley.

Waimea Bay Beach Park Waimea Bay is a beautiful, deeply inset bay with turquoise waters and a wide white-sand beach almost 1500 feet long.

Waimea Bay's mood changes with the seasons: it can be tranquil and as flat as a lake in summer, and savage with incredible surf and the island's meanest rip currents in winter.

Waimea has Hawaii's biggest surf and holds the record for the highest waves ever ridden in international competition. As at Sunset Beach, the huge north swells bring out crowds of spectators who throng to watch Waimea surfers perform their near-suicidal feats on waves of up to 35 feet.

On winter's calmer days the boogie

boarders are out in force, but even then sets come in hard and people get pounded. Winter water activities here are not for novices.

Usually the only time the water is calm enough for swimming and snorkeling is from June to September. The best snorkeling is around the rocks on the left of the bay.

Waimea Bay Beach Park is the most popular North Shore beach. There are showers, restrooms, picnic tables and a lifeguard on duty daily.

Waimea Falls Park Waimea Falls Park, across the highway from Waimea Bay Beach Park, is a botanical garden, cultural preserve and tourist park all in one.

The main park road leads three-quarters of a mile up the Waimea Valley to a waterfall, passing extensive naturalized gardens that include sections of ginger, heliconia and medicinal plants. Many of the plants are labeled for identification and there are several rare species under propagation.

The park has ancient stone platforms and replicas of thatched buildings similar to those used by early Hawaiians. Traditional hula dances, Hawaiian games and other demonstrations are given during the day.

The valley's natural beauty is nicely preserved and the park is pleasant to stroll around in, but the cost of admission is a bit steep at $19.95 for adults, $9.95 for children ages six to 12. The park is open from 10 am to 6:30 pm daily. A good discount is provided if you arrive after 4:15 pm, when the rate drops to $6.50 for adults and $4 for children – however, there are no demonstrations at that time.

A free shuttle runs from Waikiki hotels at 8 and 11:30 am daily; call ☎ 955-8276 for pick-up locations. Public bus No 52 stops at the highway, half a mile from the park entrance.

Puu O Mahuka Heiau State Monument
Puu O Mahuka is a long low-walled platform temple perched on a bluff above Waimea. It's the largest heiau on Oahu.

The terraced stone walls are a couple of feet high, although most of the heiau is now overgrown. It's scenically set and well worth a ride up for the view, which stretches from Waimea Bay out along the coast to Kaena Point.

To get to the heiau, turn up Pupukea Rd at the Foodland supermarket. The marked turn-off to the heiau is about half a mile up the road and from there it's three-quarters of a mile in.

Pupukea Beach Park Pupukea Beach Park is a long stretch of beach that includes **Three Tables** and **Shark's Cove**, two good summertime snorkeling and diving spots. In the middle of the two is **Old Quarry**, where a wonderful array of jagged rock formations and tide pools are exposed at low tide. The rocks and tide pools are tempting to explore, but be careful because they're razor sharp and if you slip it's easy to get a deep cut.

There are showers and restrooms in front of Old Quarry. The beach entrance is opposite an old gas station.

Banzai Pipeline Ehukai Beach Park is the site of the world-famous Banzai Pipeline, which curls just offshore a few hundred feet to the left of the park. The Pipeline breaks over a shallow coral reef and can be a death-defying wave to ride.

While winter waves can be enormous, water conditions mellow out in summer, when the beach can be good for swimming.

The entrance to Ehukai Beach Park is opposite Sunset Beach Elementary School.

Sunset Beach Park Sunset Beach Park, near the nine-mile marker, is Oahu's classic winter surf spot with incredible waves and challenging breaks. It's such a big name you expect a big sight, but it's just a little roadside attraction without even a sign. All the action is in the water.

Winter swells create powerful rips. Even when the waves have mellowed in the summer, there's still an along-shore current for swimmers to deal with. Portable toilets and a lifeguard tower are the only facilities.

WAIANAE COAST

The Waianae Coast is the arid leeward side of Oahu.

In 1793 Captain Vancouver, the first Westerner to drop anchor there, found a barren wasteland with only a few scattered fishing huts. Just two years later, the population jumped after Kamehameha invaded Oahu and many Oahuans who had been living in more desirable areas were forced to flee to the isolated Waianae Coast.

Today it still stands separate from the rest of the island. There are no gift shops or sightseeing buses on the Waianae Coast. When you get right down to it, other than watching surfers at Makaha, there aren't a whole lot of sights to see.

Although developers are beginning to grab Waianae farmland for golf courses, leeward Oahu remains the island's least touristed side. The area has a history of resisting development and a reputation for not being receptive to outsiders, including tourists.

Farrington Hwy (Hwy 93) runs the length of the leeward coast, with long stretches of white-sand beaches much of the way. In winter most have treacherous swimming conditions as well as some of the island's more challenging surfing.

Although the towns themselves are ordinary, the cliffs and valleys cutting into the Waianae Range form a lovely backdrop. At road's end, there's an undeveloped mile-long beach and a fine nature hike out to scenic Kaena Point.

Public bus No 51 goes up the Waianae Coast as far as Makaha Beach; there's no bus service between Makaha and Kaena Point.

Makaha

Makaha means 'ferocious' and in days past the valley was notorious for the bandits who used to hang out along the cliffs waiting for travelers to pass. Today Makaha has world-class surfing as well as Oahu's best-restored heiau.

Makaha Beach is broad, sandy and crescent-shaped, with some of the most daunting winter surf in the islands. Experienced surfers and bodysurfers both hit the waves here.

When the surf's not up, Makaha is a popular swimming beach. When the surf is up, swimming is hazardous because of the dangerous rip currents and strong shore-break.

In summer the slope of the beach is relatively flat. In winter it's fairly steep, with as much as half of the sand temporarily washing away, but even then Makaha is an impressive beach.

Snorkeling is good offshore during the calmer summer months. Makaha Caves, out where the waves break farthest offshore, feature underwater caverns, arches and tunnels at depths of 30 to 50 feet. It's a popular leeward diving spot.

Makaha Beach has showers, restrooms and a lifeguard on duty daily.

Kaneaki Heiau Kaneaki Heiau, in the center of Makaha Valley, was originally dedicated to Lono, the god of agriculture. In its final days it was rededicated by Kamehameha I as a war temple and remained in use until the time of his death, in 1819.

Kamehameha I

Restoration, which was undertaken by the Bishop Museum and completed in 1970, added two prayer towers, a taboo house, drum house, altar and god images. It was reconstructed in the traditional manner using ohia logs and pili grass shipped over from the Big Island.

To get to the heiau, turn inland onto Kili Drive opposite Makaha Beach Park. After a mile, turn right onto Huipu Drive and then after half a mile turn left onto Mauna Olu St, which leads into the heiau.

You'll first arrive at the gatehouse to Mauna Olu Estates, a private residential area. Visitors are allowed to drive through to the heiau only between 10 am and 2 pm Tuesday to Sunday. There's no admission charge.

Kaena Point State Park

Kaena Point State Park is an undeveloped 853-acre coastal strip that runs along both sides of Kaena Point, the westernmost point of Oahu.

This area was sacred to early Hawaiians, who believed that when people went into a deep sleep their souls could wander. Souls that wandered too far were drawn west to Kaena Point. The lucky ones were met here by their *aumakua* (ancestral spirit helper) who led their soul back to their body. If unattended, their soul would be forced to leap from Kaena Point into the endless night, never to return.

Until the mid-1940s the Oahu Railroad ran up from Honolulu and around the point, carrying passengers on to Haleiwa on the North Shore. The attractive mile-long sandy beach on the south side of the point is called Yokohama Bay, so named for the large numbers of Japanese fishers who came here during the railroad days.

Winter brings huge pounding waves and Yokohama is a popular surfing and body-surfing spot. It is, however, best left to the experts because of the submerged rocks, strong rip currents and dangerous shore-break.

In addition to being a state park, Kaena Point has been designated a natural area reserve because of its unique ecosystem. The extensive dry, windswept coastal dunes that rise above the point are the habitat of many rare native plants.

Seabirds common to the point include shearwaters, boobies and the common noddy. You can often see schools of spinner dolphins off the beach and in winter humpback whale sightings are not uncommon.

From Yokohama Bay, there's a 2½-mile (one-way) coastal hike that continues from the end of the paved road out to Kaena Point, following the old railroad bed. Along the trail are tide pools, sea arches, coastal views and the lofty sea cliffs of the Waianae mountain range. The trail is unshaded (Kaena means 'the heat'), so if you decide to hike take along plenty of water and don't leave anything valuable in your car.

A: View of Hanauma Bay
B: Koolau Range foothills, Kaneohe
C: Waimea Bay, North Shore

D: Surfin' USA
E: Haleiwa Alii Beach Park

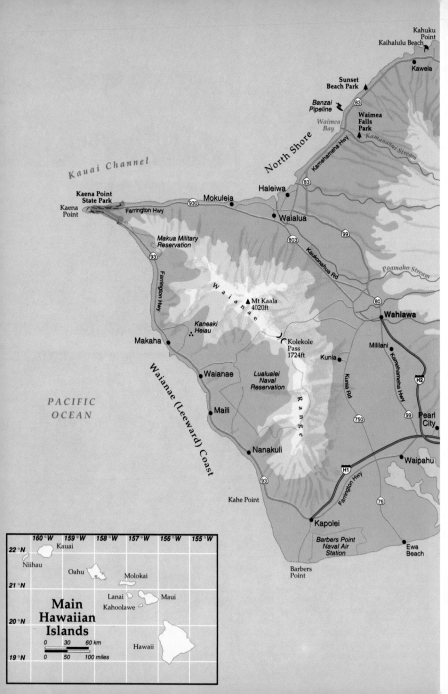

Kahuku Point

Kaihalulu Beach

Kawela

Sunset
Beach Park

*Banzai
Pipeline*

83

*Waimea
Bay*

Waimea
Falls
Park

Kamananui Stream

North Shore

Kamehameha Hwy

Haleiwa

83

Mokuleia

930

Kaena Point
State Park

Farrington Hwy

Kaena
Point

Kauai Channel

Waialua

99

803

Kaukonahua Rd

Poamoho Stream

Makua Military
Reservation

93

Farrington Hwy

Waianae

Mt Kaala
4020ft

80

Wahiawa

*Kaneaki
Heiau*

Kolekole
Pass
1724ft

Mililani

Kamehameha Hwy

Makaha

Kunia

Waianae

*Lualualei
Naval
Reservation*

Range

Kunia Rd

H2

Maili

750

99

Pearl
City

*PACIFIC
OCEAN*

Waianae (Leeward) Coast

Nanakuli

Waipahu

H1

Kahe Point

93

Farrington Hwy

76

Kapolei

*Barbers
Point
Naval Air
Station*

Ewa
Beach

Barbers
Point

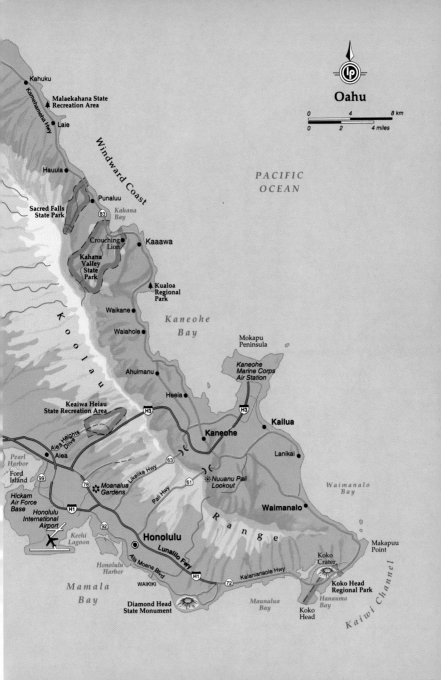

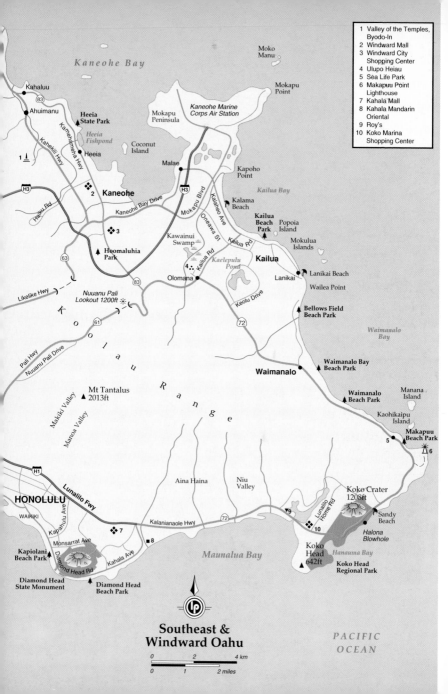

1	Valley of the Temples, Byodo-In
2	Windward Mall
3	Windward City Shopping Center
4	Ulupo Heiau
5	Sea Life Park
6	Makapuu Point Lighthouse
7	Kahala Mall
8	Kahala Mandarin Oriental
9	Roy's
10	Koko Marina Shopping Center

Kaneohe Bay

Moko Manu

Kahaluu
Ahuimanu
Heeia State Park
Mokapu Peninsula
Kaneohe Marine Corps Air Station
Mokapu Point
Heeia Fishpond
Heeia
Coconut Island
Malae
Kapoho Point
Kahekili Hwy
Kamehameha Hwy
H3
2 Kaneohe
Kaneohe Bay Drive
H3
Haiku Rd
Hoomaluhia Park
Kalaheo Ave
Kalama Beach
Kailua Bay
Kailua Beach Park
Popoia Island
Kawainui Swamp
Mokapu Blvd
Oneawa St
Kailua Rd
Mokulua Islands
63
Olomana
4
Kaelepulu Pond
Kailua
Lanikai
Lanikai Beach
83
Likelike Hwy
61
Nuuanu Pali Lookout 1200ft
Keolu Drive
Wailea Point
Koolau
Bellows Field Beach Park
72
Waimanalo Bay
Pali Hwy
Nuuanu Pali Drive
Waimanalo Bay Beach Park
Waimanalo
Range
Mt Tantalus 2013ft
Waimanalo Beach Park
Manana Island
Kaohikaipu Island
Makapuu Beach Park
5
6
Makiki Valley
Manoa Valley
H1
Lunalilo Fwy
Aina Haina
Niu Valley
Koko Crater 1208ft
HONOLULU
WAIKIKI
Kalanianaole Hwy
72
9
Lunalilo Home Rd
Sandy Beach
Kapahulu Ave
Monsarrat Ave
7
10
Halona Blowhole
Kapiolani Beach Park
8
Maunalua Bay
Koko Head 642ft
Hanauma Bay
Koko Head Regional Park
Diamond Head State Monument
Kahala Ave
Diamond Head Rd
Diamond Head Beach Park

PACIFIC OCEAN

Southeast & Windward Oahu

0   2   4 km
0   1   2 miles

Internet Directory

TOURIST OFFICES & INFORMATION

Hawaii Visitors Bureau
www.visit.hawaii.org

Hawaiian Index
www.hawaiian-index.com

Planet Hawaii www.planet-hawaii.com

BOOKS

University of Hawaii Press
www2.hawaii.edu/uhpress/uhphome.html

GAY COMMUNITY

Gay & Lesbian Community Center
www.tnight.com/glcc

Hawaii Equal Rights Marriage Project
www.xq.com/hermp

Island Lifestyle www.tnight.com/ilm

Pacific Ocean Holidays
www.gayhawaii.com

AIRLINES

Air Canada www.aircanada.ca

Air New Zealand www.airnz.com

All Nippon Airlines
www.ana.co.jp/index-e.html

America West Airlines
www.americawest.com

American Airlines www.amrcorp.com

Asiana Airlines www.asiana.co.kr

Canadian Airlines www.cdnair.ca

China Airlines www.china-airlines.com

Continental Airlines
www.flycontinental.com

Delta Air Lines www.delta-air.com

Island Air www.alohaair.com/aloha-air

Hawaiian Air www.hawaiianair.com

Japan Air Lines www.jal.co.jp

Korean Air www.koreanair.com

Mahalo Air www.islander-magazine.com/mahaloschedule.html

Northwest Airlines www.nwa.com

Qantas Airways www.qantas.com.au

Singapore Airlines
www.singaporeair.com

TWA www.twa.com

United Airlines www.ual.com

INTERNET CAFES

Cyber Cafe hawaii-cybercafe.com

Internet Cafe www.aloha-cafe.com

NEWSPAPERS

Honolulu Weekly
www.honoluluweekly.com

B&B RESERVATION SERVICES

Bed & Breakfast Hawaii
planet-hawaii.com/bandb

Bed & Breakfast Honolulu
www.travelsource.com/bnb/allhi.html

HOTELS

Hawaiian King Hotel
www.hi50.com/hawnking

Ilima Hotel www.pete.com/ilima

Manoa Valley Inn www.marcresorts.com

New Otani Kaimana Beach Hotel
www.kaimana.com

Outrigger www.outrigger.com

Hyatt Regency Waikiki
www.travelweb.com/hyatt.html

Waikiki Grand www.marcresorts.com

Glossary

aa – lava that is rough and jagged

ahi – albacore (yellowfin) tuna

ahu – stone cairns used to mark a trail; or an altar or shrine

ahupuaa – a traditional land division, usually in a wedge shape from the mountains to the sea

aikane – friend

aina – land

akamai – clever

aku – skipjack tuna

akua – god, spirit, idol

akule – bigeye mackerel

alii – chief; royalty

aloha – the traditional greeting meaning love, welcome, goodbye

aloha aina – love of the land

amaama – mullet

amakihi – small yellow-green bird, one of the more common of the native birds

ao – Newell's shearwater (a seabird)

apapane – bright-red native Hawaiian honeycreeper

au – marlin

aumakua – ancestral spirit helper

auwe – Oh my! Alas!

awa – kava, made into an intoxicating brew; milk fish

awapuhi – wild ginger

bento – the Japanese word for a box lunch

cilantro – coriander leaves (also known as Chinese parsley)

crack seed – snack foods, usually dried fruits or seeds, either sour, salty or sweet

elepaio – a brownish forest bird with a white rump

hala – pandanus; the leaves are used in weaving mats and baskets

hale – house

hana – work; or bay, when used as a compound in place names

haole – Caucasian; literally 'without breath'

hapa – half; person of mixed blood

hau – indigenous lowland hibiscus tree whose wood is often used for outrigger canoes

haupia – coconut pudding

Hawaii nei – all the Hawaiian Islands taken as a group

heiau – ancient stone temple, a place of worship in Hawaii before Western contact

Hina – Polynesian goddess (wife of *Ku*, one of the four main gods)

holoholo – to walk, drive or ramble around for pleasure

holoku – a long dress similar to the *muumuu*, but more fitted and with a yoke

holua – sled, or sled course

honu – turtle

hoolaulea – celebration, party

huhu – angry

hui – group, organization

hukilau – net fishing, with a seine, involving a group of people; the word can also refer to the feast that follows

hula – traditional Hawaiian dance

hula halau – *hula* school or troupe

humuhumunukunukuapuaa – rectangular triggerfish

iiwi – a bright-vermilion forest bird with a curved salmon-colored beak

iliahi – Hawaiian sandalwood

ilili – stones

ilima – native groundcover with a delicate yellow-orange flower

imu – underground earthen oven used in traditional *luau* cooking

kahili – a feather standard, used as a symbol of royalty

kahuna – wise person in any field, commonly a priest, healer or sorcerer

kahuna nui – high priest

kalua – traditional method of baking in an underground oven *(imu)*

kamaaina – native-born Hawaiian or a longtime resident; literally 'child of the land'

Kanaloa – god of the underworld

kane – man; also the name of one of four main Hawaiian gods

kapu – taboo, part of strict ancient Hawaiian social system

kaunaoa – a thin parasitic vine

kava – a mildly narcotic drink made from the roots of *Piper methysticum*, a pepper shrub

keiki – child, children

kiawe – a relative of the mesquite tree introduced to Hawaii in the 1820s, now very common; its branches are covered with sharp thorns

kii – image, statue

kipuka – an area of land spared when lava flows around it; an oasis

ko – sugar cane

koa – native hardwood tree often used in woodworking of native crafts

kohola – whale

kokua – help, cooperation

kona – leeward, or a leeward wind

konane – ancient Hawaiian board game similar to checkers

koolau – windward side

Ku – Polynesian god of many manifestations, including god of war, farming and fishing

kukui – candlenut tree; the official state tree, its oily nuts were once burned in lamps

kuleana – an individually held plot of land

kupuna – grandparent

kuula – fishing shrine

lanai – veranda

lauhala – leaves of the *hala* plant used in weaving

laulau – wrapped package; pork or beef with salted fish and taro leaves wrapped in leaves and steamed

lei – garland, usually of flowers, but also of leaves or shells

lilikoi – passion fruit

limu – seaweed

lio – horse

lolo – stupid, crazy

lomi – raw, diced salmon marinated with tomatoes and onions

lomilomi – massage

Lono – Polynesian god of harvest, agriculture, fertility and peace

loulu – native fan palms

luakini – a type of *heiau* dedicated to the war god Ku and used for human sacrifices

luau – traditional Hawaiian feast

mahalo – thank you

mahimahi – locally called 'dolphin,' but actually a type of fish unrelated to the marine mammal

maile – native twining plant with fragrant leaves often used in *leis*

makaainana – commoners; literally 'people who tend the land'

makaha – sluice gates, used in fishponds

makahiki – ancient annual four-month winter harvest festival dedicated to *Lono*, when sports and celebrations replaced all warfare

makai – towards the sea

makaku – creative artistic *mana*

malasada – a fried dough served warm, similar to a doughnut

malihini – newcomer, visitor

malo – loincloth

mana – spiritual power

manini – convict tang (a reef fish); also used to refer to something small or insignificant

mano – shark

mauka – towards the mountains; inland

mele – song, chant

menehune – 'little people' who according to legend built many of Hawaii's fishponds, *heiaus* and other stonework

milo – a native shade tree with beautiful hardwood

moo – water spirit, water lizard or dragon

mu – a 'body catcher,' who secured sacrificial victims for the *heiau* altar

muumuu – a long, loose-fitting dress introduced by the missionaries

naupaka – a native shrub with delicate white flowers

Neighbor Islands – the term used to refer to the main Hawaiian islands outside of Oahu

nene – a native goose; Hawaii's state bird

nisei – people of Japanese descent

noni – Indian mulberry; a small tree with yellow, warty, smelly fruit, used medicinally

nuku puu – a native honeycreeper with a bright-yellow underbelly

ohana – family, extended family

ohelo – low-growing native shrub with edible red berries related to cranberries, said to be sacred to *Pele*

ohia lehua – native Hawaiian tree with tufted feathery pompomlike flowers

okole – buttocks

olo – surfboards used by the *alii*

onaga – red snapper

ono – delicious; also the name of the wahoo fish

opae – shrimp

opakapaka – pink snapper

opihi – edible limpet

pahoehoe – type of lava that flows quickly and smoothly

pakalolo – marijuana; literally 'crazy smoke'

pali – cliff

palila – native honeycreeper

paniolo – a Hawaiian cowboy; the word is derived from the Spanish *español*, as Hawaii's first cowboys were Mexican

pau – finished, no more

Pele – goddess of fire and volcanoes, who lives in Kilauea volcano

pho – a Vietnamese soup of beef broth, noodles and fresh herbs

piko – navel, umbilical cord

pili – a bunch grass, commonly used for thatching houses

pilikia – trouble

pipikaula – a salted, dried beef served broiled

poha – gooseberry

poi – a gooey paste made from taro roots, a staple food of the Hawaiian diet

poke – chopped raw fish marinated in soy sauce, oil and chili peppers

Poliahu – goddess of snow

pua aloalo – a hibiscus flower

pueo – Hawaiian owl

puka – any kind of hole or opening

pupu – snack food, hors d'oeuvres; shells

puu – hill, cinder cone

puuhonua – place of refuge

saimin – a Japanese noodle soup

tabi – Japanese reef-walking shoes

talk story – to strike up a conversation, make small talk

tapa – cloth made by pounding the bark of the paper mulberry tree, used for early Hawaiian clothing. In Hawaiian: *kapa*

taro – a plant, with green heart-shaped leaves, cultivated in Hawaii for its edible rootstock. The root is mashed to make *poi*. In Hawaiian, taro is called *kalo*.

teishoku – Japanese word for fixed-plate meal

teppanyaki – Japanese style of cooking with an iron grill

ti – common native plant; its long shiny 'multipurpose' leaves are used for a variety of things, including plates and *hula* skirts. In Hawaiian: *ki*

tutu – aunt, older woman

ukulele – a stringed musical instrument derived from the 'braginha,' which was introduced to Hawaii in the 1800s by Portuguese immigrants

ulu – breadfruit

ulu maika – ancient Hawaiian game

wahine – woman

wana – sea urchin

wikiwiki – hurry, quick

Index

SIDEBARS

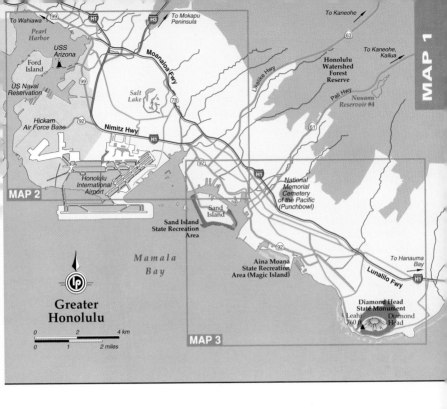

MAP 1

To Wahiawa
To Mokapu Peninsula
To Kaneohe

Pearl Harbor
USS Arizona
Ford Island
US Naval Reservation

Moanalua Fwy

To Kaneohe, Kailua

Honolulu Watershed Forest Reserve

Likelike Hwy
Pali Hwy
Nuuanu Reservoir #4

Salt Lake

Hickam Air Force Base

Nimitz Hwy

MAP 2

Honolulu International Airport

National Memorial Cemetery of the Pacific (Punchbowl)

Sand Island

Sand Island State Recreation Area

Mamala Bay

Aina Moana State Recreation Area (Magic Island)

To Hanauma Bay

Lunalilo Fwy

Greater Honolulu

| 0 | | 2 | | 4 km |
| 0 | 1 | | 2 miles | |

MAP 3

Diamond Head State Monument
Leahi 760 ft
Diamond Head

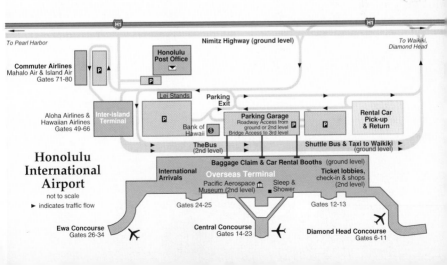

Honolulu International Airport

not to scale

▶ indicates traffic flow

To Pearl Harbor

Nimitz Highway (ground level)

To Waikiki, Diamond Head

Commuter Airlines
Mahalo Air & Island Air
Gates 71-80

P

Honolulu Post Office

P

Lei Stands

Parking Exit

Aloha Airlines & Hawaiian Airlines
Gates 49-66

Inter-island Terminal

P

Bank of Hawaii $

Parking Garage
Roadway Access from ground or 2nd level
Bridge Access to 3rd level

P

P

Rental Car Pick-up & Return

TheBus
(2nd level)

Shuttle Bus & Taxi to Waikiki
(ground level)

Baggage Claim & Car Rental Booths (ground level)

International Arrivals

Overseas Terminal

Pacific Aerospace Museum (2nd level)

Sleep & Shower

Ticket lobbies,
check-in & shops
(2nd level)

Gates 24-25

Gates 12-13

Ewa Concourse
Gates 26-34

Central Concourse
Gates 14-23

Diamond Head Concourse
Gates 6-11

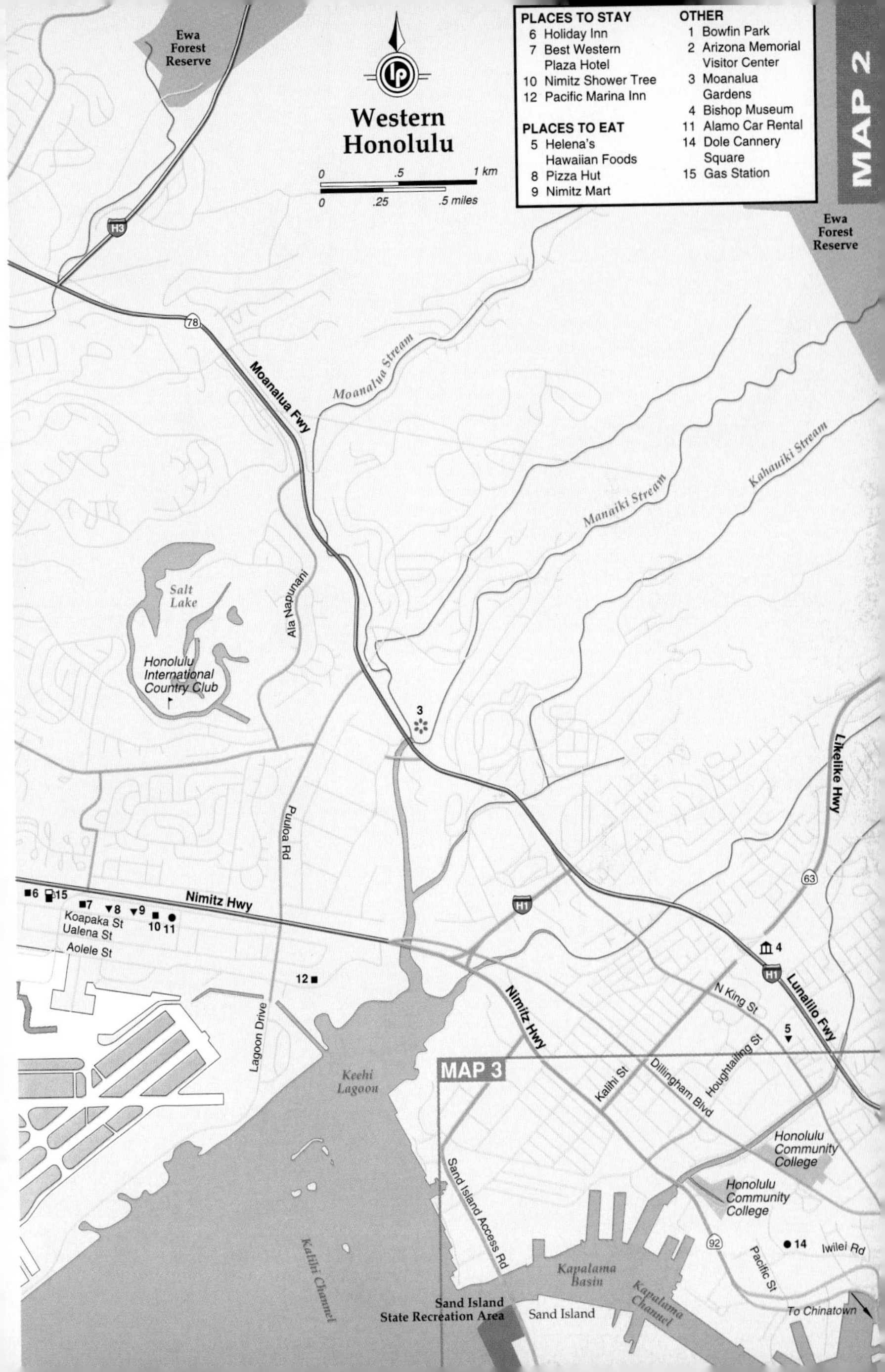

MAP 2

Western Honolulu

0   .5   1 km

0   .25   .5 miles

Ewa
Forest
Reserve

Ewa
Forest
Reserve

H3

78

Moanalua Fwy

Moanalua Stream

Manaiki Stream

Kāhauiki Stream

Likelike Hwy

Salt
Lake

Ala Napunani

Honolulu International
Country Club

3

Puuloa Rd

63

Nimitz Hwy

H1

6 15
7 8 9
   10 11
Koapaka St
Ualena St
Aolele St

12

Lagoon Drive

Keehi
Lagoon

MAP 3

Nimitz Hwy

Kalihi St

Dillingham Blvd

Houghtailing St

N King St

4

H1

Lunalilo Hwy

5

Honolulu
Community
College

Honolulu
Community
College

Sand Island Access Rd

Kalihi Channel

Kapalama
Basin

Kapalama Channel

Sand Island
State Recreation Area

Sand Island

92

Pacific St

14

Iwilei Rd

To Chinatown

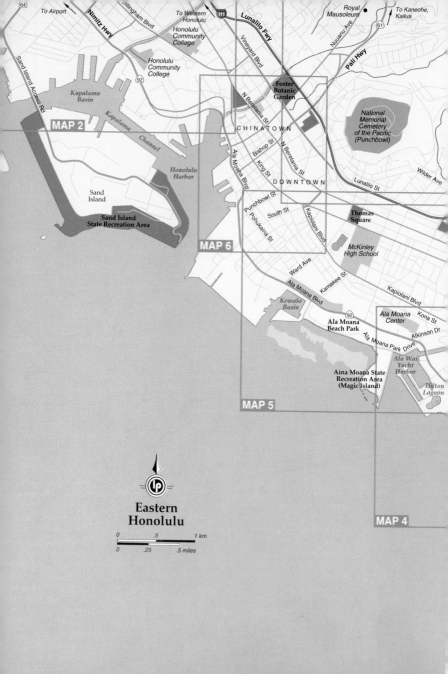

**Eastern
Honolulu**

MAP 3

Tantalus Drive

**Honolulu
Watershed
Forest Preserve**

Oahu Ave

Manoa Rd

M A N O A
V A L L E Y

Lowrey Ave

**Puu Ualakaa
State Park**

Round Top
1048ft ▲

Round Top Drive

Makiki Heights Drive

Manoa Rd

E Manoa Rd

Oahu Ave

Makiki St

**Honolulu
Watershed
Forest
Preserve**

MAP 8

Punahou St

**Makiki
District
Park**

H1

*Punahou
School*

Dole St

Lunalilo Fwy

University Ave

Maile Way

Manoa Stream

**Palolo Valley
District Park**

S Beretania St

S King St

*University
of Hawaii*

Kalakaua Ave

**Moiliili
Park**

Pensacola St

Kapiolani Blvd

Date St

University Ave

*St Louis
High School
& Chaminade
University*

**Mau'u Mae
Nature Park**

Kapiolani Blvd

Kapiolani Blvd

MAP 7

Waialae Ave

Kapahulu Ave

Lunalilo Fwy

Ala Wai Canal

Ala Moana
Blvd

Ala Wai Blvd

Kalakaua Ave

Manoa-Palolo Drainage

Kuhio Ave

Kaiulani Ave

Ala Wai Blvd

12th Ave

To Hanauma Bay

H1

Kalia Rd

Saratoga Rd

**Fort
DeRussy
Military
Reservation**

W A I K I K I

*Ala Wai
Golf Course*

Kalakaua Ave

Kalakaua Ave

Kapahulu Ave

Liliuokalani Ave

Paki Ave

Alohea Ave

Makapuu Ave

Kilauea Ave

Pahoa Ave

Kapahulu Ave

Monsarrat Ave

**Honolulu
Zoo** 🐘

**Kapiolani
Park**

Diamond Head Rd

*Kapiolani
Community
College*

18th Ave

22nd Ave

Hunakai St

Kilauea Ave

Hunakai St

Elepaio St

**Diamond Head
Memorial Park
(Cemetery)**

Kalakaua Ave

**Diamond Head
State Monument**

Diamond Head

760 ft ▲

Diamond Head Rd

Diamond Head Rd

Kahala Ave

Kuilei Cliffs

**Kupikipkio
Point**

MAP 9

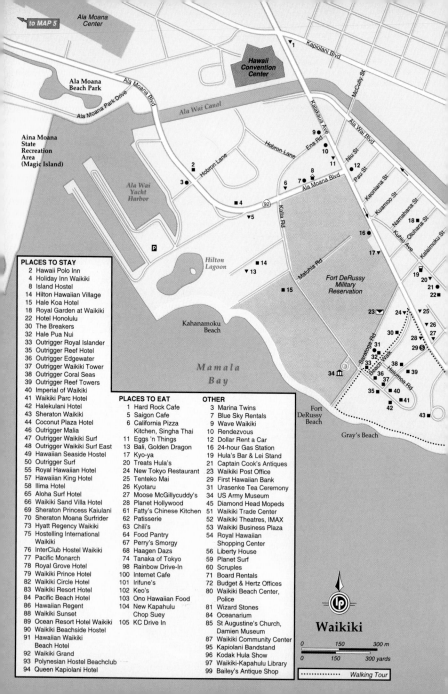

to MAP 5

Ala Moana Center

Hawaii Convention Center

Kapiolani Blvd

McCully St

Ala Moana Blvd

Ala Moana Beach Park

Kalakaua Ave

Ala Wai Blvd

Ala Moana Park Drive

Ala Wai Canal

Hobron Lane

Niu St

Aina Moana State Recreation Area (Magic Island)

Hobron Lane

Paul St

Keoniana St

Namahana St

Kalaimoku St

Ala Wai Yacht Harbor

Ena Rd

Kuamoo St

Kuhio Ave

Olohana St

Ala Moana Blvd

Kala Rd

Matuhia Rd

Hilton Lagoon

Fort DeRussy Military Reservation

Saratoga Rd

Beach Walk

Hekimoa Rd

Kahanamoku Beach

Mamala Bay

Fort DeRussy Beach

Gray's Beach

Waikiki

PLACES TO STAY

2 Hawaii Polo Inn
4 Holiday Inn Waikiki
8 Island Hostel
14 Hilton Hawaiian Village
15 Hale Koa Hotel
18 Royal Garden at Waikiki
22 Hotel Honolulu
30 The Breakers
32 Hale Pua Nui
33 Outrigger Royal Islander
35 Outrigger Reef Hotel
36 Outrigger Edgewater
37 Outrigger Waikiki Tower
38 Outrigger Coral Seas
39 Outrigger Reef Towers
40 Imperial of Waikiki
41 Waikiki Parc Hotel
42 Halekulani Hotel
43 Sheraton Waikiki
46 Coconut Plaza Hotel
46 Outrigger Malia
47 Outrigger Waikiki Surf
48 Outrigger Waikiki Surf East
49 Hawaiian Seaside Hostel
50 Outrigger Surf
55 Royal Hawaiian Hotel
57 Hawaiian King Hotel
58 Ilima Hotel
65 Aloha Surf Hotel
66 Waikiki Sand Villa Hotel
69 Sheraton Princess Kaiulani
70 Sheraton Moana Surfrider
73 Hyatt Regency Waikiki
75 Hostelling International Waikiki
76 InterClub Hostel Waikiki
77 Pacific Monarch
78 Royal Grove Hotel
79 Waikiki Prince Hotel
82 Waikiki Circle Hotel
83 Waikiki Resort Hotel
84 Pacific Beach Hotel
86 Hawaiian Regent
88 Waikiki Sunset
89 Ocean Resort Hotel Waikiki
90 Waikiki Beachside Hostel
91 Hawaiian Waikiki Beach Hotel
92 Waikiki Grand
93 Polynesian Hostel Beachclub
94 Queen Kapiolani Hotel

PLACES TO EAT

1 Hard Rock Cafe
5 Saigon Cafe
6 California Pizza Kitchen, Singha Thai
11 Eggs 'n Things
13 Bali, Golden Dragon
17 Kyo-ya
20 Treats Hula's
24 New Tokyo Restaurant
25 Tenteko Mai
26 Kyotaru
27 Moose McGillycuddy's
28 Planet Hollywood
61 Fatty's Chinese Kitchen
62 Patisserie
63 Chili's
64 Food Pantry
67 Perry's Smorgy
68 Haagen Dazs
74 Tanaka of Tokyo
98 Rainbow Drive-In
100 Internet Cafe
101 Irifune's
102 Keo's
103 Ono Hawaiian Food
104 New Kapahulu Chop Suey
105 KC Drive In

OTHER

3 Marina Twins
7 Blue Sky Rentals
9 Wave Waikiki
10 Rendezvous
12 Dollar Rent a Car
16 24-hour Gas Station
19 Hula's Bar & Lei Stand
21 Captain Cook's Antiques
23 Waikiki Post Office
29 First Hawaiian Bank
31 Urasenke Tea Ceremony
34 US Army Museum
45 Diamond Head Mopeds
51 Waikiki Trade Center
52 Waikiki Theatres, IMAX
53 Waikiki Business Plaza
54 Royal Hawaiian Shopping Center
56 Liberty House
59 Planet Surf
60 Scruples
71 Board Rentals
72 Budget & Hertz Offices
80 Waikiki Beach Center, Police
84 Oceanarium
84 Wizard Stones
85 St Augustine's Church, Damien Museum
87 Waikiki Community Center
95 Kapiolani Bandstand
96 Kodak Hula Show
97 Waikiki-Kapahulu Library
99 Bailey's Antique Shop

0   150   300 m
0   150   300 yards

·········· Walking Tour

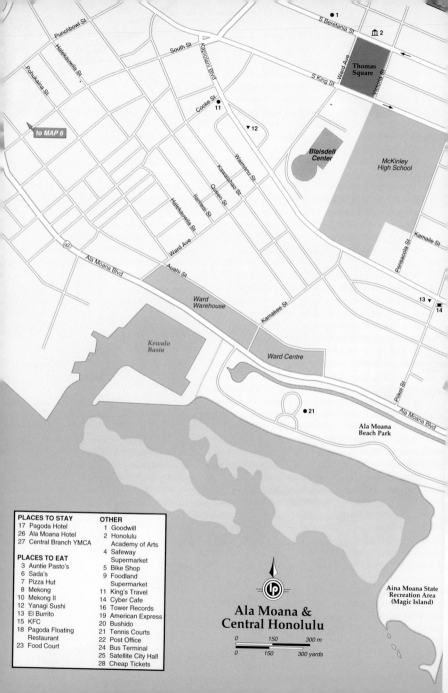

Ala Moana & Central Honolulu

to MAP 6

Thomas
Square

Blaisdell
Center

McKinley
High School

Ward
Warehouse

Kewalo
Basin

Ward Centre

Ala Moana
Beach Park

Aina Moana State
Recreation Area
(Magic Island)

Punchbowl St
S Beretania St
Halekauwila St.
South St
Kapiolani Blvd
S King St
Ward Ave
Victoria St
Pohukaina St.
Cooke St.
Waimanu St.
Kawaiahao St.
Queen St.
Ilaniwai St.
Halekauwila St.
Ward Ave
Ala Moana Blvd
Auahi St.
Kamakee St.
Kamaile St.
Pensacola St.
Piikoi St.
Ala Moana Blvd

0   150   300 m
0   150   300 yards

MAP 5

Downtown & Chinatown

MAP 6

to MAP 5

to MAP 5

LP

0   75   150 m
0   75   150 yards

········· Walking Tour

PLACES TO STAY
11 Nuuanu YMCA
36 Executive Centre Hotel

PLACES TO EAT
4   Doong Kong Lau
5   Buddhist Vegetarian
    Restaurant
7   Ha Bien
8   To Chau
9   Ba Le
15 Wo Fat
16 Shung Chong Yuein
20 Kung Thai
25 Indigo
28 Ba Le, Fort Street Cafe
29 Pizza Hut, Taco Bell
30 Kozo Sushi
31 McDonald's
32 Mandarin Express
33 KFC

12 Antique Shops
13 Bank of Hawaii
14 Cindy's Lei Shop
17 Nature Conservancy
18 Ramsay Galleries
19 Chinese Chamber of
    Commerce
21 Lai Fong Department Store
22 Pegge Hopper Gallery
23 Police Station
24 Abacus Studio
26 Former Pantheon Bar
27 Hawaii Pacific University
34 Woolworth
35 Longs Drugs
37 Delta & Aloha Airlines
38 Hawaiian Airlines
39 Honolulu Book Shops,
    Northwest Airlines
40 United Airlines
41 Federal Express
42 Kinko's

43 Bandstand
44 Queen Liliuokalani Statue
45 War Memorial
46 Post Office
47 Kamehameha Statue
48 AAA
49 Kamaka Hawaii

OTHER
1   Kuan Yin Temple
2   Izumo Taisha Shrine
3   Taoist Temple
6   Sun Yat-sen Statue
9   Yat Tung Chow
    Noodle Factory
10 Main Bus Stop

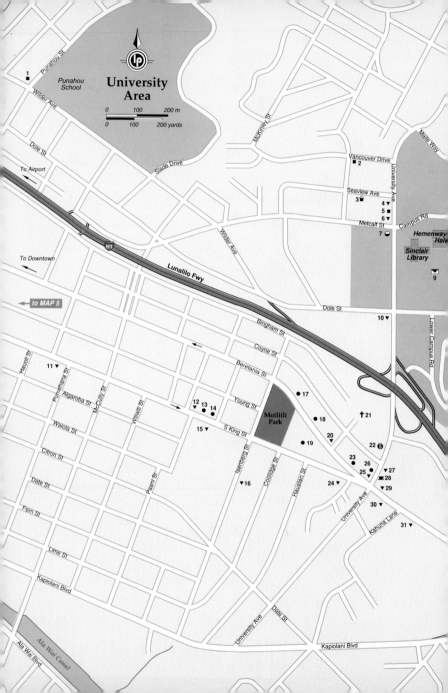

University Area

University Area

1

Punahou St

Wilder Ave

Dole St

Punahou School

Slade Drive

To Airport

H1

To Downtown

Lunalilo Fwy

to MAP 5

McKinley St

Vancouver Drive
2

Seaview Ave
3

4 ▼
5 ■
6 ▼
Metcalf St
7 ⚲

University Ave

Manoa Way

Campus Rd

Hemenway Hall

Sinclair Library

9

Lower Campus Rd

Wilder Ave

Dole St

10 ▼

Bingham St

Coyne St

Beretania St

Harding St

11 ▼

Punehana St

Algaroba St

McCully St

Wiliwili St

12 ▼ 13 ● 14

Young St

15 ▼

S King St

17 ●

Moiliili Park

18 ●

20 ▼

19 ●

† 21

22 Ⓢ

Waiola St

Citron St

Date St

Fern St

Lime St

Kapiolani Blvd

Pumehana St

Isenberg St

Coolidge St

Hausten St

▼ 16

23 ●

26
25 ● ●
● 24 ▼

▼ 27
■ 28
▼ 29

University Ave

30 ▼

Kahuna Lane

31 ▼

University Ave

Date St

Kapiolani Blvd

Ala Wai Canal

Ala Wai Blvd

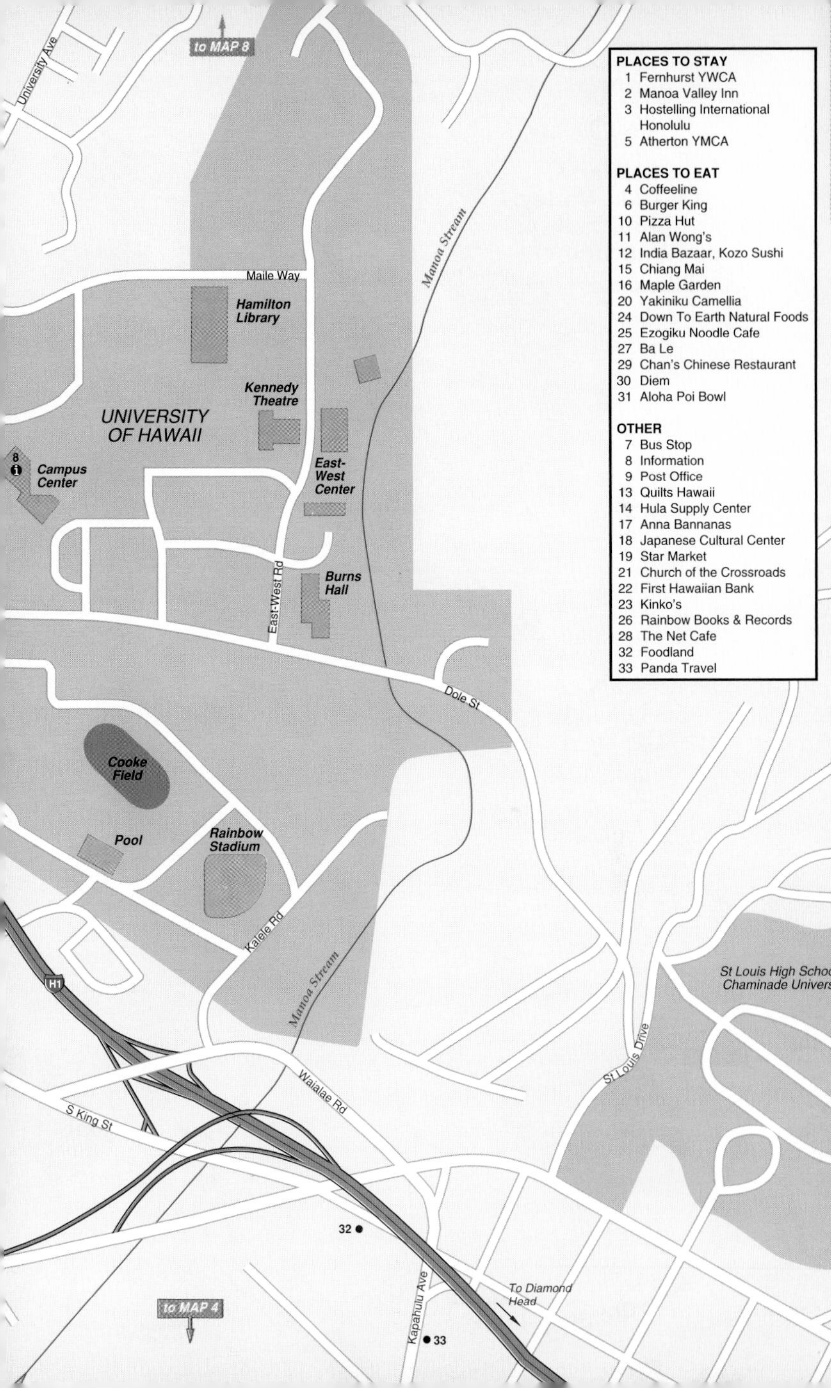

MAP 7

to MAP 8

University Ave

Manoa Stream

Maile Way

Hamilton Library

Kennedy Theatre

UNIVERSITY OF HAWAII

8 ℹ️ Campus Center

East-West Center

East-West Rd

Burns Hall

Dole St

Cooke Field

Pool

Rainbow Stadium

Kalele Rd

Manoa Stream

H1

St Louis High School & Chaminade University

St Louis Drive

S King St

Waialae Rd

Kapahulu Ave

32 ●

To Diamond Head

● 33

to MAP 4

PLACES TO STAY
1 Fernhurst YWCA
2 Manoa Valley Inn
3 Hostelling International Honolulu
5 Atherton YMCA

PLACES TO EAT
4 Coffeeline
6 Burger King
10 Pizza Hut
11 Alan Wong's
12 India Bazaar, Kozo Sushi
15 Chiang Mai
16 Maple Garden
20 Yakiniku Camellia
24 Down To Earth Natural Foods
25 Ezogiku Noodle Cafe
27 Ba Le
29 Chan's Chinese Restaurant
30 Diem
31 Aloha Poi Bowl

OTHER
7 Bus Stop
8 Information
9 Post Office
13 Quilts Hawaii
14 Hula Supply Center
17 Anna Bannanas
18 Japanese Cultural Center
19 Star Market
21 Church of the Crossroads
22 First Hawaiian Bank
23 Kinko's
26 Rainbow Books & Records
28 The Net Cafe
32 Foodland
33 Panda Travel

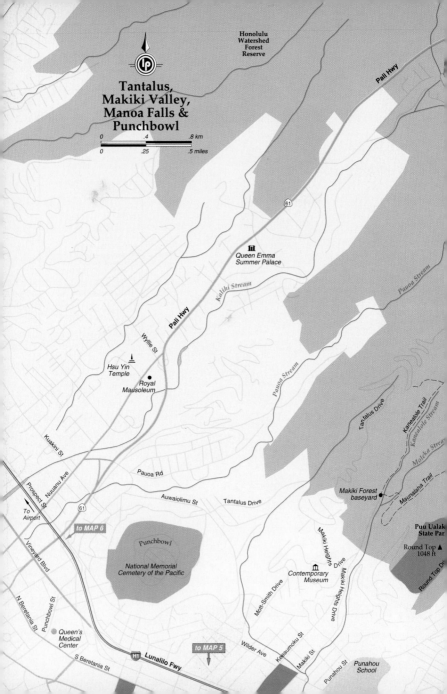

Tantalus,
Makiki Valley,
Manoa Falls &
Punchbowl

0   .4   .8 km
0   .25   .5 miles

Honolulu
Watershed
Forest
Reserve

Pali Hwy

61

Queen Emma
Summer Palace

Kalihi Stream

Pauoa Stream

Pali Hwy

Wyllie St

Hsu Yin
Temple

Royal
Mausoleum

Pauoa Stream

Tantalus Drive

Kaneaole Trail

Kanealole Stream

Moleka Stream

Kuakini St

Nuuanu Ave

Pauoa Rd

Auwaiolimu St

Tantalus Drive

Makiki Forest
baseyard

Maunalaha Trail

Prospect St

To
Airport

61

to MAP 6

Punchbowl

National Memorial
Cemetery of the Pacific

Makiki Heights Drive

Mott-Smith Drive

Contemporary
Museum

Puu Ualak
State Par

Round Top ▲
1048 ft

Round Top Dr

Vineyard Blvd

N Beretania St

Punchbowl St

Queen's
Medical
Center

S Beretania St

H1   Lunalilo Fwy

to MAP 5

Wilder Ave

Keeaumoku St

Makiki St

Punahou St

Punahou
School

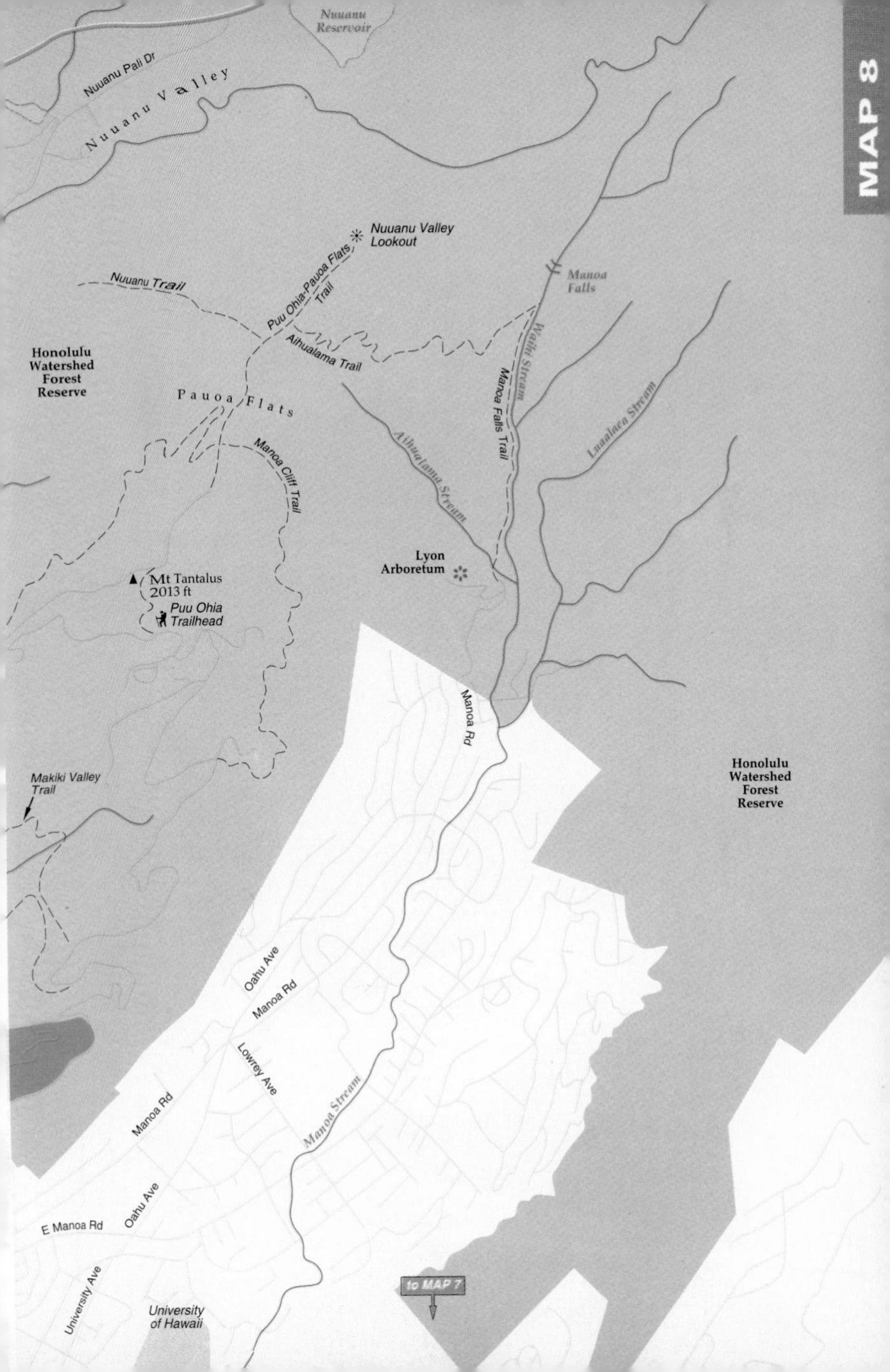

MAP 8

Nuuanu
Reservoir

Nuuanu Pali Dr

Nuuanu Valley

Nuuanu Valley
Lookout

Manoa
Falls

Nuuanu Trail

Puu Ohia-Pauoa Flats Trail

Aihualama Trail

Honolulu
Watershed Forest
Reserve

Pauoa Flats

Waihi Stream

Manoa Falls Trail

Laaaloa Stream

Manoa Cliff Trail

Aihualama Stream

Lyon
Arboretum

▲ Mt Tantalus
2013 ft

Puu Ohia
Trailhead

Manoa Rd

Honolulu
Watershed
Forest
Reserve

Makiki Valley
Trail

Oahu Ave

Manoa Rd

Lowrey Ave

Manoa Rd

Manoa Stream

Oahu Ave

E Manoa Rd

Oahu Ave

University Ave

University
of Hawaii

to MAP 7

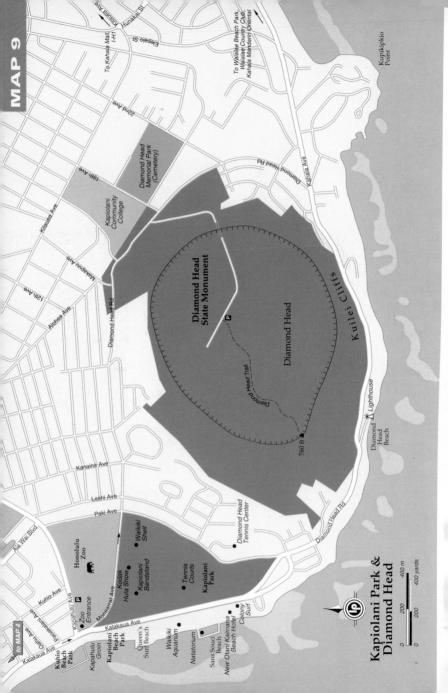

MAP 9

Kapiolani Park & Diamond Head

Kapikpkio Point

To Wailae Beach Park,
Wailae Country Club,
Kahala Mandani Oriental

Kahala Ave

Diamond Head Rd

Diamond Head Memorial Park (Cemetery)

18th Ave

Kapiolani Community College

Kilauea Ave

22nd Ave

To Kahala Mall, I-H1

Kilauea Ave

Hunakai St

Elepeio St

Diamond Head State Monument

Diamond Head

Kuilei Cliffs

760 ft

Diamond Head Trail

P

Lighthouse

Diamond Head Beach

Diamond Head Rd

Makapuu Ave

12th Ave

Alohea Ave

Diamond Head Rd

Kanaina Ave

Leahi Ave

Paki Ave

Diamond Head Tennis Center

Ala Wai Blvd

Honolulu Zoo

Kapahulu Ave

Zoo Entrance

Monsarrat Ave

Kodak Hula Show

Waikiki Shell

Kapiolani Bandstand

Tennis Courts

Kapiolani Park

Kalakaua Ave

Kuhio Ave

Kapahulu Groin

Kuhio Beach Park

Kalakaua Ave

Oahu Ave

Koolauwai Ave

Kapiolani Beach Park

Queen's Surf Beach

Waikiki Aquarium

Natatorium

Sans Souci Beach

New Otani Kaimana Beach Hotel

Colony Surf

to MAP 4

0   200   400 m
0   200   400 yards